AVIATOR EXTRAORDINARY

Sidney Cotton in 1941

AVIATOR EXTRAORDINARY

THE SIDNEY COTTON STORY

as told to

RALPH BARKER

1969

CHATTO & WINDUS

LONDON

Published by
Chatto & Windus Ltd
42 William IV Street
London, W.C.2

*

Clarke, Irwin & Co. Ltd
Toronto

W869

SBN 7011 1334 0

© Ralph Barker 1969

Printed in Great Britain by
Cox & Wyman Ltd
London, Fakenham and Reading

Contents

Illustrations

PLATES

FIGURES IN THE TEXT

ACKNOWLEDGEMENTS

The letter appearing on page 132 is reproduced by permission of the Right Hon.
The Earl of Halifax, D.L., J.P., those on pages 199–200 and 209; which are Crown
Copyright, by permission of the Controller of Her Majesty's Stationery Office; that
on page 206 by permission of Air Chief Marshal Lord Dowding, G.C.B., K.C.B.,
G.C.V.O., C.M.G.

AVIATOR EXTRAORDINARY

If a man does not keep pace with his companions, perhaps it is because he hears a different drummer. Let him step to the music that he hears.

THOREAU

1

Learning to Fly

'GOOD morning, Cotton–how are you getting along with your hops?'

I was standing in front of the Farman Longhorn trainer at Chingford, then the main training station for pilots of the Royal Naval Air Service. It was early 1916, and only a few weeks earlier I had arrived from Australia on the *Maloja* and joined up as a sub-lieutenant. So far I hadn't even had a chance to taxi a plane to get the feel of it, let alone fly one, and I had hardly seen the inside of a cockpit. But I had been allocated to an instructor named Warren Merriam. It was Merriam who had phrased the question.

Merriam was one of the great flying instructors of the early years of aviation. He had been an instructor since before the war. He had also, some years earlier, survived a very bad accident, and his eyesight was said to have been affected, and sometimes even his memory. He was reputed to be able to take off, fly and land a machine virtually without looking. And his method with cadets was reputed to be a tough one – make 'em or break 'em.

I knew what he meant by 'hops'. The trick was that several sparking plugs were removed from the engine to reduce power. Beginners then taxied about the airfield and by opening the throttles fully were just able to lift the aircraft off the ground for a few yards. Then it would settle back gently on the ground. In this way trainees got some idea of how an aircraft handled without much risk.

I had, of course, done no hops, but I thought perhaps I was supposed to have done, so I made my answer fairly non-committal. 'Oh, I'm getting along fine, sir.' I had thought the question was little more than a pleasantry, another way of passing the time of day, but Merriam treated my answer seriously.

'Good. You can take your ticket today. Come up with me for a couple of circuits and we'll see how you are.'

The shock was appalling. My mind worked quickly enough, but my tongue was paralysed. Could it be that Merriam was simply calling my bluff? I didn't think so. I remembered the things people said about his eyesight–he must have mistaken me for someone else. Or it might be his memory–he had confused me with someone else. But above all I remembered his reputation for making or breaking. It was about to happen to me.

I suppose it would have been the easiest thing in the world to correct the false impression I'd given, to explain that I was getting on all right but that I hadn't actually done any hops, but I thought it would make me look silly. I allowed myself to be led into the rear seat of the Longhorn. I was petrified, hardly able to speak or move, but I had the presence of mind to watch Merriam closely to see what he did. He sat just in front of me, and after he had taken off I leaned over his shoulder at his bidding and was just able to touch the handlebar control with the tips of my fingers while he did the flying. There was no dual control, so I couldn't get the feel of the rudder bar. We went round the airfield several times, and he showed me how to come in over a particular tree just by the end of the reservoir. 'If you cut the engine at 500 feet over that tree,' he shouted back at me, 'you'll touch down nicely just inside the aerodrome and come to a stop in the white circle. You've got to do that to get your ticket.' A few moments later he landed and stopped in the circle just as he said he would.

I knew that if I tried to go solo now I should almost certainly break my neck. Well, I should just have to break it, that was all. I couldn't own up now. But instinctively I started to delay matters. I found several rusty bracing wires and had them replaced. Then I had all the plugs changed. The mechanics seemed to work with remorseless speed and it was torture to watch them. I walked across the airfield to steady my nerves. Most of the other trainees were making their way to the Mess, and I followed. It was lunchtime.

I didn't eat much lunch. When I came out again Merriam was running up the engine, apparently about to take off. He had forgotten all about me! At least, that was what it looked like, and I could hardly believe my good luck. Then he closed the throttle and climbed out of the cockpit, spotted me and strolled across.

'All right, Cotton. Everything's ready for you now.'

He hadn't forgotten me at all. In my imagination his figure took on the black robes of an executioner. I still hadn't got the sense to tell him that I'd never even taxied a plane before, and I got into the pilot's seat. Merriam helped to strap me in. 'Push the throttle fully open,' he was saying, 'and when you reach forty miles an hour, ease the stick back until the machine leaves the ground. Keep the controls steady until you've gained height, then feel them out quietly until they give you confidence.' My teeth chattered something back at him and he disappeared over the side of the cockpit. A few moments later he reappeared in front of me, and then he moved across to my right, signalling for me to go. It was make 'em or break 'em all right. There was nothing I could do now but open the throttle and go to my death.

The machine gathered speed rapidly and I was soon racing across the grass field. I sat rigidly braced in my seat, my hands clenched on the controls, every muscle taut, waiting for the inevitable crash. Suddenly I saw the hedges on the far side of the field swinging into focus. I tightened up like a screw and cringed against the back of my seat.

A few yards from the hedge the plane lifted gently, and to my utter astonishment I sailed safely over. In my instinctive recoil from the crash I had eased back the stick. I kept perfectly still, eyes fixed straight ahead, uncertain for a moment what had saved me. I was airborne, and climbing steadily.

I began to move the handlebars very gently, up a little on one side and down on the other, keeping my eyes on the horizon. I was still in a gradual climb. The gentle movement of the plane from one side to the other was a miracle to me. I tried moving the controls a little farther each way and found that I was actually controlling the plane laterally. I relaxed ever so slightly as I began to gain confidence.

I pushed the control column forward, and nearly collapsed with fright as the nose dipped and the plane dived towards the ground. I pulled it back again and tried more gently. It seemed that I had been up a long time already, and I began to look for the coastline, but I discovered that I had flown no more than about four miles. I decided to try a gentle turn back towards Chingford.

The time I had spent as a schoolboy making model gliders and rubber-driven aircraft may not have been good for my general education, but as a result of it I probably knew more about the theory and practice of flight than the average trainee of my time. I began to feel thoroughly at home, to handle the machine with confidence, and to exult in the power it gave me. I hadn't wasted my schooldays after all. For another minute or two I cruised around in triumph. I had fully expected a crash, and I almost gloated over my escape. But I was careful to keep the Chingford reservoir, on the northern edge of the airfield, well in sight.

I had watched the other trainees carrying out the various man-oeuvres that were demanded for the coveted 'ticket', and I had them well fixed in my mind. I knew I had to do figures-of-eight to the right and left, and one of the pilots on the war flight had explained to me how these were done. I flew over the centre of the airfield and tried one out. It worked perfectly. I was so excited at this that I completed my figures-of-eight by doing what were called 'split-arse' turns – one banked the plane over until the wings were vertical and then pulled on the elevator control, using the elevator as a rudder. By this time I felt I had shown Merriam and anyone else who happened to be watching that I could fly an aeroplane. It was time to make the landing.

I remembered Merriam's instructions about coming in over the tree at 500 feet, but I didn't judge the distance too well and I was still at 600 feet when I crossed over the tree. I thought I knew what to do about this, and I put the nose down to lose height, but as soon as I did this my airspeed went up. I passed well into the field and only touched down in the middle of the circle. I knew this wouldn't do, so I opened the throttle and took off again. I carried out the rest of the manoeuvres required for the 'ticket' and then brought the machine down to 500 feet again some distance from the field. Now all I had to do was hold it steady and cut the engine when I crossed over the tree. It worked as Merriam had said and I made a perfect landing, coming to a stop in the middle of the circle.

I taxied across to the hangar, where Merriam was waiting for me. I was sure I had done all that was expected of me, but I couldn't help wondering to what extent I had given myself away by my behaviour before and during the take-off.

'Congratulations, Cotton!' called Merriam, as I climbed down from the cockpit. 'I didn't realize you were so far advanced!' I still wasn't sure how much he knew of the truth, but I told him that after the first few minutes I'd felt perfectly at home and that I'd like to go up again. Merriam shook his head. 'No,' he said, 'that's enough for today.' I wondered if perhaps he'd guessed the truth from my take-off and been almost as frightened as I was.

The incident taught me just how far it's possible to go on sheer bluff. But it taught me, too, that it's essential to have something solid to fall back on in case one's bluff is called. Although I hadn't realized it, I already had quite a fair if elementary knowledge of the science of aeronautics.

2

Boyhood in Australia

I WAS born on a cattle station at Goorganga, Queensland, on 17th
June 1894. My first memory is of when I was about four years old.
I used to play with my younger brother Victor, then aged about a year,
on the veranda of our home. There was a hole under the edge of the
veranda, and we found to our delight that by putting our hands through
this hole we could pull out fluffy white round balls which were great
fun to play with. We always put them back in the hole after the game.
Victor had reached the crawling stage, and one day, in another part
of the house, my mother lost sight of him. She asked my sister Vera
and myself to help her find him. When we went out on to the veranda
we found him crawling after a black snake. My mother held us back.
'Don't move,' she whispered. She had recognized it as a tiger snake.

The snake was moving slowly down the veranda, closely followed
by Victor. Every few feet the snake would turn its head and stop for
a moment until Victor caught up, then move on again. At last it disappeared over the edge of the veranda.

My mother let go of our hands and rushed after Victor, grabbing
him just as he toppled over the edge of the veranda after the snake. He
was cooing happily, delighted with his new playmate.

Had the snake bitten Victor he would have been dead within
minutes. It had come out of the hole where we had been putting our
hands. The fluffy white balls were its eggs.

Goorganga is situated about five miles from a little village called
Proserpine, near the Pacific coast. Forty miles to the north-west is the
port of Bowen, the whole stretch of coastline being protected by the
Great Barrier Reef. We often used to drive into Proserpine in the buggy
with my mother to do the shopping, and on one of these visits something happened that made such an impression on me I have never forgotten it, something that has certainly played a part in moulding my
life. It was about a year after the snake incident, so I was about five,

I was walking round the little general store, hand in hand with my sister Vera, when I saw a toy boat that took my fancy. It was marked 1/6, though I had no idea what that meant. I could not resist this boat and I took it, leaving Vera behind and hiding the boat as best I could while walking quickly back to the buggy. I kept the boat concealed on the way back, and then found a hiding-place for it at home. I used to take it out surreptitiously and play with it on the lagoon on the banks of which our house was built, and hide it again afterwards. It was an exciting possession and I imagined that I was quite safe so long as I kept it out of sight.

Some days later we were having lunch when my mother looked out of the window. 'Look,' she said, 'there's someone riding up to the house. Who can it be?'

'That's Paddy the policeman from Proserpine,' said my father. 'I think he's come to inquire about a boat that somebody took from the store.'

I stopped eating, and as soon as I could I left the table quietly and went upstairs. I was terrified, choked with guilt and shock. It never occurred to me that my father and mother had staged their conversation for my benefit, and I felt the awful weight of secret guilt. I had heard the dreadful stories about policemen coming to take little boys away when they weren't good, and I sat on my bed dreading the summons to go.

The visitor stayed for an hour or so and then left. I went downstairs, partly out of relief, partly to hear what had happened. 'By the way,' my father said quietly to my mother, soon after he saw me come in, 'they haven't found out who took the boat yet, but they're still looking.' Thus I was condemned to further uncertainty and fear of discovery. For weeks I was so miserable that after a time, like the Jackdaw of Rheims, I must have looked ill.

I think my father would have kept me in torment until I finally owned up, to make sure the lesson was thoroughly learnt, but eventually my mother decided that I ought not to be punished further in this way. She told me that she had seen me take the boat and had paid for it at the time. Paddy the policeman had come on a social visit.

The suffering I went through in those weeks is still a vivid memory. From then on, opportunist and adventurer though I may have been, I have always applied an unorthodox but strict moral code. I can't live with a bad conscience.

.   .   .   .   .

My father and mother were both strong characters, descended from long-established European families, whom fate had led towards a meeting in a new colony. My mother's story really starts at Loxley Park in Staffordshire in 1775, when Mary Kynnersley, fourth daughter of a Staffordshire squire, went on a trip abroad with a party of friends. At Dunkirk she met and fell in love with a young German nobleman named Baron von Boden. There was just enough opposition from Mary's family to test her determination, and the young couple were married in London in the same year.

The Baron's relations retaliated by subjecting Mary's pedigree to a close scrutiny. They were duly informed that the Kynnersley family was 'one of the most ancient in England, and nobly allied during eight hundred years'. This was good enough, and they gave the couple an affectionate welcome.

A son Clement was born, and then the new Baroness, having registered Clement's birth in England and thus assured his British nationality, joined her husband abroad. The Baron, changing his name to de Bode, obtained the Fief of Sultz in Alsace, and the family's future looked assured; they had had twelve children by the time the French Revolution drove them out.

The Baroness was resourceful as well as determined; she obtained letters of introduction to Catherine the Second of Russia, and drove with her coachman to St Petersburg to meet her. It must have been a considerable test of endurance in the 1790s. She became such a favourite that within a year or two Catherine had given her vast properties in the newly-conquered Crimea as well as other properties near St Petersburg. The Baron de Bode then brought the children across Europe to the Crimea, but two years later he died there of a fever. The Baroness returned to Moscow with her children and did what she could to develop her estates from there, but her position was now threatened by the military adventures of Napoleon. She died in Moscow a year before he entered the city.

Meanwhile the French Government had remitted £7,000,000 to the British Treasury to reimburse the British owners of estates confiscated during the Revolution. Fortunately the Baron de Bode had registered the title deeds in the joint names of himself and his eldest son Clement, who was of course a British subject, and Clement came to England to press his case with the Treasury. His name headed the reimbursement list with a sum of half a million pounds. But the Treasury had spent the money, and neither Clement, nor his sons, nor his grandsons in their turn, could induce them to pay up. By 1859 the family had become so impoverished by protracted legal actions that two of Clement's grandsons emigrated to Australia. One of them took up a cattle-raising property at Bromby Park, near Bowen, and seven years later, in 1866, a daughter Annie Jane Elizabeth was born to a couple styling themselves 'Mr and Mrs Bode'. Annie Bode was later to become my mother.

Fifty years before the Norman Conquest a family called de Coton settled in Derbyshire and founded a village of that name which is still there. In succeeding generations the name became anglicized and became simply 'Cotton'.

The most distinguished of the Cottons was probably Sir Robert Cotton—Robert Bruce Cotton, to give him his full name, because of his descent from Robert Bruce. Born in Huntingdonshire in 1570, he was educated at Westminster and Cambridge and later settled down at a house on the site of the present House of Lords, where he began the collection of books, coins and other antiquities for which he is famous. Many priceless collections of manuscripts had been broken up and scattered as a result of the dissolution of the monasteries, and Robert Cotton dedicated his life to the task of gathering as many of these manuscripts as he could trace into his personal collection. But for his dedication, most of these manuscripts would almost certainly have been lost to posterity. He could hardly have indulged such a passion had he not been a wealthy man; but in those days not all the manuscripts he collected were recognized at their true worth. His greatest finds were two of the four surviving copies of Magna Charta, one of which he is reputed to have bought from a tailor for fourpence just as it was about to be cut up for stiffening a collar.

In helping James I to find a means of raising revenue, Robert Cotton stumbled on records of the extinct honour of baronetcy, which James promptly revived. Cotton was then himself made a baronet. He was not so popular with Charles I, who was suspicious of his views on national liberty, imprisoned him on a trumped-up charge, and confiscated his possessions including his library. Later he regained his liberty, but not his library. It was one of three collections which formed the foundation of the British Museum library, where it is still known as the Cottonian Library.

All this is especially interesting to me because it shows that both branches of my family have been the victims of high-handed injustice from the ruling authority. It is only comparatively recently that I have discovered all this, and I have certainly never had a chip on my shoulder about it. But there's no doubt that this was the sort of background which many of the early settlers in Australia left behind them when they left England, and it helps to explain the distrust of long-established institutions which is characteristic of many Australians. Something of this must have been deeply ingrained in me from birth, accounting for my persistent refusal throughout my life to accept or obey the orders of established authority when I felt them to be wrong.

By the nineteenth century the Cottons were flourishing again, this time as 'merchant princes', as they were then known. It was the habit of the more affluent people of those days to go to Jersey for the summer to get away from the English climate, and it was in Jersey that my father was born, in 1861. In the 1870s my grandfather, Charles Cotton, had gone out to South Africa to develop land. Some years later his health broke down and he had to sell the land. He returned to England a broken man both financially and physically, and he died soon afterwards. The family were left in low straits, and at the age of fourteen my father was apprenticed to a firm of shipowners. He went to sea in a 700-ton barque carrying coal to China, and he spent six years at sea before settling in Australia. There he soon showed a flair for handling horses and cattle, travelling all over Queensland droving cattle from one station to another. In this way he arrived one day at Bromby Park, near Bowen, and met a girl called Annie Bode. They married four years later.

In 1900 we moved from Goorganga to a new 10,000-acre property called Jost Vale, forty miles from Brisbane. I shall never forget the magnificent view as we emerged from the trees into open country approaching the property. We had driven about four miles from the railway station by buggy when we suddenly found ourselves on the top of a hill looking down across a valley. My mother exclaimed, 'What a wonderful surprise! We must change the name from Jost Vale to Hidden Vale. It's one of the loveliest views I've ever seen.' The Liverpool range, rising to several thousand feet, lay to our right; and the whole valley was ours, our nearest neighbours, the Morts, being three miles away. The homestead was in the valley, about a mile down from the crest of the hill, and it became almost a habit to walk up to the top of the hill to see the magnificent changing colours on the Liverpool range as the sun went down. When the sun dipped into the horizon the shades became deeper and deeper, changing rapidly from the gold of the sunset into blues and purples and then suddenly into an inky blackness as night fell. It was something we could never tire of.

The Morts—Arthur Mort, his wife and their children—were an important part of our lives. They were our only near neighbours. We would help in mustering and dipping each other's cattle, and always when more hands were wanted for any particular task we would join forces. Once a week we used to go to their home at Franklyn Vale for dancing lessons, and we often picnicked together. As the years passed I grew more and more attached to Olive, the youngest of the four daughters. She was some years younger than me, but we enjoyed each other's company.

After two or three years my father built a new homestead on the top of the hill, as my mother said that the beautiful view was being wasted. She felt that if we lived at the top of the hill and awoke daily to the wonderful panorama of Hidden Vale it must have an uplifting effect on our characters. I don't know whether she was right or not, but we certainly loved our new home.

In 1904 I was sent to Southport Grammar School, fifty miles south of Brisbane along the coast, and I stayed there for the next six years. Southport was a small seaside resort which abounded in magnificent beaches, most of them without a house in sight. I didn't like schoolwork, but the games, the boating and the swimming appealed to me. There was an oyster bed just in front of the school and we used to swim out and dive for oysters. What feasts we used to have! But most of all I loved the holidays, and the wonderful free life at Hidden Vale, riding and working the cattle.

In 1910 my father got the idea that it would do us all good if we went to school in England. He decided to our sorrow to sell Hidden Vale, and he booked passages for the whole family on the *Waratah*. Fortunately he was unable to wind up his business affairs in time to sail on the *Waratah* and we had to catch a later boat. On clearing Durban for Cape Town the *Waratah* disappeared with all hands and no trace of her was ever found.

When we arrived in London we stayed at Berners Hotel. A few months earlier Bleriot had flown the Channel, and flying had become a craze. I made friends with the head porter at Berners and he told me how to get to Brooklands. I found my way down there and spent a day trying to get close to the bits of wood, wire and linen that then passed for aeroplanes. My father reprimanded me for going there without his permission, but thereafter I was allowed to go daily. At fifteen I was too shy to do more than help push the machines out of their sheds and watch them trying to take off, but I became thoroughly obsessed with aeroplanes.

My father rented an estate in Scotland of some 1,200 acres called Warthill, eighteen miles from Aberdeen, and while we were there he took us to a flying meeting at Lanark. Colonel Cody was the hero of the meeting, and headlines in the local paper reported that he had 'got up to the clouds'. Henry Farman, however, could not get very much lift, and while he was circling at low level he ran into a down-current above the trees and slowly descended into the topmost branches. There he stayed until someone went up with a ladder and got him down. I remember that I could not understand why these men kept pulling out little boxes and striking matches, until I was told that they held the match up to test the strength of the wind. I noticed, too, that before flying they would wet a finger and hold it up in the air, to check the wind direction. There were no windsocks in those days.

My father arranged for my two brothers and me to go to Cheltenham College. I went to the senior college and my two brothers to the preparatory section. I spent two years at Cheltenham, and I enjoyed them, mainly because of the facilities for making model aeroplanes. I spent nearly all my time building models instead of learning my lessons, and my biggest excitement was a six-foot model of bamboo and linen which the carpenter from the school carpentry shop helped me to build. Work on it, and anticipation of the joy of flying it, filled my days. We fitted a small single-cylinder petrol-engine into this model, and just before the summer holidays of 1911 it was ready. We made several short test flights on the cricket field, and then I packed it up carefully and sent it to Warthill, ready for the holidays.

The first thing I did when I got to Warthill was to reassemble the aeroplane and prepare it for flight. I set the rudder so that the plane would fly in a wide circle, and it took off beautifully, clearing the trees on the edge of the field comfortably. But now, instead of going into a turn, it flew on and on and was soon lost to view. I knew it wouldn't stay up for more than a few minutes and I followed it hopefully, but I never found it. It must have come down on top of one of the many fir trees on the estate. On its first real flight I had lost the toy upon which I had lavished six months of my school life, and I was inconsolable. I believed afterwards that I had not allowed enough for the torque of the propeller when I set the rudder.

During that summer term I was swimming one day in the pool for exercise, and after covering two or three lengths I climbed out for a rest. Several of the seniors met me as I came out of the water and asked me to swim two lengths as fast as I could. I suppose I was tall for my age, and fairly strong. I dived in and began swimming, and towards the end of the second length I was conscious of a commotion ahead of me. When I grabbed the rail at the finish the excitement was terrific. I had broken the school record.

I had never been considered a fast swimmer in Australia, but now I was asked to swim in the school team. I remember thinking that the standard must be much lower in England than back home, but it gave me an interesting outlet for the rest of my stay at Cheltenham.

At the end of that year my father went back to Australia. We missed him very much and it grew on us that we could not adjust ourselves more than temporarily to what we felt was the restricted life in England. We all pressed very hard to go back to Australia, and eventually, in 1912, my father agreed to our return. On our arrival to our great delight he bought back our old home at Hidden Vale.

We at once picked up the threads of our friendship with our neighbours the Morts, and particularly, so far as I was concerned, with Olive. I interested Arthur Mort in buying his first car, an Overland, and he gave me the job of teaching his children to drive it. This threw us all very much together, and I spent a lot of time at Franklyn Vale. Then they would go back to school and I would miss them terribly.

On the whole, though, I thoroughly enjoyed myself in the next eighteen months, riding about the cattle station, or travelling sometimes for weeks on end through the outback areas between New South Wales, Queensland and the Northern Territory, visiting properties with my father. Yet I did not feel that cattle, as a life's work, was the thing for me. It was too slow.

Early in 1914 my father arranged for me to 'jackeroo' on a big sheep station at Cassilis in New South Wales. A jackeroo is someone who is apprenticed to a cattle or sheep station to learn the business. My father must have realized by this time that I was bored with cattle, and he hoped I might take an interest in sheep. I didn't doubt that I would find sheep much the same, but my father was adamant. 'I want you boys to follow in my footsteps,' he would say, and then, if he thought we looked defiant, he would remind us that one day we would have to earn our own living, and threaten to leave all his money to a sailors' home if we failed to carry out his wishes. We had no doubt that he meant what he said.

After I had been at Cassilis for about a fortnight, Fred McMaster, the owner, asked me how I thought I would like the job. I was callow enough to say that I thought I would like it very much.

'You don't have to kid *me*,' said McMaster. 'I've been watching you. What do you really want to do?'

'I'm very keen on engineering,' I said, 'but my father wants me to follow in his footsteps and become a station owner. That's why he sent me here.'

McMaster put his question to me again. 'We all have to carve out our own futures. What do you really want to do?'

'I'd like to build a motor-car.'

He looked hard at me for a moment. 'All right, why shouldn't you? You'd better go down to Sydney and get all the materials you want, and then come back here and build it. Charge everything to my account.'

During the next eight or nine months I built the car, with much good advice and help from the perceptive Fred McMaster, and at the end of that time I drove it across 150 miles of country to the main railway and trucked it to Queensland. My father was not at all pleased when he realized how I had been spending my time at Cassilis. It was our first real clash of wills. There were many more to come.

I had driven the car with a soap-box for a seat because I hadn't had the time or the materials to build a body at the sheep station. But when the Willys Overland agent in Brisbane saw the chassis he was delighted with it, and his factory built a streamlined body for it, which we designed together. I used dog clutches to change the drive between one shaft and the next, and then a final V-belt drive to the rear wheels. The drive between the shafts was very similar to that used some years later in England by Fraser Nash. The belt pulleys were variable so I had an infinite range of gears. I had built cantilever springs for the rear wheels and half elliptic underslung springs for the front. My brothers and I got a great deal of pleasure out of this car.

The war had now started, and I asked my father if I could go to England to join up. The answer was no. My father said he had been advised that the war would not last more than a few months, so it would be all over before I could get there. Secondly, my mother had been unwell and for that reason alone he didn't want me saying any-thing about joining up. Lastly, he was planning a motor trip to Brunette Downs and he couldn't do without my help. So in April 1915 I left with him once again on a 1,200-mile drive to the Northern Territory.

It was on this trip that we heard of the sinking of the *Lusitania*, and the news so incensed me that I told my father I was determined to go to England when I got back. I was close on twenty-one and I knew he couldn't stop me. Eventually he promised to discuss it with my mother on our return. Back at Hidden Vale, my mother drew me aside and told me that she quite understood and wouldn't stand in my way. My father asked me what regiment I would like to join, and I told him I wanted to fly and that as Australia had no flying corps I would have to go to England. He booked a passage for me on the P. & O. liner *Maloja*.

I had one other matter to attend to–I had to say good-bye to Olive. We had never discussed the future, though I felt we had an under-standing. Now she was away at school. I wrote to say good-bye to her and told her of my feelings, and her reply seemed in much the same vein. I thus left Australia in a mood of some elation, and after that I had little time to be miserable.

Several other volunteers had taken passage on the *Maloja*, and we got together soon after sailing from Sydney to practise Morse code and signalling. The ships' officers advised me to join the Royal Naval Air Service, and as I was also very fond of the sea, that was my decision.

3

With the Royal Naval Air Service

THREE days after my first solo flight at Chingford I was posted to the Central Flying School at Upavon on Salisbury Plain. There I ran into an old neighbour from a sheep station in Australia named Cox, and he turned out to be my instructor on the B.E. 2c. Three weeks later Cox gave me my final passing-out test, which included flying, navigation, plotting and Morse code. I managed all right on the first three, but then came the Morse code. We had practised on the boat on the way from Australia, but I was still a poor sender and even worse at receiving. Most pilots were the same.

'What are you like on the radio?' asked Cox.

I thought there was a chance he might let me off the Morse test, so I said I was pretty good. 'Then you're probably better than I am,' said Cox, sitting down at the desk and picking up the headphones. 'I'm no good at all and I've got to pass you out!' This gave me my cue, and I rattled the Morse key as fast as I could. Cox was so baffled that he gave me a 100 per cent pass on the strength of it, not liking to ask me to take down his own halting Morse. I was posted to the B.E. 2c flight at Dover. I had five hours solo in my log and felt like a veteran.

A new squadron was forming at Dover with Breguet biplanes. These aircraft had a free tail-plane with no fixed portion and were extremely sensitive to the use of the elevator and very difficult to control. The slightest pressure on the stick put too much movement on the elevator and the plane would 'hunt' madly. One day the squadron commander told me that he'd heard good reports of me as a pilot and asked me if I'd like to try one. It seemed he was looking for pilots. He warned me about the delicate handling the plane needed, and for the take-off I used the same tactics as I had used on my first solo at Chingford, although that time I had done it from fear. I held the control stick tightly between my knees and eased it back very gently until the plane rose. This got me over the airfield boundary without any 'hunting', but after a few minutes the engine started to backfire and I had to land in a field. After cleaning the carburettor I managed to get the engine going, and soon I was airborne again. This happened several times and each time I managed to cure the trouble and get off again only for the engine to peter out and force me down. (Forced landings weren't quite such serious matters as they later became: at C.F.S. I had pancaked a B.E. 2c on a tennis-court surrounded with wire netting and the machine was flying again that afternoon.) By the time I got back to the airfield I had been away for several hours and had been up and down four or five times. The squadron commander had been looking out for me, and he asked me where the devil I'd been with his Breguet. I told him about the forced landings, and how I had kept tinkering with the carburettor until at last I'd coaxed her back. He must have approved, because this flight landed me in the Breguet squadron.

A few days later I was on patrol over the Channel when I saw a large ship directly below me. Suddenly a plume of water arose beside her hull and the vessel stopped and began going astern. I didn't understand what was happening but I kept circling. Then people began to drop over the side, the ship continued to go astern, it began to list, and finally it sank. Meanwhile boats were putting out from Dover and destroyers were hurrying to the scene. The ship had struck a mine. When I landed I heard it was the *Maloja*, on her way from Australia with another load of volunteers. One hundred and two lives were lost.

It was a tragedy that seemed very close to me. Since arriving in England on the *Maloja* I had fulfilled my life's ambition in learning to fly, and in that time the *Maloja* had been out to Australia and back again. Now I had been on patrol over her and she had been sunk. It made me determined to get into the fighting as soon as I could.

The chance came a few days later when the squadron moved to an airfield near Dunkirk. Spenser Grey, leader of many early bombing raids on German targets, was the squadron commander, and Reggie Marix, who had scored a direct hit on a Zeppelin shed at Dusseldorf eighteen months earlier, destroying at least one Zeppelin, was one of his flight commanders. I was sent to St Pol, the main base for the various Naval wings in France, to collect a Breguet, and it was such a beautiful day that on the way back I decided to fly up the coast to get an idea of what the surrounding country was like.

I kept going until I came to a place where there was an oval lake just inland and a town with a port on the left. Deciding that I had probably gone far enough, I turned back towards Dunkirk. Immediately I did so I saw a little black cloud with white edges form below me and to the right, then another and another. I had never seen clouds form so quickly before, nor had I seen them form in such strange shapes. Then one appeared suddenly very close to me, and in the centre was a purple flash, which was followed by the sound of an explosion. I suddenly realized that I was being fired at. Nobody could have been more surprised – I had not been told about this sort of thing. I was, of course, off Ostend. I put the nose down and hedge-hopped back to Dunkirk. There were no hits on the machine, but the experience had thoroughly frightened me.

Soon afterwards we were ordered to make a mass attack against one of the Ostend aerodromes. Apart from being told to take off and get there just before dawn, we weren't briefed in any way. Pilots who had been on raids talked about their experiences and answered questions, but that was all. After my earlier experience I hedge-hopped all the way. We were late in getting away and it was after dawn when we reached the aerodrome, so I was glad I had stayed low.

As I approached our main objective, the hangars, I was suddenly aware that splashes of earth were spurting up in all directions around me, inside and outside the aerodrome. I kept straight on until I was almost on top of the hangars, and then I looked up. There was an absolute flock of Breguets and Caudrons directly above me; I was picking my way through a rain of bombs dropped by my own squadron. I made for the nearest hangar, hastily unloaded my bombs, and veered off out to sea as fast as I could.

When I had reached a point three to four miles off-shore the battery of 15-inch naval guns in Ostend opened up at me. Their gunnery was good and the near-misses threw me all over the sky. There were several hits from shrapnel and my engine coughed and spluttered. They kept firing at me until I was out of sight of the coast.

Straight ahead of me I saw a destroyer. I noted its sloping stern and recognized it as British. Fortunately they for their part recognized me. I circled the destroyer for half an hour trying to gain sufficient height to give me a sporting chance of reaching the French coast. I didn't want to come down beside the destroyer and lose my new plane. Eventually I set off at about 700 feet, but I ran out of altitude fairly soon and was forced to land on the beach.

I phoned Spenser Grey and he sent an engineer out to examine the plane. When the engineer saw it he roared with laughter, somewhat unpleasantly it seemed to me. 'I'll bring the C.O. out to have a look at this,' he said, 'he won't half be mad. It's in ribbons.' He seemed to think that the whole thing was my fault. The fabric was shot to pieces and one shell splinter had gone right through the seat and lodged in the cushion. Fortunately it hadn't reached me. To my chagrin the engineers burned the plane where it stood after taking out the engine.

Next day I had to go to St Pol to get another Breguet. Forty planes were to take part in a night raid on Ostend docks and aerodrome. I took off with my observer but we hadn't got very far when the engine started to cough. I estimated that we must have crossed the German lines. Following my usual habit I was hedge-hopping, so I had no choice but to land. It was quite dark, but to my left I could see the white fringe of surf where the water lapped on to the beach. I knew it was low tide, and I decided that if I aimed to the right of that line of surf I would land on the beach.

My observer was in the front cockpit, and I tapped him with my foot and shouted to him. 'Next time I kick you, fire a Verey light at the ground. It's the only way I'll be able to judge my height.' When the white fringe seemed close underneath me to my left I kicked him and he fired the pistol. The Verey light bounced straight up in front of the machine and I knew I must be very close to the beach. I pulled the stick hard back and next moment we touched the ground and quickly rolled to a stop.

We had to work quietly and quickly to get that engine working and get off again before we were discovered. It was carburettor trouble, and after a tense half-hour we managed to fix it. The combination of saving our machine and getting away from enemy territory made us highly elated, and we had visions of a commendation and perhaps even a decoration. But as we climbed away into the darkness I recognized a long building to my right. It was the Belgian hospital at La Panne; we hadn't crossed the lines after all.

Soon after this, volunteers were called for to form a new wing whose task it would be to bomb southern Germany. With several of the other squadron pilots I put my name down, and we were sent back to Manston for training and to work up our machines. After a false start on converted Short seaplanes we were given Sopwith one-and-a-half-strutters, a faster and better aeroplane in every way. The bomber and the fighter versions were very similar, but we of course had bombers. The fighter could only be identified by the gun-ring mounted behind the pilot.

We were to be based at Luxeuil, a French health resort about fifty miles from the German and Swiss borders, and we flew there in two hops, staging at Paris on the way. Reggie Marix was to lead us, and one of the other squadron pilots was a fellow Australian named Charles Kingsford-Smith. Also with us was Chris Draper, one of our squadron commanders, who set a wonderful example by his superb flying and courage. We called him 'Mad' Draper even then; it was as 'Mad' Draper that he hit the headlines in the fifties when he made his famous unauthorized flight under the Thames bridges, to draw attention to the plight of so many men of his age-group who could not find worthwhile work.

I fitted a gun-ring to my plane immediately behind the cockpit, and painted a large black blob at the point along the fuselage where the gunner sat in the fighter version, to fool the Germans into thinking that my bomber was a fighter. They held the fighter version in great respect, and they seldom attacked a bomber if it was accompanied by a fighter. I also fitted a Lewis gun behind my back, firing backwards, and I filled the trays with tracer bullets to make sure that anyone who got on my tail knew it was firing. We were trained to fly in V formation, and I always took up position at the tail-end of the V. Any fighter coming in to attack would suddenly see tracer bullets coming at him and would think – or so I hoped – that there was a fighter guarding the rear.

Our first task was to raid the Mauser factory at Stuttgart, 150 miles to the north-east. Our route lay across the Vosges mountains south of Strasbourg. Fifty planes were to take part, which convinced us that it must be an important target. We got off in good order, but for many of us the strain of climbing over the mountains with a bomb-load proved too much for our engines. I couldn't get above the mountains myself so I flew between two peaks. As I got abreast of them, guns opened up on me from either side. I had reached the German border. My engine was still faltering and the only sensible thing to do was to turn back. It was just as well I did because within a few minutes my engine petered out altogether and I had to force-land in a field. The plane ran over the top of a small drop in the ground and crashed on the far side. The bombs were still on board and I jumped out and ran – unnecessarily as it turned out, as the bombs were set safe and did not explode. Of the fifty planes which set out, thirty-seven failed to return, but most of the pilots got down safely and were taken prisoner.

A few days later I was one of a small party detached to an aerodrome at Ochey, near Toul, about seventeen miles west of Nancy, with the object of bombing the Saar valley. Things went smoothly enough until we were sent one day to bomb the blast furnaces at Thionville in bad weather. The formation was quickly broken up and soon we were all flying on our own. I kept going for some time and actually reached the Saar valley, but the fog was getting worse and I couldn't find Thionville. I dropped my bombs on an important-looking factory and headed back towards Toul.

The fog was still thick and although I was flying only just above the tree-tops I couldn't get any check on my position. I went on flying south until I was quite sure I must be past Nancy and well behind our own lines. Suddenly I realized that I was flying right over the top of an aerodrome. I immediately cut my engine and landed, then taxied through the fog in the direction in which I thought I had seen a hangar. As I approached it I passed two parked aircraft. On the rudder of each, quite unmistakably, was the emblem of the Iron Cross.

I turned my machine round as quickly as I could and took off in the opposite direction. I was completely lost. All I could do was continue to fly south, and this I did until I ran out of petrol and came down in a field. I had landed near Epinal, fifty miles south of base. I phoned for some petrol and flew back to Ochey. All the other pilots had also force-landed away from base.

I always personally supervised the maintenance work on my plane, and one day in the middle of the very cold winter of 1916 I was tuning up my engine, dressed in dirty blue overalls, when we got an enemy approach warning. There were several one-and-a-half-strutter fighters based at Ochey, and I took off with them and we searched the sky for an hour. We saw nothing and returned to the aerodrome. When we collected afterwards in the Mess everyone seemed to be frozen stiff. Everyone, that is, except me. One of the other pilots remarked on this.

'Cotton,' he said, 'you don't seem to be cold at all. Why's that?'

'That's funny,' I said, 'I'm quite warm. And I didn't even have time to put my flying kit on! I was simply wearing my dirty overalls.'

I thought a lot about this, and I went to my room to puzzle it out. On examining my overalls I found they were thick with oil and grease, and I decided that they must have acted as an airtight bag and kept the body heat in. At this time, pilots in their open cockpits were suffering severely from the cold, and it seemed that I had a ready-made idea for a flying suit. Largely because I hated the thought of anyone else flying my plane, I hadn't taken leave since I went to France, but now I asked for leave and went to London, where I got Robinson and Cleaver to make up a flying suit to my design. The suit had a warm lining of thin fur, then a layer of airproof silk, then an outside layer of light Burberry material, the whole being made in one piece just like a set of overalls. The neck and cuffs had fur pieces inside to prevent the warm air from escaping. I had deep pockets fitted just below either knee so that pilots could reach down into them easily when sitting in the cockpit. I asked Robinson and Cleaver to register my design, and for a name I took the first three letters of my Christian and surnames – 'Sidcot'.

After twenty-one days' leave I returned to Ochey with several of the new flying suits, and I was able to report shortly afterwards to Robinson and Cleaver that the requirement had been fully met. I was the envy of the other pilots and several of them ordered their own suits from Robinson and Cleaver, who then tried to interest the R.F.C. and R.N.A.S. in them officially. After searching tests the Sidcot suit later came into general use. It was the first flying suit to fly the Atlantic – Alcock and Brown wore them – and hardly a man who flew in the Royal Air Force in the Second World War didn't wear one at some time. Baron Richthofen, of the famous Richthofen Squadron, was wearing one when he was shot down in the First World War.

My father had drilled it into his family that none of us should ever try to make money out of our country's need in war, so I never made a penny out of the Sidcot flying suit, nor did I make any kind of claim after the war.

When I got back to France I found that No. 8 (naval) fighter squadron was being formed and I volunteered for it. We were given the new Sopwith Pup, a magnificent little fighter, easy to fly and wonderfully manoeuvrable. We started training and practising at Couderquerque – the same airfield near Dunkirk where I had been stationed with the Breguet squadron – but we were continually harassed by the attentions of a German Taube bomber which came over to bomb us twice daily at dusk and dawn. I got tired of this, and just before dawn and just before dusk I used to take off to intercept him. For some days he avoided me, but one morning I was patrolling at 18,000 feet when I spotted him about 8,000 feet below. I pulled the nose of my Pup right up and flicked over into a dive. Then I passed out.

I came to at 3,000 feet, spinning rapidly, and with blood pouring from my nose and ears. My first thought was that the Hun had got me, and I looked round expecting to see him on my tail. But he had disappeared. I soon felt all right apart from a pain in my ear. When I landed I was told that I had spun down past the Taube and that it had made off.

'You're to go on extended leave,' the doctor told me after he had examined me. 'You've cracked an ear-drum.' So, somewhat crestfallen, I came back to England.

I was soon fully fit again, but my next posting was to Hendon, where I spent several months as second-in-command. One of my tasks was to help in the preparations for a secret long-distance flight by a giant Handley Page 0/400 bomber. The plane was to carry over six tons of luggage, tools and spares, and the chief pilot was to be Flight-Lieutenant K. S. Savory. I persuaded the R.N.A.S. to fit Savory and his crew with Sidcot flying suits to give them a thorough test.

By the end of May–it was 1917–the plane was ready to go, and when we opened the sealed orders we discovered that Mudros, on the Greek island of Lemnos in the Aegean, was the destination. The 0/400, only the second of its kind to be built, had been earmarked for the task of the surprise bombing of Constantinople and of two German warships, the *Goeben* and the *Breslau*, which were lurking in the Bosphorus, forcing us to hold a fleet in readiness in case they broke out. Constantinople was far outside the range of any known bomber in that area, so the flight of the 0/400 had to be kept secret if surprise was to be achieved.

Just as the plane was being got ready for take-off, one of the petrol tanks was found to be leaking. It was essential to get the plane away on schedule, but a spare fuel tank had simply not been thought of. I went with a small party to the Handley Page factory at Cricklewood, but it was a Saturday and the whole place was locked and barred. So I put the guard under protective custody and broke into the factory and took a fuel tank. When the deed was done we released the guard. The plane then got away on schedule. I was upbraided by Frederick Handley Page himself for my offence of breaking and entering, but he saw the sense of it when I produced a special document which ensured that he got paid.

Savory and his crew set up a record in their flight to Mudros, covering the distance in fifty-five flying hours spread over ten days. Their bombing of the German warships and of the Turkish capital was a brilliant success, which was followed up later in the same machine by Jack Alcock. No doubt Alcock first encountered the Sidcot during Savory's visit. When Savory got back–to be awarded the D.S.O.–he reported that the Sidcot suit was too hot!

Inspired perhaps by Savory's expedition, I put up a plan to the Admiralty to bomb Berlin. I was sent for by Commodore Godfrey Paine, head of operations in the R.N.A.S., and interviewed by him in the presence of the Master of Sempill, his chief of staff. I proposed to use D.H. 4 planes fitted with Napier R.A.F. engines, as the Rolls-Royce engine normally fitted in the D.H. 4 used too much fuel for such a long flight. My idea was to bomb Berlin and then land in Russia. My proposal was accepted in principle by Commodore Paine and I was promised all the facilities I wanted.

The first thing was to get a couple of the new engines tuned up and thoroughly tested by Napier's before fitting them to the aircraft. There were a number of teething troubles, and I was relieved of my duties at Hendon so that I could spend most of my time at Napier's. I was given two D.H. 4s for the job. Unfortunately the cooling system gave us a great deal of trouble, the water in the radiator continually boiling away, and we couldn't attempt any long-distance flights until this fault was cleared. The Admiralty then lowered their sights and decided that the planes should be used for photographing Wilhelmshaven. The plan was that we should move to Yarmouth and carry out anti-Zeppelin patrols until the troubles in the cooling system were overcome.

When we got to Yarmouth I could see at once that we were going to be unpopular. The facilities we had been promised were not forthcoming and the commanding officer made it clear that he did not approve of 'special units'. Sempill arranged for me to take over a small flying station at Bacton, thirty miles to the north-west, and I staffed this station with picked engineers. Sempill found another pilot for me named Fane and the unit was complete.

The water in the cooling systems continued to boil away, and in desperation I fitted an extra tank under the seat of my plane carrying another ten gallons of water. I fitted a gauge to the radiator, and when the water level began to get low I topped it up from the extra tank by means of a hand pump. In this way I made several long practice flights covering a greater distance than the return flight to Wilhelmshaven.

Once again the Admiralty changed their minds, deciding this time that the planes were to be used for long-range anti-Zeppelin patrols. We fitted pilot-operated twin Lewis guns firing upwards from the centre section of the plane, the idea being to manoeuvre into position underneath the Zeppelin and fire tracer and incendiary bullets into the gas-filled cells. The guns in both planes were working well when I suddenly had an order from the Admiralty that Fane was to take off in his plane on a patrol to Terschelling, in the Frisian Islands. Fane's plane hadn't been modified with the extra water tank, so I signalled the Admiralty to this effect and added that I proposed to do the patrol myself in my own plane. Back came a peremptory signal telling me to obey the original order.

I went straight to London and saw Commodore Paine. He was extremely angry with me. 'When senior naval officers give orders,' he said, 'they are to be carried out.'

'My plane is capable of doing the flight,' I said. 'Fane's isn't. With your approval I propose to go in my plane, but I'm perfectly willing for Fane to take it if that's what you want.'

'Are you refusing orders?'

'What I'm doing is refusing to accept an order that Fane's plane is to go. I'm the man you put in charge, and I estimate that if Fane's plane goes it will come down about half-way between Terschelling and Bacton on the return trip. I see no point in throwing away a plane, and probably a crew as well, when we've got one perfectly capable of doing the job.' But all my arguments only made Paine angrier still, and when he insisted that Fane's plane must go I felt I had no alternative but to offer my resignation from the R.N.A.S. 'You'd better stay in London for a few days,' said Paine, 'and then come and see me again.'

I went back to my hotel and wrote a report amplifying what I had said, describing the difficulties we'd had with the cooling systems and confirming that our range tests had proved that my plane could make the trip but that Fane's in its present state could not. I made the report factual and impersonal and said nothing about resigning my commission. But the next thing I heard was that Paine had appointed another officer to take over my unit. His name was Gilligan–A. H. H. Gilligan, the well-known cricketer and brother of a later England captain–and his orders were unchanged. Gilligan was reluctant to send Fane in a machine he knew was unlikely to get back and without further reference to the Admiralty he took it himself. He reached Terschelling Island and sighted a Zeppelin, but as soon as he climbed to attack it his engine overheated and he had to break off. Half-way back to Yarmouth his engine failed completely and he came down in the sea. He was missing for three days, but was eventually picked up in an exhausted state by a cruiser. A flying-boat which attempted to rescue him was also lost, although this crew, too, was saved.

I heard all this from Sempill, and I went back to see Paine. 'Couldn't we let bygones by bygones, sir?' I asked. 'What about putting me back on the job, so that I can do it properly?' But he shook his head. 'You disobeyed orders at Bacton,' he said, 'and I'm not sending you back there.' I told him that if that was the way the Admiralty was going to run the war I would certainly resign my commission. 'I've got a job for you, Cotton,' he said. 'I want you to go to Mudros, where you'll get another chance.' This was an unfortunate choice of words, as I felt I had been entirely vindicated by what had happened, and I was furious at being offered 'another chance'. I was ready to meet Paine half-way, and I would have gone to Mudros but for this taunt. Now my mind was made up. 'No, sir,' I said. 'You have my resignation here and now. I shall go back home and join the Australian Air Service. We've lost a perfectly good machine, plus a flying-boat, whereas if my advice had been taken we'd have bagged the Zeppelin and we'd still have our aeroplanes. You were wrong and I was right and it's no thanks to you that Gilligan isn't dead.' I knew I was finished with the Royal Naval Air Service, bitter as this realization was for me, and I saluted, turned on my heel, and left.

Sempill came to see me and tried to persuade me not to resign. He told me he had argued my case with Paine and had even volunteered to join my unit and serve under my command, but Godfrey Paine was not a man who could admit that he had been wrong. I appreciated Sempill's gesture, but I told him that I could not continue in a Service where men at the top brought disaster by refusing to accept the advice of those they put in command.

This great disappointment and upset in my Service career came on top of an even bigger personal blow. Olive Mort and I had corresponded regularly when I first came to England, but then Olive wrote to say that she had made a mistake about her feelings for me and that she would not be writing any more. I suspected that her mother, who I felt had never been over-keen on our friendship because Olive was so young, had persuaded her to write the letter. I wrote back to her many times, but I never got another letter from her. I discovered after my return to Australia that my letters had never reached her.

While I was at Hendon I had gone to see a play at the Golders Green Empire called *The Enemy Within*, and there I was introduced to an attractive Scottish girl who was playing a leading part. She reminded me a good deal of Olive. A young Englishman named David Plaistowe, who was stationed with me at Hendon and with whom I had done a lot of flying, was with me, and we were invited out to supper. From that time on I saw this girl fairly frequently, and our friendship ripened rapidly. I had never had anything to do with women, I was rather out of my depth, the situation with Olive Mort looked hopeless and the hurt was still fresh, and the outcome was that we got married and left for Australia together. We travelled via America. I had introduced her to some of my father's relations in London, and I'm afraid they may have given her rather extravagant ideas about my father's land holdings in Australia. Anyway, I ran short of money on the way across America and had to cable home for more, and I remember telling her that we had spent rather a lot of money and would have to go easy. She said she had understood that I had plenty of money – an innocent remark, no doubt, but it put rather a damper on things.

We sailed from Vancouver to Sydney, where I was met by my family, and we went straight on to Tasmania, where my father had a summer home. The Australian Flying Corps had recently been formed, and I wrote to them to say that I had resigned from the R.N.A.S. and would like to volunteer. Several weeks later I got a letter to say that they had now contacted London but regretted that they could not accept me. My father, who knew a good many influential people in Melbourne, made a personal inquiry on my behalf and was told that the Admiralty had said I had given trouble in England and that I was of a difficult temperament and unsuitable for employment in a uniformed service. The Australian air authorities, much more dependent in those days on the home country, felt they could not ignore such a warning.

I had assumed that there would be no difficulty in getting into the Australian forces, and I was extremely upset. I felt that my record in the R.N.A.S. had certainly not been a bad one. Had I thought when I was in England that I might have this difficulty I suppose I should never have resigned. I was still very keen to do my part in the war. But I was beginning to see how the 'machine' worked. Authority does not like its incompetence to be shown up, and it can hit back most vindictively. But I just had to resign myself to the situation and make the best of it.

4

The 1920 Aerial Derby

THE summer home which my father had bought in Tasmania consisted of several hundred acres, on which he had planted a very fine apple orchard and erected an apple-drying factory. He asked me to operate the factory, and having nothing else in mind and still feeling frustrated at being out of the war I agreed. I ran the factory for a full season, and in addition to drying the apples I got a contract from the manufacturers of I X L jams for an unlimited quantity of dried vegetables. I had asked for a contract for 300 tons, but they scoffed at this and said I could not possibly dry that many in my factory. I thought I knew better and I kept pressing them, and eventually they gave me a contract for as much as I could deliver. I went across to Sydney and bought some of the latest automatic American machinery, and at the end of the season I had delivered nearly 1,000 tons.

Up to the time I took over, the peelings and cores had been fed to the pigs, but I found an old recipe for apple jelly which used all the skins and cores. The jelly came out a beautiful pink colour, absolutely clear, and I developed a market for it throughout Australia. I also experimented in making soup from the dried vegetables. I powdered them down and put them in packets. The powder needed only a few minutes boiling to make an excellent soup. I sent some to the English market, and I got requests for a lot more the following season.

This was the summer of 1918, and inevitably there were times when I had unhappy thoughts. But I cannot say that I did not enjoy that summer. However, I couldn't see any real future in the factory. There was a limit to the distance the fruit and vegetables could be brought economically, and I couldn't see how a profit of more than about £5,000 a year could be made. I had big ideas and this wasn't enough for me.

When the war finished I told my father that if he would put up a plant in Victoria, where vegetables and fruit would not have to travel so far to the factory, I would stay in the business and try to make a big thing of it. He countered by offering me the Tasmanian home to

live in, the factory, his yacht and a new car if I would stay where I was.
But I didn't have the interest in it and I declined. My mind was set
on machinery and land development.

I had been seeing a lot of an old school friend named Geoffrey
Chapman. Financed by my father, Geoffrey had bought a large
property in Tasmania and then cut it up and sold it to small farmers
on the never-never. His method was to sign contracts with the farmers
one by one and then sell the contracts *en bloc* to one of the big land
companies for cash at a discount. In this way he had made nearly a
quarter of a million pounds in three years. Geoffrey told me he was
moving his business to Melbourne and planned to tackle some of the
big properties in Victoria and New South Wales. He was keen for me
to join him in partnership, first because he said the Cotton name would
help a lot, and secondly because he thought it would speed up the
transactions and save precious time if he could get someone to fly
prospective buyers to inspect the properties. I liked the sound of it
and we drew up a contract.

At this time there was a conflict of principle between the Australian
Government and the big landowners. The Government's policy was to
give everyone a chance to own land, and this meant the compulsory
breaking-up of a percentage of the larger properties, to which the big
landowners naturally objected. Geoffrey Chapman's methods, as it
happened, fulfilled the Government's policy painlessly. Our first venture was to buy a big property in Victoria, and within a month we had
sold it all to small farmers. The contracts were then sold to a land
development company at 75 per cent of their face value, showing a
handsome profit. Everyone was happy, and there was only one snag.
When my father heard about it he was most irate.

'All my life,' he said, 'I've taken up new country and developed it
into something big. I won't have the Cotton name connected with the
breaking-up of properties.' In vain did I point out that we were doing
what the Government was trying to do and at the same time making
it unnecessary for them to expropriate the big estates; we were doing
something worthwhile and businesslike and helping in the development of Australia. He demanded that I cancel my agreement, and
when I refused he went to Geoffrey. As my father had started him up
in business, Geoffrey could hardly refuse him, and he came to me in
great distress to say that he would have to cancel our contract.

I fought my father as hard as I could on this, using every possible
argument, and I finally threatened to leave Australia. I was very fond

of my home and my family and I certainly didn't want to go, but neither was I bluffing. My mother suggested that I go away for a while to give my father time to change his mind, and I did this, but when at length I went back to Hidden Vale it was a sad visit; my father hardly spoke to me. I had several long talks with my mother, who said it was clear that with my independent temperament I would always clash with my father and that much as she regretted the separation it would be better for me to carve out my future elsewhere. When my father realized that I was just as adamant as he was, he drove me back to the railway station. On that journey he didn't speak to me, nor did he say good-bye. Yet I knew that his action in driving me to the station was as near as his obdurate nature could get to a conciliatory gesture. In our mutual obstinacy we understood each other. I was after all his eldest son.

Shortly afterwards my wife and I sailed for England. I was leaving everything that I loved and wanted, I was still seeking some way of changing my father's mind, and I wrote to him during the voyage. After setting out my case yet again, I reminded him how essential it was to complete the inspection and sale of the properties quickly, because of the expense of holding a property once it was bought, and of the role that had been planned for me in flying prospective buyers out to the properties. While I was confident of my own flying ability I knew that Geoffrey's brother, who would be taking my place, was quite inexperienced, and I warned my father that if there was an accident the blame would be partly his. I wrote this in a last attempt to persuade. Perhaps there was something intuitive in it, too–I did genuinely fear for Geoffrey. My father never answered my letter, but some months later there was a terrible vindication of what I had written. Geoffrey, flying with his brother, lost his life.

When we reached England I found that my father had instructed the Bank of New South Wales to put a regular credit through to my account of £1,000 a year. It was a generous gesture, but I did not feel that I could accept it. It was just this sort of insistence on my filial dependence that I had left Australia to escape. Still, I had to have some money, and I decided to go and see Napier's. I had got to know them pretty well when I was working on their engines in 1917 and I thought I might be able to persuade them to open an aviation department to exploit and publicize their engines. They accepted my proposal and put me in charge of the department at £1,000 a year. With the un-graciousness of youth I cabled my father to say that I had got myself a job and did not want his money.

Big sums were being offered at this time for trans-oceanic and trans-continental flights and I was keen to attempt a flight to Australia. Boulton and Paul offered to build me a plane and Napier's agreed to provide the engines. But then two young pilots who were about to set out for Australia were killed in an aircraft that was powered by Napier engines, and the chairman, Mr H. T. Vane, was so upset that he de-cided to close down the aviation department. He didn't mind making and selling engines, but he drew the line at sponsoring and encouraging pioneer flights.

I had lost my chance of the Australia flight for the moment, and also my job, and I went home to break the news to my wife. I found a note from her to say that she had been offered a stage engagement in America by Basil Dean and had left at short notice for New York. I was left with our twelve-months-old son. I got in touch with my wife's parents and they looked after the boy for me while I tried to work things out. Later I allowed him to join his mother in America as I believed that young children needed most of all a mother's care.

I was still determined to fly to Australia, and I went to see Sir Sefton Brancker and asked him if his firm, the Aircraft Manufacturing Com-pany, would let me have the D.H. 14A which they had built for an attempt at flying the Atlantic. Alcock and Brown had beaten them to it and the plane, which had a single Napier Lion engine, lay idle. Brancker, whom I knew from the war years, agreed. I was at Hounslow getting ready for the flight when news came through that Keith and Ross Smith had reached Darwin. So the Australia flight was dead too.

Soon afterwards Brancker sent for me and told me that the route from London to Cape Town had been declared open and his firm wanted one of their aircraft to attempt the flight. One of the conditions was that the D.H. 14A would be mine if I succeeded. Napier's lent me an engineer named Townsend, and after various tests we took off from Hendon in January 1920 for Cape Town.

Things immediately began to go wrong. We hadn't been airborne more than a few minutes when the oil pressure valve blew out and we force-landed at the Handley Page aerodrome at Cricklewood, covered in oil. We put this right and made another start, and this time we got as far as Paris, where we were forced down with more engine trouble. Napier's sent one of their chief engineers over, the trouble was put

right, and on we went to Rome. Next day when I was pulling the propeller over to start the engine it felt loose, and when I pushed it backwards and forwards it moved nearly an inch at the tip of the blades.
We removed the propeller, pulled down the reduction gear and found
that the roller race behind the propeller had been starved of oil and
was badly worn. We were all that day and most of the next putting
it right, and it was after lunch on the second day before we were
ready to take off. I decided on a short hop to Catania, in Sicily–about
325 miles. There were no proper lighting facilities on Catania aerodrome and we were warned not to try to land there after dark because
of a cluster of high wireless masts on one side of the airfield, but I
thought we would just about get there before dark. If we didn't look
like making it, there was a reserve landing strip, we were told, at San
Paola, in the Gulf of St Euphemia, near the toe of Italy, which we
would certainly reach in daylight.

Soon after take-off we ran into a strong headwind, and after checking
progress as we passed Naples it became obvious that we would never
reach Catania before dark. We made for the reported position of the
San Paola airstrip but there was no sign of it and it was clear that we
had been given the wrong position. The only alternative was to land
on the beach. It looked a fairly hard surface and we landed gently
enough, but the sand was soft, a tyre burst, and the plane turned over
on its back.

We were unhurt, but I was very upset at our failure. I should never
have started off for Catania so late in the afternoon. But when I found
that no one succeeded in finishing the African flight except two South
Africans who were given a new plane by their government every time
they crashed, I didn't feel so badly about it. We got the plane back in
a packing-case, Brancker took the disappointment well, and he sold
me the wreck for £500 and then repaired it for me for nothing.

While the plane was being repaired I met up again with David Plaistowe, who had read about my crash in Italy and tracked me down. He
was sitting in my flat reading a copy of the *Aeroplane* when something
attracted his notice. 'Listen to this,' he said, 'here's a strange advert.'
And he read out the following advertisement: PILOT WANTED –
PLENTY OF RISK, GOOD PAY. I read it through several times, trying
to imagine what sort of job might be on offer. I had entered my plane
in the 1920 Aerial Derby, and after that I was planning to take it to

Australia to open up an air route in the Northern Territory, but this advertisement intrigued me. I wrote to the box number with details of my experience and asked what the proposition was, and I received a reply from a Major Clayton-Kennedy inviting me to meet him at his club.

Clayton-Kennedy, small, neat, well-dressed, quick-witted and a fast talker, struck me straight away as being a first-class salesman. He certainly told a fascinating story to me. I learned that he had landed a substantial contract to organize a seal-spotting service in Newfoundland. The seals were to be located by air. The Newfoundland Government, it seemed, had been given two airships by the British Government after the war, and Clayton-Kennedy had contracted to operate them. To back them up he had also bought a small aeroplane.

Every year at the beginning of March, so Clayton-Kennedy told me, thousands of seals appeared on the ice-floes off the north shores of Newfoundland to give birth to and tend their young. The areas were broadly known, but the precise positions of the largest concentrations varied each year, according to how wind and current affected the ice-floes. The sealing ships steamed out through the ice-floes, but they had nothing to guide them to the seals. The transatlantic flight attempts of 1919 had impressed the Newfoundland merchants, who had had a close-up view of the planes, and they were ready to be persuaded that the element of chance that attended every seal hunt could be removed by the use of airship or plane to spot the herds and signal to the ships.

Clayton-Kennedy warned me of the difficulties of operating in the sub-zero temperatures of Newfoundland, beset by winter gales and other weather hazards. Airship and plane (it was a D.H. 9) would have to fly several hundred miles out over the ice, and the people he had consulted so far all felt that to operate any sort of air service in these conditions would be impossible. What, he asked, was my opinion? I said I would think about it.

I had no experience of really cold conditions, but I discussed the project with my friends in aviation and all agreed that it was a mad venture, likely to end in disaster. I couldn't imagine, they said, what I would be up against in the Newfoundland climate. One word kept recurring again and again – 'impossible'. I think it was the constant repetition of that word that finally decided me, and I told Clayton-Kennedy that I would go. I signed an agreement with him, and I further undertook to supply my own aeroplane, as I didn't think the

1(a). The Cotton family in 1913. From left to right (*sitting*) my father, my brother Douglas, and my mother; and (*standing*) Victor, Vera, and myself

1(b). The homestead at Hidden Vale

1(c). The car I built at Dalkeith sheep station, Cassilis, in 1914

2(a). The Maurice Farman Longhorn trainer on which I qualified as a pilot

2(b). The B.E. 2c on which I completed my training

2(c). My Sopwith 1½-strutter, showing rearward-firing gun

2(d). My D.H.4 the camouflage my own idea

D.H. 9 would be suitable for long-range work over the sea. I intended taking my D.H. 14A.

We were not due to leave for Newfoundland, though, until late in the year, and meanwhile there was the Aerial Derby. The repairs to my plane were completed only the day before the race, but early next morning I gave it a thorough air-test, everything was in order and I landed at Hendon and lined up for the start. This time I took the precaution of insuring my machine.

There was a big crowd at Hendon, almost as huge as that for the first Hendon Air Pageant a fortnight earlier, and the space in front of the hangars was lined with bookmakers. Betting on the result was heavy. There were fourteen starters, most of them small racing machines capable of more than 150 miles an hour, and there were two first prizes, one for the winner of the speed section and the other for the handicap. The D.H. 14A had been handicapped to average 114 miles per hour and to complete the 200-mile course in 1 hour 48 minutes. Apart from two Baby Avros, one piloted by Bert Hinkler and the other by Captain H. A. Hamersley, it was the slowest machine in the race. The Baby Avros were to start an hour before me and the other machines would start at intervals varying from twelve to forty minutes after me. Among these were three Sopwith Snipes, two Martinsydes, the Avro Schneider, converted from the seaplane that had raced in the Schneider contest of the previous year, and a Sopwith A.B.C. piloted by Harry Hawker. If we all ran true to form and the handicappers achieved perfection, we would all cross the finishing line together.

'The Airco 14A,' said *Flight*, 'entered and flown by F. S. Cotton, is, perhaps, the most interesting machine in the field, inasmuch as it is by no means a racer but a "cruiser", carrying a pilot and three passengers and fuel for 18 hours, and having a range of 1,600 miles.' I was not, of course, carrying three passengers for this race, nor any great quantity of fuel, but I did have with me an observer named Harwood, an employee of Brancker's, who had volunteered to come with me, the only passenger in the race. I felt it would be useful to have someone to check on the navigation. And in other respects I felt I had given myself a good chance to outwit the handicappers. By various perfectly legitimate methods, which I had made a study of and which I was to employ again with great success in the Second World War – such as using a dope that gave the external fabric a hard, shiny finish instead of the normal rough surface, and streamlining all projections with light wood or fabric – I had succeeded in increasing

c

my actual cruising speed to 130 miles per hour. On paper this gave me a winning margin.

The course had been plotted round London to give the maximum number of people a chance to see something of the race. We began by flying south-west from Hendon to Brooklands, where we turned east-south-east for Epsom, looking out for the grandstand on the racecourse, which was our next turning point. From there we flew north-east via Croydon, Bromley and Dartford to our next landmark, a large cement works at West Thurrock, then turned north-west through Epping to our final turning point at Hertford, and thence back to Hendon. The distance was exactly 100 miles and we were to fly the circuit twice.

I got off right on time at 3.15 and climbed quickly to 800 feet. All the competitors were flying fairly low. Visibility was good, I had no difficulty in finding the turning points, the D.H. 14A was going well and I knew that nothing had caught up with me. I had covered about 185 miles and was approaching the last turning point, a meadow with a white circle painted in the middle of it just north of Hertford, when I saw the two Baby Avros dead ahead. I was passing Bert Hinkler and was about to take the lead from Hamersley fourteen miles from home when my engine suddenly burst into flames.

I managed to put the fire out by cutting off the petrol and continuing on full throttle until the petrol in the carburettor was exhausted, but I was flying at only about 800 feet and I had to look quickly for a place to land. My chance of winning the 1920 Aerial Derby had gone. I picked out a long narrow strip of field to my right, pulled the plane completely round in a sharp left-hand turn, floated in over a high railway embankment and then side-slipped to lose height. But I lost too much speed and the plane started to spin. I pushed the nose down to regain flying speed until I almost hit the ground, then pulled back on the stick. I was now flying at right angles to the field and a row of trees lay right across my path.

I had no power so I couldn't pull up again. There was nothing for it but to aim to pass between two of the trees, hoping to do no more than pull off the wings as I went through, thus reducing the shock in the fuselage. I aimed for the centre point between two trees that looked about twenty feet apart. My wing-span was fifty-five feet. I lined the plane up nicely and waited for the crash.

I heard the swish of branches brushing against the wings, but to my astonishment I passed safely between the two tree-trunks and across a main road, where I flew straight into some telegraph wires, carrying them with me. Ahead of me was a field of barley into which I had to land. The landing itself was all right but the long barley acted as a brake and the plane turned over on its back.

I was unhurt but Harwood hadn't strapped himself in and he was thrown out. He lay on the ground beside the plane. He said he was all right but complained of being hungry and asked for something to eat. By an extraordinary coincidence a doctor had told me only a few days earlier that if anyone asked for food after an accident the likelihood was that his back was broken and he should not be moved on any account. I refused to let anyone touch him until the doctor came and this probably saved his life as he had indeed broken his back. After a spell in hospital his injuries mended and apart from a plate in his back he was as good as ever.

When the ambulance had taken him away I measured the distance between the trunks of the two trees. They were sixty feet apart—a clearance of thirty inches either side. Those few inches probably saved our lives.

I was bitterly disappointed at having failed with the race almost won, but I did have one piece of luck. The plane was so badly damaged that the insurance company called it a write-off and paid up. From being virtually penniless I thus acquired the sum of £5,000.

5

Winter in Newfoundland

I WAS now in something of a quandary. I had contracted to take my plane to Newfoundland with Clayton-Kennedy but I had written it off. I saw an announcement about a Westland plane that had just won a Government competition for the best enclosed-cabin passenger plane, so I contacted Westlands and visited them at Yeovil. I tested the plane and found it suitable. The pilot's head still stuck out of the top of the plane but all the passenger seats were enclosed. The engine was a Napier Lion, which pleased me because I had managed to salvage the engine from the D.H. 14A. I was thus able to buy the Westland without an engine and save money.

On 5th November 1920 I left Liverpool for Newfoundland on the S.S. *Digby*, full of the joy of adventure. With me I had my old friend David Plaistowe as second pilot and two rigger/mechanics named Wallace and Cleaver. Our aircraft and equipment, together with the airships, their crews and ground engineers, had gone ahead on another ship. Nine days later we were met at St John's by a Captain Sydney Bennett, a son of the Colonial Secretary to the Newfoundland Government, and he installed us in a local hotel and advised us on weather conditions and flying equipment. 'There's only one flying suit that's any good out here,' he told us, 'and that's the Sidcot.' I had a quiet chuckle over this. I got on well with Syd Bennett, and he later joined us as pilot and general factotum.

There were five different sealing companies supporting Clayton-Kennedy's venture, and after several meetings with the principal ones, Job Brothers, Bowring Brothers and Bairds, we left for a small village called Botwood, some 180 miles north-west of St John's. Botwood was the port used by the Northcliffe Paper Mills at Grand Falls, twenty-three miles inland, and it was sheltered and easy of access, suitable for both summer and winter operations. In the summer we could use the water for seaplane work and in winter when the water froze we could use the ice to operate on skis.

There were soon rumours, however, that all was not well at St

John's, and I received a telegram asking me to go back there. Clayton-Kennedy's plans were probably too extravagant; anyway he was in financial difficulties. His contract provided for a single payment from the sealing companies of 50,000 dollars at the start of the season, and on the strength of this he had secured a Bank overdraft. But the overdraft was mounting, the Bank were getting concerned, and all Clayton-Kennedy's efforts to get a bigger payment out of the sealing companies failed. Negotiations continued for the whole of December and most of January, while preparations at Botwood stood still.

The whole operation turned very much on the question of confidence, since the sealing companies, like ourselves, had been told again and again that they were on to a madcap scheme. Eventually the companies revoked the contract, and the Bank then gave Clayton-Kennedy three days to clear his overdraft. Since he had borrowed the money against the contract he hadn't a hope of repaying it.

All our personal contracts foundered if Clayton-Kennedy went under; and in any case I was most reluctant to see the expedition fail before it had had a chance to prove itself. I therefore offered to take over the contract – if the sealers would give it to me – and pay off the overdraft provided all the existing equipment was turned over to me. Clayton-Kennedy accepted, and the Bank, who had no hope of getting any of their money back except by selling off the equipment, which nobody else wanted, agreed, though the sealers took the opportunity to knock down the sum payable under the contract from 50,000 to 40,000 dollars. As Clayton-Kennedy's overdraft was already 26,000 there wasn't much left, but I was prepared to lose money in the hope that we'd make a success of it and that the sealing companies would take up the option they had for the following year.

As soon as I got control I dispensed with the airship party, though I kept on a radio operator named Heath; and the following year Williams, the airship pilot, returned to work with me. But for the first season there were only five of us – Plaistowe and myself, Heath, and the two rigger/mechanics. On 20th January, less than six weeks before the seals were due to appear, the sealing companies advanced me the 40,000 dollars and I cleared off the overdraft and bought a piece of land at Botwood on which to erect a hangar. I engaged a St John's firm to build it with the aid of my party.

The ground at Botwood was frozen solid to a depth of eighteen inches and the holes for the main posts of the hangar had to be chipped out with an ice-pick. It took many hours of hard work. Heavy blizzards delayed us still further. They were so bad that our supply line by rail from St John's was cut off. I had ordered a supply of the special petrol-benzole mixture that we needed for the Napier Lion engine in the Westland, but it was snowbound at St John's. Meanwhile, as soon as the hangar was ready, we trundled the Westland from the shed where we had stored it to the hangar, assembled it and got the engine ready for testing. There was still no sign of the petrol.

I decided to try to reach St John's and tackle the problem from there. It meant going by air. I acquired some petrol locally that I hoped would do, and I made several engine tests in which the performance seemed all right. Then I had a path cut through the snow to a clear patch of ice in the bay and prepared to take off. Nobody in Botwood had ever seen an aeroplane and an enormous crowd came out to see the fun.

On this my first flight in Newfoundland, David Plaistowe came with me as passenger with a brief to listen in the cabin for any unwanted noises from the engine. They were not long in coming. I managed the take-off quite well and we had climbed to 500 feet when there was a loud bang and black smoke poured from the engine and filled the cabin. Something was seriously wrong and I did a quick turn and landed straight back on the ice. When we examined the engine we found that one piston had a hole the size of a penny burnt right through it. We had no spare pistons, so that meant cabling to England. There would be a delay of at least a fortnight. The sealing ships were due to sail in three weeks.

While we were waiting for the pistons I had the D.H. 9 erected; this was the aircraft I had taken over from Clayton-Kennedy and it proved to be a very old and well-used aeroplane. It had a range of 300–400 miles, but its single Puma engine was known to be unreliable and I had never felt it would be suitable for seal-spotting. Nevertheless I thought it would be useful for communications and small contracts inland. I fitted it with home-made wooden skis, which after a few modifications worked well on both thin layers of snow and on the solid ice of the bay, and I managed to get a small contract to deliver mail to the islands in Notre Dame Bay. We dropped our first mails by hand without landing, and it gave us something to keep our minds off the trouble with the Westland. Meanwhile the snowploughs cleared the railway and we got the special petrol through. The pistons arrived late in February, just before the sealing ships were due to go out, but they were lighter in weight than the originals which meant that the engine would be un-balanced and would run roughly. We cursed Napier's but it was too

NEWFOUNDLAND

ST. ANTHONY

HAWKES BAY

BONNE BAY

FOGO IS.

DEER LAKE

BOTWOOD

GRAND
FALLS

PORT-AUX-BASQUES

ST.
JOHNS

PLACENTIA BAY

scale: miles   0   50   100

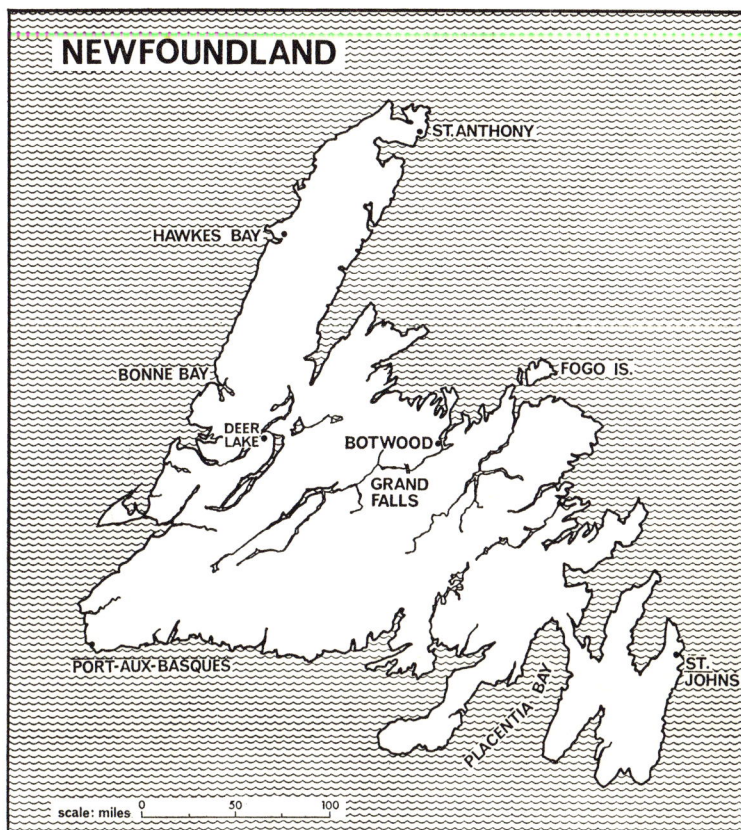

late to do anything about it. The sealing season had started, the ships were on their way to the ice-fields and we simply had to show them what we could do.

I took the Westland out for flying tests but at full throttle the engine started to misfire and wouldn't develop full power, so back it had to go into the hangar while we looked for the trouble. The solution defied our combined efforts for a week, and we worked night and day in conditions of almost unbearable cold. At last we traced the trouble to a tiny crack on the inside of the carburettor intake. I blanked off the water inlet to this carburettor and ran the engine with one carburettor hot and the other cold. It was a desperate measure but time was desperately short. The sealing fleet was already in the ice-fields.

After several local flights I made a trial flight to Fogo Island, an island about sixty miles north-east of Botwood. There would be ice beneath us the whole way in case we had to land. The engine ran rather roughly but all things considered it went pretty well and we landed at Fogo and returned to Botwood without incident. The sealing fleet was reported to be about a hundred miles north-east of Fogo Island and I decided that if the weather was at all suitable we would go out and look for the seals next day.

The weather turned out to be fine and bright, with an off-shore wind of 80 m.p.h. at 8,000 feet. It was 29th March, the sealing fleet would be returning to St John's in another day or so and this was our last chance to prove our worth. I took off early that morning, and behind me in the cabin of the Westland I had David Plaistowe, Captain Kean, a veteran sealing captain lent to me by the sealing companies to advise us and to identify the seals, and Heath for the radio. We had a flight ahead of us of about 150 miles to the reported position of the ships, and having found them we should then have to search for the seals.

We flew up to Fogo, then turned north for the ships. We were about ninety miles out from Fogo and were beginning to look for the ships when I suddenly noticed small pieces of ice flying past the cockpit. I guessed almost at once what had happened: we had cracked a water-jacket. The hot water from the leak was freezing instantly as it came in contact with the air, and this accounted for the splinters of ice. How long the water in the cooling system would last depended on how bad the leak was: it might be half an hour, it might be only a few minutes. Eventually the engine would overheat and seize up.

Should I carry on, try to find the fleet, and land near them on the ice, or should I turn back into the 80-m.p.h. off-shore wind and try to get back to Botwood? The off-shore wind had been blowing for some days and had opened a ten-mile ditch of water between the land and the ice, which suggested that it might be better to go on. Against that, Heath had not yet been able to make contact with the ships and we had only an approximate idea of their position. This for me was the deciding factor and I turned for home. We were still flying at 8,000 feet so I put the nose down and built up to a steady 120 m.p.h. indicated, which gave us a ground speed of 40 m.p.h. This ground speed increased steadily as we lost height – the wind was not so strong lower down. I was enormously relieved when I got within gliding distance of the mainland. We got to Botwood safely, but the engine was nearly dry when we landed.

I was determined to try again if it was at all possible before the sealing fleet started back, otherwise I feared that the companies would simply write us off for next year. There was no internal damage to the engine that I could see, so we sealed the crack in the water-jacket and then, taking only Heath with me this time to work the radio, I took off and set course for the second time. I had flown no more than six miles out over the bay ice, however, when there was a horrible metallic crash in the engine, after which the propeller stopped dead. I was able to glide down and land on the ice without difficulty, but it was obvious that the engine was finished. Plaistowe was watching the progress of the Westland from the hangar, and when he saw me come down with the propeller stopped he flew after me in the D.H. 9, landed beside me and towed me back across the ice to the hangar. When we removed the engine cowling from the Westland we found a sorry sight; a wrist-pin had seized up in one of the pistons, the connecting rod had sheared off and pushed its way through the crankcase, and there was much incidental damage, quite beyond our capacity to repair. It was a depressing end to our first seal-spotting season.

Because of the protracted negotiations with the sealing companies when Clayton-Kennedy withdrew and our own mechanical troubles, we had gone out into the ice-fields far too late, but we had felt bound to make every possible effort. At that stage we had really had no chance, yet we had learned many lessons and had proved, at least to our own satisfaction, that there were no insuperable difficulties to operating aircraft in Newfoundland. We had flown with water-cooled engines under conditions which all the experts had described as impossible, and I was determined to build on this achievement.

I went back to St John's to see the sealing companies, but we had not done enough to convince them and they were evasive about renewing our contract. They did, however, agree to pay the wages owing to my employees, and I believed that I could ultimately win their confidence. Meanwhile if I was to keep my team together I had to have more capital. The engine from the Westland had to go back to Napier's for repair and I decided to go back to England with it.

6

We Find the Seals

WHEN I reached London I went to see my lawyers and told them of my problems and my need for financial backing, and they mentioned a client of theirs named Alan Butler. He was young, a qualified pilot, and had just sold his late father's coal briquette business for over £4½ million. They thought he might help. He was leaving London next morning by train for Devon, but my lawyers gave me a note of introduction to him and the following morning I got on the same train. Before we reached Torquay Butler had promised to join me in the venture and put up what money I needed, up to a total of £100,000. Two days later we returned to London and agreements were drawn up under which Butler got just over 50 per cent of the profits. He then advanced me an initial sum of £8,000.

I could now look around for more suitable machines and I chose the Martinsyde, powered by a Rolls-Royce engine, on which I knew I could rely. It had a four-passenger enclosed cabin, the pilot sitting, as in the Westland, with his head in the open. I bought one Martinsyde and ordered another, and felt much better equipped for the task ahead. I also visited Napier's and they were so upset at the way their engine had let us down that they rebuilt it for me at a special price.

David Plaistowe had joined me in England after completing the caretaker work at Botwood, and finding that his family wanted him back in their business he had to give up the idea of returning to Newfoundland. I was very sorry indeed as he had been a great help, not least in his ability to keep everyone in good spirits under difficult circumstances. I knew he would be hard to replace, but I was lucky in that back in Newfoundland I had been joined by Syd Bennett, who was to become my right-hand man. I was lucky, too, in meeting up while I was in London with an engineer called Stannard who had been in my Bacton flight and who had worked with me on the special engine at Napier's in 1917, and I took him back to Newfoundland with me.

I was anxious that we should be able to operate from St John's as well as from Botwood, St John's being the business centre as well as the seat of government; I felt I needed closer contact with both. So when we got back to Newfoundland we spent the rest of that summer of 1921 building a hangar at the Quidi Vidi Lake at St John's, as well as getting our planes ready for the winter's operations and hunting up what business we could. The attitude of the sealing companies seemed to have hardened, and while they did not turn us down they made all sorts of excuses. Finally they said they would wait and see what we could report in the coming season and discuss a contract with us then. I didn't like this much but I had to accept it. How Clayton-Kennedy ever sold the companies the idea of aerial seal-spotting in the first place was a mystery to me. He must have been some salesman.

Meanwhile we had to get some income from somewhere and I asked the Postmaster-General in St John's for a contract to fly mails. I pointed out that in the winter months we could deliver mails in a matter of hours which occupied dog-teams for weeks. I stressed the prestige that Newfoundland would gain by introducing an air mail service. And having discovered that he was a keen philatelist I tried to interest him in the possibilities of air mail stamps. Eventually we were given one mail route as a test, from Botwood via various islands to Fogo and then back to Botwood.

We made this run on the Tuesday of each week, stopping at three or four places *en route*, the whole flight taking about two and a half hours. We acted as a travelling post office, collecting letters at each stop, franking and sorting them, and delivering them where necessary. We soon had friends in all the villages where we dropped and picked up mail. Our success with this small contract did not seem to impress the sealers, but in December we got a second contract to fly mail from St John's to Halifax, Nova Scotia, for which we were to be paid a thousand dollars. We were preparing the Martinsyde for this job when we had an accident. Water had come through on top of the ice, but the surface of the water had frozen into a thin crust which had all the appearance of permanence. One ski of the Martinsyde went through the top layer, twisting the undercarriage on that side, and I could see it would take a week or more to repair. We decided to use the D.H. 9, which we had been unable to use during the summer because it had no floats. We gave it a quick overhaul and a thorough air-test, and on the morning of 10th December 1921 Syd Bennett and I took off from Botwood on the first air mail run from Newfoundland to Nova Scotia.

We soon ran into bad weather, but we were coming through it well enough and had covered about a hundred miles when suddenly we saw water seeping from the cylinder head of the engine. We landed near Deer Lake in western Newfoundland and found that the water-retaining ring in the top of the cylinder head had perished. We had a new one sent from Botwood next day, but after we'd fitted it we simply couldn't get the engine to start. Bennett and I spent the rest of that day pulling the propeller over, completely exhausting ourselves, and late in the afternoon I was still at it, with Bennett in the pilot's seat. He twirled the exciter magneto handle while I waited in front of the engine to see if it kicked over. When it didn't I reached up and pulled the propeller. We were on the point of giving up when I decided to have one more try. I heard the exciter magneto being turned over, the engine still didn't kick, and I leaned forward once more to catch hold of the propeller blade. As I did so the engine started. I fell into the blade and it threw me to the ground, catching both my elbows as I went down.

I was completely incapacitated and could not move my arms. We were quite near Deer Lake Railway Station and Bennett used the telegraph to get word to the nearest hospital, who sent a doctor up at once by special train. The doctor said I must be taken to the hospital in St John's for treatment and X-ray, and the Government very kindly put the train at my disposal to take me there. I was laid up for several weeks.

Meanwhile Bennett waited at Deer Lake to fly the D.H. 9 back to Botwood while the mail went on by rail and steamer. Once installed in the hospital at St John's I was able to direct affairs to some extent and I sent some mechanics up to Deer Lake to help Bennett. On the way back to Botwood he ran into bad visibility and had to fly low to keep contact. Fifteen miles out of Botwood the engine packed up again and this time it cut out completely. He was forced to make a quick landing on the snow. The surface was soft and rough and the machine was wrecked. Bennett and his mechanic pulled themselves out of a snow-bank uninjured, but it was the end of the D.H. 9. Quotations to cover flying risks in Newfoundland were unobtainable in 1921 and there was no insurance to collect this time.

I took advantage of my enforced rest in hospital to renew negotiations with the sealing companies, but without success, though I did manage to get another Government mail contract. These mail contracts, although small at first, were remunerative.

In spite of the loss of the D.H. 9 I felt that possession of the Martinsyde meant that we were much better equipped than the year before. I was expecting delivery of the second Martinsyde in the New Year, and I had also ordered two small Westland aircraft with Rolls-Royce engines, for which I would have to engage two more pilots. But it was in the fight against sub-zero conditions that I felt I was now especially well prepared. I had designed an engine-cover on the same principle as the Sidcot flying suit, using balloon fabric which I had inherited from the airship equipment, and these covers fitted tightly round the nose of the plane and covered the engine compartment completely. The propeller itself stayed out in the open. I had also bought a number of catalytic lamps, and two of these, placed at the base of the engine under the crankcase, prevented the engine from getting cold. (In fact we always used six for safety as the lamps had a habit of going out.) As a result we never lost an engine from freezing. Our aircraft would stay for days on end in temperatures of from 30 to 50 below zero but when we pulled our covers off the engines would start up immediately. And when we landed anywhere for a short time to collect or deliver mails we fitted the nosebag as soon as we landed and this kept the engine warm for up to two hours without any help from the lamps.

We added alcohol to the water in the aircraft radiators to prevent freezing, but we soon found that the alcohol evaporated before the water got hot. One of the local Newfoundlanders told us to boil the water up in a wooden barrel and then add the alcohol, and to repeat the process three times, when we would find that the alcohol would no longer boil off and the mixture would not freeze. For the life of me I couldn't see why it should work, but we tried it and work it did. From then on all the water for our radiators was treated in this way.

Another danger that worried me was the problem of survival if we made a forced landing in winter, when temperatures could be extreme and winds of gale force. I felt that if the trappers could live in these conditions so could we, and with the help of a trapper named Hart whom I engaged and who worked for me continuously from then on, I equipped each plane with special survival gear, including airproof silk tents and sleeping bags. Hart came with us on most of our longer trips.

I left hospital early in the New Year and returned to Botwood, by which time the Martinsyde had been repaired and the new hangar on the Quidi Vidi Lake at St John's was ready to receive it. I flew back to St John's in the Martinsyde, hoping to create confidence among the sealing companies by doing so. Next day, while I was bargaining with Bert Job of Job Brothers, he mentioned that he wanted to speak to

a Mr Brooks, one of his directors, urgently. It transpired that Brooks
had left an hour or so earlier to ski to Murray's Pond, a well-known
fishing and skiing club about eleven miles to the west. 'Here's your
chance to prove what you can do,' said Bert Job.

I drove out to the Quidi Vidi Lake and took off immediately in the
Martinsyde. We hadn't flown more than three miles when we saw two
figures skiing across a lake. We landed on the lake just ahead of them
and one of them proved to be Brooks. Within an hour I had him back
in his office at St John's. But even this did not seem to convince the
sealers, and in desperation I offered to do the sealing job on the basis
that they pay us a dollar a head for every seal they got over an 80
per cent shipload. For a load of 80 per cent or less they would pay us
nothing. They wouldn't even bite at this offer, and we were left with
the vague promise that they would see what we could do when the
season started.

Early in March the ships went out as usual on the seal-hunt. A few
days later, when they were out in the ice-floes, we flew out to them in
formation in the Martinsyde and the Westland. Alan Butler had now
joined us at Botwood and he flew the Westland with Syd Bennett and
Heath while I flew the Martinsyde with Stannard. I was carrying the
sealing crews' mail and the plan was that I should land on the ice and
deliver it. The Westland would accompany us to Fogo and some distance beyond, then land back at Fogo and wait for us. We duly found
the ships and then made a wide circuit looking for seals, discovering
one fairly large group several miles away from the ships. The Westland
then turned back while I landed on the ice alongside a ship called the
Sagona, delivered the mail and discussed the position of the seals with
the captain. After staying for about an hour I flew back to Fogo and
then on with the Westland to St John's. This was the first time an aircraft had landed beside the seal fishery vessels when they were stuck
out in the ice and the seal captains were so impressed that they radioed
St John's asking for their mail to be flown out every two or three days.
The time seemed ripe to talk to the owners again about a contract, but
the owners were still evasive. Alan Butler offered to charter the whole
sealing fleet and direct them to the seals, but even this offer was refused.

Although the information we were capable of providing was obviously useful I realized that it might not greatly affect a good season;
at such times the owners would be reluctant to pay for it. What we
wanted was a really bad season up to about half-way through, with the

ships searching for the seals in vain. Then the owners might panic and give us a contract.

I decided to bet on something like this happening, keeping our whole party right out of the way for a week or so, and I accepted a contract to fly mails to Labrador which would take us away for several days. While we were at Cartwright, on the southern Labrador coast, we organized a partidge hunt, and we killed two hundred brace. As soon as they died they froze solid, and in that condition we flew them back to St John's. We had been delayed at Cartwright by a blizzard, and at St John's we had been given up for lost, so that half the population turned out on the frozen lake to meet us. As we came in to land we were astonished to see the whole black swarm of people rush from the lake to the shore as though blown there by a mighty wind, and we learned afterwards that the ice had shuddered with a tremendous crack under their weight and they had made a dash for safety.

I sold the partridges at four dollars a brace. They were out of season, and the fact that they had been brought direct from Labrador by air no doubt added to their value. But I got into trouble with the chief of police at St John's. 'Do you realize,' he asked, 'that you're liable to a heavy fine for killing partridge out of season?' I answered that I thought it must be all right as the birds had only just come out of cold storage. This went down well, and I gave him a brace for himself and heard no more about it.

I learnt with some satisfaction that the sealing ships had had very little luck while I was away. There was only about a week of the season left, so I flew out in the Martinsyde with Stannard, found the fleet, which was not very far off Fogo Island, and started to search farther out. About ten miles north-east of the ships I found a big herd of seals.

A quick survey showed that the area between the ships and the seals was jammed with great hummocks and ridges of ice and that there was no possible way through. It seemed to me that the ice was drifting north-west, then north. After a long search I found a loose lead to the north-west through which the ships could round the great mass of ice that confronted them and find their way south-east again to the seals. I flew back to St John's and reported that I had found the main herd of seals.

Even now the shipping companies wouldn't offer me a contract. They wanted me to tell them where the seals were so they could check up and see if I was right. If my information proved accurate they wouldn't make use of it until they had discussed a contract with me.

This clearly wasn't good enough and I told them so, but they still refused to give me a contract.

The information that I had was no use to me unless I could sell it to the sealing companies, so I decided to take them a good deal further into my confidence. I told them how the ice was drifting north-west then north, I described the great mass of heavy ice that lay between the ships and the seals, and I warned them that there was only one way through. 'If your ships try to get through direct to the seals,' I said, 'they'll get jammed in the ice.' I then produced a map and showed them exactly where the seals were. I felt quite safe because I was sure the ships would never find the open lead to the seals without my help. This was the vital piece of information that they must have to succeed, and this was the one piece of information that I withheld.

Unfortunately the cupidity of the shipowners overcame their caution and sense of fair play and they wirelessed their ships immediately, giving them the position of the herd. They may, of course, have intended to pay me later for the information if it proved correct. But the ships steered straight for the spot, or as straight as they could, and as I had anticipated they got jammed in the ice. The shipowners still refused to accept my help to guide the ships through the leads and I still wouldn't tell them without a contract. The result was that the main herd was not found at all that year and the ships and their owners had a bad season. The owners told me afterwards that they had distrusted my information because I told them that the ice had wheeled north-west then north, something which no one could remember happening in the history of sealing. When the ships returned to harbour all their log-books recorded that for the first time in living memory the ice had wheeled north-west then north.

The whole affair was a bitter disappointment to me, but I still obstinately refused to give up hope of working with the sealing industry.

7

Engine Failure over the Ice-floes

B Y this time I had flown over most of Newfoundland and I was impressed by the fact that, while there was a great deal of timber in some areas, other areas on which I knew the papermill firms were counting were very thin. A thorough aerial survey would therefore be of immense value. During the war I had met a pilot named Hemming, nicknamed 'Lemnos', who had had considerable experience in mapping and photography. Tall and thin, but jovial, he had a flair for expressing himself on paper and a wonderful memory. I wrote to Hemming and asked him if he would care to join me, and he came out to Newfoundland to run my aerial survey department.

I went to see the manager of the Northcliffe Papermills at Grand Falls, but I was unable to interest him or anyone else in Newfoundland in my project so I came back to England and saw Lord Northcliffe. He agreed to give me a contract. On the same visit I negotiated two other important contracts–one with Sifton Praed and Co., the mapmakers, to supply aerial photographs of various parts of Newfoundland so that they could correct their maps, and the other with a Welsh coal-mining firm for a large quantity of pit-props. So we were now in the timber business as well.

We made a number of overlapping photographs of the Grand Falls area, joined them together into a mosaic, and then photographed the whole on one plate, thus producing a complete aerial picture of the area. We repeated the process with other important areas, and this for me was the real beginning of my interest in aerial photography. Northcliffe's firm were delighted with our pictures, and so were Sifton Praed's, who told us the existing maps of Newfoundland were clearly inaccurate. Both these contracts paid off a nice royalty, though the contract for the pit-props was the one with the biggest possibilities.

The previous winter, flying mail up the west coast of Newfoundland, I had had an opportunity to study the whole area, which was completely undeveloped and contained some fine stretches of timber that had not been taken up. On several occasions I had dropped mail at

Port Saunders, at the entrance of Hawkes Bay, and I had noted the fine natural outlet for shipping provided by the bay. There was an old whaling factory in the bay and I decided to make this my headquarters, forming a company with Alan Butler which we called the Hawkes Bay Trading Company. I intended to develop Hawkes Bay as a centre for the west coast, to make an aeroplane base there to carry mails and supplies north during the winter, and to use the centre for development of Labrador. This coast was virtually deserted in winter. I soon got a licence on the areas I wanted. I enlisted the help of some timber experts from Canada, and in May 1922 cutting operations began.

Another man who was seeking his fortune on the west coast of Newfoundland was a Professor Henry, who had already made a name for himself in the Baku oilfields, about which he wrote several books. He was drilling for oil, and he had in fact found high-grade oil in small quantities to the south of Hawkes Bay, which he sold to fishermen for use in their motor-boats. In the winter Professor Henry retired to his bungalow in Hawkes Bay and rejoined his wife and youngest daughter. The bungalow had originally been built as a fishing camp, the fishing in and around Hawkes Bay being among the finest in the world. On the East river, where the Henrys' bungalow was situated, we used to catch salmon of ten to fifteen pounds weight at the rate of four or five an hour, each fish taking ten or fifteen minutes to play and bring in. If we wanted a change of diet we went a hundred yards down-river to catch sea trout of between five and eight pounds, and if we wanted larger salmon we went by motor-boat to the Torrent river, a mile and a half across the bay. There were very pretty falls where the river entered the bay, and the salmon we caught there were up to forty-five pounds in weight. They were not quite so numerous as in the East river, but one could rely on catching two or three in a morning's fishing.

The acknowledged expert in all this was the fifteen-year-old Joan Henry. She used to shame us by catching salmon using a long crooked piece of wood for a fishing rod, with flies made from feathers out of her mother's hat. She was a most attractive young girl, with pale blue eyes and long blonde hair down to her waist. She knew a great deal about woodcraft and she had a wonderful way with animals and birds. Wild birds would come and settle round her at her call, and she was quite fearless with dog-teams. An owner of a dog-team would never go in amongst the dogs to stop them fighting, but Joan Henry would go straight in and cuff the dogs and they would stop fighting at once. She was greatly admired by all the dog-team drivers along the coast, most of whom were pretty tough types, and she had her own dog-team which she drove better than any man. The only schooling she got was from her mother, and I thought it a great shame that such an attractive and intelligent girl should not have a better opportunity for education. I asked the family if they would let me arrange for her to go to school in England, and after considering the matter for some time they consented. On my next visit to England I took her with me to an aunt of hers in London and she started shortly afterwards at a school in Bournemouth.

Early in the summer of 1922 I bought a 60-foot twin-engined yacht to use in and around Hawkes Bay in connection with our work. She had a speed of about twenty knots and turned out to be a very good sea-boat, and we called her the *Hawke* after our new headquarters. We had two steamers in the bay loading pit-props before the end of that summer, the *Hawke* was purring around busily, and the bay had changed from its natural state of wild desolation into a hive of industry. We were also carrying out logging operations 100 miles farther south at Bonne Bay, where a third steamer was loading.

Our contract with the Welsh coal-mining firm called for payment against shipping documents, and when the ships were ready I planned to fly down to St John's with the documents, present them at the bank, and make sure that our account had been credited before releasing the ships. The two steamers in Hawkes Bay were ready first, and I collected the shipping documents and flew down to St John's. It took me about two hours. When I got to the bank I found that no money had been transferred and that the Welsh firm had not deposited any credit which could be released, so I asked the Customs to hold the ships in Hawkes Bay, cabled the shipowners telling them why their ships were held up, and cabled the principals of the coal firm reminding them that I would require payment before the ships could leave. They had overlooked the fact that I had an aeroplane and could get quickly to and from St John's.

I flew back to Hawkes Bay to keep an eye on things, and a day or so later I got a cable from Wales to say that the credit would be remitted immediately. On the strength of this I let the ships go. I should have known better. The credit never came, and it was several years later, after we had gone to arbitration, that we were paid.

However, most of our contracts were flourishing as we approached the winter of 1922–3. We had a skilled Canadian lumberman at Hawkes Bay, supervising the cutting of pit-props for shipment as soon as the ice went out of the bay in the following spring. Alan Butler and Syd Bennett were flying the original Westland on the mail contracts from Botwood, where I now had five aircraft in all, and I was flying the long-distance mail deliveries and getting up to Hawkes Bay whenever I could. Things were working out pretty well, yet during that winter it became apparent that Butler and I were not always seeing eye to eye. I was obsessed with the importance of making the business pay, whereas Butler with his great wealth was not always so concerned on that score. His chief interest was flying, and so long as he was in the air regularly he was happy. I was so keen to develop the business that I had refused to take a holiday, and it may well be that I was tired and inclined to be irritable. At length we decided that since our outlooks were so different we ought to separate, and we agreed to divide the business, Butler taking the timber side at Hawkes Bay while the Aerial Survey and Communications side came to me. I had many regrets about this because I felt there was a wonderful future in both sides of the business: between them they would open up the country. But my main interest had always been to build up a well-organized air service.

At the same time I was getting more and more depressed at the general lack of interest shown by the Newfoundland Government towards us. It was costing them nearly a million dollars a year to distribute the mails through local dog-teams in winter and steamer services in summer, besides taking weeks and even months to do it, yet they rejected my tender for carrying all these mails at half the existing figure. Their objection, I discovered, was political: if they took the business away from the steamers and dog-teams they might lose votes. Several times we were able to move doctors quickly to the outposts in emergency, and we were fulfilling many small contracts without incident, some as far afield as Labrador, but still the main contracts eluded us. I had a long talk with a high Government official in which I expounded my views on the future of flying in Newfoundland, and this exalted public servant offered to get me the exclusive flying rights in Newfoundland for twenty-five years if I would give him a 10 per cent interest in my company. This incensed me. I was young and I hadn't yet heard of *baksheesh*.

Early in 1923 I decided to make one last attempt to get a contract out of the sealing companies, and this time I did at least manage to sell them an idea. I had heard that the small Avro which had been specially built for Shackleton's last expedition might be available. Shackleton had died in Georgia, the expedition had returned, and the Avro was for sale. I suggested to the sealing owners that the Avro could be carried on the deck of one of their ships, that it could be dropped on the ice, and that it could then take off on local searches and return to the ship. I did not think this would interfere with the longer-range work that suited the Martinsyde. After discussions between the ship-owners and the Government, who agreed to pay half the cost, the owners asked me to buy the plane and operate it for them, and I agreed. They still offered only vague promises for the Martinsyde.

I brought over a pilot from England specially to fly the Avro and he went off with one of the ships, and as the season progressed I made several flights out over the ice-floes on my own account in the Martin-syde, searching for the big herds. But I didn't have the luck of the previous year. Towards the end of the season I decided to make one more flight. I was far out over the ice-floes, 200 miles from land, when my engine coughed and hesitated and began to run roughly. It looked as though I would have to come down. No one knew where I was or what route I had taken and I had no radio.

I suddenly realized what an absolute fool I had been. I'd been taking this sort of risk for three years and so far I had been lucky, but now the prospect of freezing to death on the ice-floes stared me in the face. Why had I done it? All the time, as I coaxed the engine along and it gave more and more trouble, I was thinking these miserable thoughts. The sealing people had still not grasped the importance of aerial seal-spotting and perhaps they never would. If the Avro proved successful they would cut me out and run it themselves. Even the air mail con-tracts, it seemed, were stifled by politics and threatened by corruption. There and then, as the engine missed and spluttered, I made a vow that if I ever got back to Botwood I would give up seal-spotting, and that if I couldn't get a promise of constructive support from the Government I would leave Newfoundland.

I managed to keep the engine going, and after a very worrying trip I eventually got back to Botwood. Many a flier has promised himself this sort of thing in a tight corner and forgotten it later, but this time I had learnt my lesson. Nothing was forthcoming from the Govern-ment, so I went to Canada and sold my three Westland aircraft, and later I sold the two Martinsydes and the yacht. By August 1923 all my transportable equipment had been moved out of Newfoundland, and what was left was turned over to Alan Butler at Hawkes Bay – except for the hangars, which I tried unsuccessfully to sell.

For three years all my interests had been in Newfoundland and it was a terrible wrench to cut myself adrift in this way. I loved the country, I liked its people, and I felt that there were tremendous possibilities there, but I disliked the existing political outlook. After so many frustrations I thought it would probably be best to get out, and in the autumn of 1923 I found myself in New York, my assets now in cash, trying to make up my mind what to do next. The Aerial Survey Company had been worth much more as a going concern than in liquidation, and when I had paid my debts I found I was worth no more than about 25,000 dollars.

8

The Search for Nungesser and Coli

WHERE the Northern Territory of Australia was concerned my father was a visionary. He saw the importance of populating this vast area, and he urged the Australian Government to encourage small farmers and immigrants to settle there. In the autumn of 1923 he was planning to acquire 20,000 square miles of the Northern Territory to add to his company's existing holding of 10,000 square miles of Brunette Downs. It was all good sheep- and cattle-rearing country and it had never had a drought in living memory. Unable to raise the finance in London, my father was advised to try America. We met in New York. I had not seen him for four years, and we laughed about our old differences. When he told me about his new project I was enthusiastic; he said he needed me, and I was keen to go. But the project foundered when the National City Bank of New York, which had been prepared to come in, was advised by the Bank of England that Australia was London's preserve and that American investment would be considered an unfriendly act. My father and I were both incensed at this dog-in-the-manger attitude, which could only arrest and hinder the tide of Australian development.[1] It was a great blow to my father, and for me it meant that there was nothing to attract me back to Australia. My father went back on his own.

I had begun to take an interest in the possibility of introducing new American inventions into Britain and vice versa, and I toured the principal American cities picking up inventions which I thought might have a commercial application in England. Then for some months I travelled backwards and forwards on what proved to be the profitable business of introducing the inventions of one country to another. But after my father's return to Australia it became apparent from my mother's letters that she had been very disappointed that I had not accompanied him back. Then towards the end of 1924 I learned that she had been paralysed by a stroke, so I decided to go out to see her.

[1] Today America is providing most of the foreign capital for the development of Australian projects.

My mother's illness saddened me greatly; she could not speak, she could not move her limbs, and she had to be helped in every way. Yet there was no doubt that seeing me did her good. The doctor told me that the news that I was coming had strengthened her perceptibly; at that time they had not expected her to live.

The old homestead at Hidden Vale, and the way of life in Australia, attracted me as always, but it soon became evident that my father was as dominating as ever and that it would be unwise for me to remain long in Australia. After spending a few weeks with my family I returned to America.

In October 1925, soon after my return to America, my divorce came through in New York. By this time it was a mere formality, as I had not seen my wife since 1920 except for one brief visit that I made to New York in 1922. I had felt then that for the boy's sake we ought to try to work things out together, but when this became impossible I felt it was better that one or other of us should have him and take full responsibility. I felt that joint control of a child by separated or divorced parents could only have a bad effect on the child. My wife said that she could not possibly live without her son, and I agreed that she should bring him up. I did not see him again until he was fourteen, when I arranged for him to go out to my family in Australia. By then his mother had remarried and had other children, who by that time perhaps had a greater claim on her. I believe now that my original decision, which deprived my son of a father's influence and guidance while he was young, was a mistaken one and I have never ceased to regret it. It is better, I think, for a separated couple to share a child equally for so many months of the year, unsettling though this may be, rather than one parent only having care and custody, especially if the child is a boy.

Whenever I went to London I used to go down to Bournemouth to see how Joan Henry was getting on at school. She always seemed to be enjoying it very much, but although she was doing a great deal of riding I knew she was missing the open-air life she was used to in Newfoundland. In December 1925 I was in London, and I went down to Bournemouth at the end of the school term to take Joan back to her aunt's for the Christmas holidays. While I was at Bournemouth we went for a walk along the beach. The tide was well out and there was a fine stretch of wet, firm sand. I noticed vaguely that Joan was drawing pictures in the sand with a stick, and when we walked back up the beach and looked down at the sands from the top of the cliffs I could see what she had written. Spelt out boldly in the sand in large capitals were the words 'I love you'. I suddenly realized that I felt the same way. We were married in January 1926, David Plaistowe witnessing our wedding. Joan was then eighteen.

At about this time I received a letter from my father telling me that he had at last been able to get an option from the other two share-holders in his Brunette Downs company to buy their shares, which if taken up would give him a free hand to develop the property. This was a very big project, and he wanted me to join him in it. As it gave me another opportunity to live and work in Australia, I accepted. Then when my family got the news of my wedding they begged us to visit them, so we decided that as soon as I could get away we would travel to Australia via Canada as part of our honey-moon.

My mother's health had improved sufficiently for her to be moved to our summer home in Tasmania, and when we arrived in Australia towards the end of 1926 we went straight there. The Brunette Downs deal, however, fell through, so there was nothing after all to hold me in Australia.

When we finally left my mother must have realized that she would probably never see us again, and although she was still severely paralysed she was actually able to lift herself up and lean forward on the veranda rail to see us drive away. I wanted my father to stop the car and let me go back for a moment, but he refused. 'She will be happy that she was able to make the effort to say good-bye,' he said. I never saw her again, but the memory of her strength of will in adversity has remained with me as an inspiration.

Passing through Canada on our way to Australia I had been offered a very fine timber property of 145,000 acres near Vancouver for £15,000. I liked the idea of settling in Canada and I arranged for the property to be checked over while I was away. I decided to return to London via Canada, and when we got to Sydney I made a brief study of my financial position and cabled my brokers, Messrs Hamilton, Mackay, of London, to ask how my account stood. They replied that there was a credit of £8,800. I had about the same sum available in cash, so if I sold my shares I would have enough ready money to buy the property.

I cabled my brokers instructing them to sell all my shares–which were Dunlop's–at once, and then we sailed for England.

Our first stop was Auckland, and just as the boat was about to sail I got a cable from my brokers to say that they had bought more Dunlop's for me on the strength of some good information they had received, but that the shares had fallen and unless I put up a further £20,000 immediately they would have to sell out my account. I was unable to cable a reply until we got to Fiji, but from there I cabled that I had instructed them to sell my shares at Sydney, that whatever they had done was their own responsibility, and that unless they paid the £8,800 into my account I would take the matter up with the Stock Exchange committee on my return.

When I got to London I asked my brokers what they thought they were doing. The sole partner, with whom I had become very friendly over a number of years, told me a hard luck story to the effect that he had heard that a big bid had been put in to buy Dunlop's and to do me a good turn he had bought a lot more for me instead of selling. Unfortunately it had been no more than a rumour, the shares had dropped, and instead of my account showing a profit of £8,800 it showed a loss of £13,500. I told him he owed me £8,800 and I wanted the money, but he said if I pressed my claim he would have to go bankrupt. So I had no chance of getting the money. I liked the man, I believed he had genuinely tried to help me, and I finally decided to take no action. I did, however, demand a written statement from him to the effect that I did not owe him the money and that he would never make any claim against me, and this he gave me.

Meanwhile I had had news from Canada that the title to the property I was interested in was so tangled that there was no point in my going any further, so I wasn't as upset as I might have been. Later I heard that the whole area had had to be burnt down because of the discovery of death-watch beetle in the timber, so I had had a lucky escape. Some years afterwards Hamilton, Mackay did in fact go bankrupt, so my gesture did not save them for long. It did, however, subsequently have the most unpleasant repercussions for me.

In the course of my patent introduction business I had become interested in a new type of snow tractor, built by a firm in Detroit, and based on the Ford tractor. Instead of the normal caterpillar track it had two torpedo-shaped drums, pointed in front and blunt at the back, with a thin steel blade welded around the drum to form a corkscrew. Each drum was about 2 feet 6 inches in diameter and as it turned it screwed its way through the snow. I thought this tractor might be very successful in Canada and Newfoundland, and I decided to take it up to Newfoundland for testing. I arranged for a model to be shipped to the Ford agent at St John's, who could supply me with spares for the tractor, and from there I transported it by rail to Deer Lake. I then started out on the drive north-west across country covered in deep snow to Bonne Bay on the west coast, where three years earlier I had been cutting pit-props. There was no made road but we followed a rough track that was used in summer and was only recognizable because it lay between gaps in the trees. It was a good test. I took Joan with me, and a woodsman to help as general handyman, and we towed a sleigh behind us carrying our tents and equipment so that we could stop *en route* at various logging camps to demonstrate the tractor.

Nearing the first camp on our itinerary the snow at the edge of the track gave way and the tractor tilted to the left. The revolving drum dragged my foot into a two-inch gap between the drum itself and the steel chassis and crushed it. Fortunately my foot had fallen into a flat space where there was just enough room to clear the knives of the screw. I immediately stopped the tractor and reversed it and this brought my foot out again. I couldn't feel much except a numbness, and Joan and my assistant helped me up the slope to a flat space in the middle of the track, where Joan pulled off my sealskin boot and socks. My foot fell into a flabby mass which Joan found she could hold in her cupped hands. All the bones appeared to have been crushed.

There was nothing we could do but get to a doctor as quickly as possible. It was three miles to the nearest lumber camp, and no one else knew how to drive the tractor. It was extremely cold, well below zero, it was impossible to get my foot back into the sealskin boot, so Joan wrapped it up in woollen scarves and tied a bag over it. They helped me back on to the tractor and we drove on. Fortunately the pedals were worked by the right foot. We were fortunate again when a dog-team passed us on its way to the lumber camp and we told the driver of the accident, so that when we arrived an hour or so later they were ready for us. By this time I was in agony. The nearest doctor was at Bonne Bay, but they promised to take me on next morning to Lomond, a lumber camp in the Bonne Bay area, and to get the doctor to come out from Bonne Bay meanwhile.

I found that if my foot was propped up above my heart the pain was not too severe. Next morning the lumbermen propped me up in the same way on a mattress on the dog-team sleigh and in two hours we reached Lomond, where the doctor was waiting for me. But when he got the bandages off he could see very little. No toes were visible and the foot was the size and shape of a rugby football. He told me he could do nothing until the swelling subsided and that this might take a week or more, but added that I would do no harm if I travelled on the sleigh meanwhile.

I telegraphed the chief engineer of the Ford Company in St John's and asked him to come out and drive the tractor. He arrived two days later and we set off to visit the lumber camps. In a week of demonstrations we sold the snow-motor we had with us and took orders for several more. Then we took the train from Deer Lake to Corner Brook, forty miles to the south-west, where the nearest hospital was situated. They told me I would do no harm if I travelled back to St John's, and after a number of X-rays taken at the hospital at St John's I was told that the shape of the bones was all right but that I would have to wear a steel strap to keep my foot from moving. The local blacksmith made up a wonderful contraption for me and I returned to New York and then went on to Detroit to discuss improvements and modifications to the tractor.

While I was in Detroit a doctor to a big insurance company showed great interest in my foot and wanted to know the whole story. He then made X-rays from all angles and finally declared that, because I had got back on the tractor and put the foot down, the blood had built up pressure in the foot, the pressure had pushed the bones back into shape, and they had knitted. He made a proper brace for me and after a few weeks I was able to get about without much trouble.

I was still working on the snow-motor project when I read in the papers about the disappearance of the two French fliers Nungesser and Coli, who had been attempting to fly direct from Paris to New York. A substantial money prize had been offered for the first men to complete the direct flight, and at least two other contestants were preparing to take off and fly in the reverse direction, from New York to Paris, an easier proposition because of the prevailing winds. The Atlantic had never been flown from east to west by aeroplane. Charles Nungesser was one of the leading French aces of the First World War, third on the list with forty-five victims, a man with an insatiable desire for combat that was not shaken by an amazing succession of wounds and injuries that had left him crippled for life. François Coli, too, was a distinguished French pilot. They left Paris in their plane the *White Bird* on 8th May 1927 and were seen crossing Southern Ireland, but in spite of many reports that they had been seen crossing the Newfoundland coast in cloudy weather there was no more definite news either of them or their plane. A constant vigil was kept by coastal wireless stations, while Government patrol boats and seaplanes searched the waters between Canada and Newfoundland and an airship of the United States Navy combed the area east of New York. Nothing was found, but there was a general air of conviction that the two men had got across the Atlantic safely but had been forced down in some isolated spot, probably not very far inland.

I was approached by a member of the Dupont family, the American industrialists, who are of French descent, to know if I could think of anyone who knew Newfoundland well enough to take an aerial expedition up there to look for the missing fliers. They may well have guessed what my reaction would be–it was just the sort of venture that appealed to me. I was offered anything I wanted, but I said I'd be happy to go if all expenses were paid and I was given a free hand. I was pleased to be able to help, and glad of the chance to do some flying again. I was later asked to take a journalist with me who would also act as co-pilot and whose task it would be to keep up a flow of reports back to a news syndicate.

I arranged to buy a new Fokker monoplane, seaplane version, and I got an oil company to lay down caches of petrol at various points in Newfoundland where I thought I might need it. While I was waiting for delivery of the Fokker I was introduced to Harry Guggenheim, the copper magnate, who had joined in sponsoring the expedition, and he invited me out to his home on Long Island. There I met a young mail pilot who had just flown up from San Diego in a single-engined Ryan monoplane and who had announced his intention of flying solo from New York to Paris. The newspapers were calling him the 'flying fool', but his flight from San Diego, a record one, had shaken them. Less than a week later this young man was in Paris. His name was Charles Lindbergh.

I had not flown for nearly three years, but when the Fokker was handed over to me I took it up for a test flight and found that it handled well. The steel strap on my left foot, however, got in the way of the rudder bar, so I unstrapped it and threw it overboard. My foot was still weak but by using the heel I was able to operate the port rudder bar well enough. Towards the end of May we were ready, and then, as fog abounds at that time of year in the area I was heading for, I decided it would be safer and probably quicker to go up to St John's by sea. This didn't much suit my co-pilot, Cy Caldwell of the *Aero Digest*, who wanted something more exciting for his first dispatch, but I had to remind him that the prime object of the expedition was to look for Nungesser and Coli and not to make a stunt flight to the frozen north.

Immediately on arriving at St John's we put the Fokker over the side of the ship and into the water and I flew it to my old hangar at Lake Quidi Vidi. That same afternoon we left on a flight to the south-west round Placentia Bay, one of the areas where the *White Bird* was supposed to have been seen. All my old friends had crowded round us in St John's and pressed us to accept their hospitality but I told them this would have to wait until the expedition was over.

For the next few weeks we combed Newfoundland without finding any trace of the missing plane. One day after a long search we were getting short of petrol and I decided to make for Port-aux-Basques in the south-west corner of Newfoundland, where a cache had been put down for us. We didn't quite make it, running out of fuel and being forced down on a lake about five miles short of the town. But the lake was right by the railway and we could soon get some petrol sent out to us. I was still having some difficulty with my left foot and I asked Cy Caldwell to walk into Port-aux-Basques to organize the petrol. He was a most amusing fellow but he could be very obstinate at times, and this time he put on one of his cranky moods and refused to go. I didn't bother to argue but started straight away to walk the five miles to the town. When I got there two hours later I was limping badly and my foot felt just about finished.

Next morning I collected a drum of petrol, borrowed a railway hand-cart, and got some railwaymen to work it back to the lake for me. Caldwell had put himself up for the night very comfortably in the Fokker cabin and was as fresh as a daisy. I told him that as I had walked in for the petrol he could do the refuelling, which he did. But I didn't feel that this made the scores anything like even. I had sent the railwaymen back with the handcart, and just as Caldwell finished the refuelling I got into the cockpit and called to him from the window. 'I'm afraid the lake's a bit short for a take-off with two of us on board. See you at Port-aux-Basques.' And I opened up the engine and took off. Some hours later a very angry Cy Caldwell rejoined me in the village.

Everyone in Newfoundland wanted to be helpful and there were many rumours of wreckage and flares, but after nearly two months of continuous searching, during which we covered about 15,000 square miles, we came to the conclusion that Nungesser and Coli couldn't possibly have come down in Newfoundland. Since evidence had been given earlier that the plane had been seen crossing Ireland and then heading out to sea, it now seemed likely that the fliers had been lost in the Atlantic. The sponsors finally decided to abandon the search.

On the way back to New York in the Fokker, Cy Caldwell produced a very nice example of his particular brand of wit. We ran into bad weather, great banks of fog swirled around us and we had no way of checking our position. There was no communication between the cockpit and the cabin, where Cy Caldwell sat, except a small hole through which one could put one's hand to pass a note. Half-way across the Straits between Newfoundland and Nova Scotia I was feeling very uncertain and apprehensive when I felt a nudge on my shoulder, and I turned round to see Caldwell's outstretched hand and a note. I took the note and read it. 'At last we look like finding Nungesser and Coli,' it read. I appreciated his grim sense of humour.

Caldwell had been sending reports from Newfoundland throughout the expedition, some of which I thought were a little colourful to say the least, and we were the centre of interest when we got back to New York. After my years in Newfoundland it had been very much a routine job for me, but I didn't spoil Cy's story. I wrote a short report on the expedition for the sponsors and then left for London, where I had some business to attend to.

Two months later a Glasgow priest, on returning from a holiday in County Kerry, told the French vice-consul in Glasgow that he had heard reports during his holiday that people in the Kerry Head district had not only seen the *White Bird* flying west on Sunday 8th May, the day Nungesser and Coli left Paris, but had also seen what they believed to be the same machine returning from a westerly direction the following morning, until it reached a point about three miles from Meanoghan. There, they said, it fell into the sea. A boat put out later but although oil was found on the surface there was no sign of wreckage. Could this have been Nungesser and Coli, trying to reach Ireland after being driven back by bad weather and headwinds in mid-Atlantic? It seems quite possible that it was. Yet the belief that the two fliers had been seen over Newfoundland was strongly held. It was thirty-four years before the smallest corroboration came, and then in January

1961, the instrument panel of an aeroplane which from its design and vintage could well have belonged to the *White Bird* – although this was never conclusively proved – was fished up by lobstermen from the sea-bed in Casco Bay, on the Maine coast, 120 miles north of Boston. Either way, it is not surprising that Caldwell and I should have combed Newfoundland in vain.

3(a). Upside-down on an Italian beach – my D.H. 14A

3(b). Cooking a meal after the crash

3(c). The start of the 1920 Aerial Derby at Hendon, showing the D.H. 14A

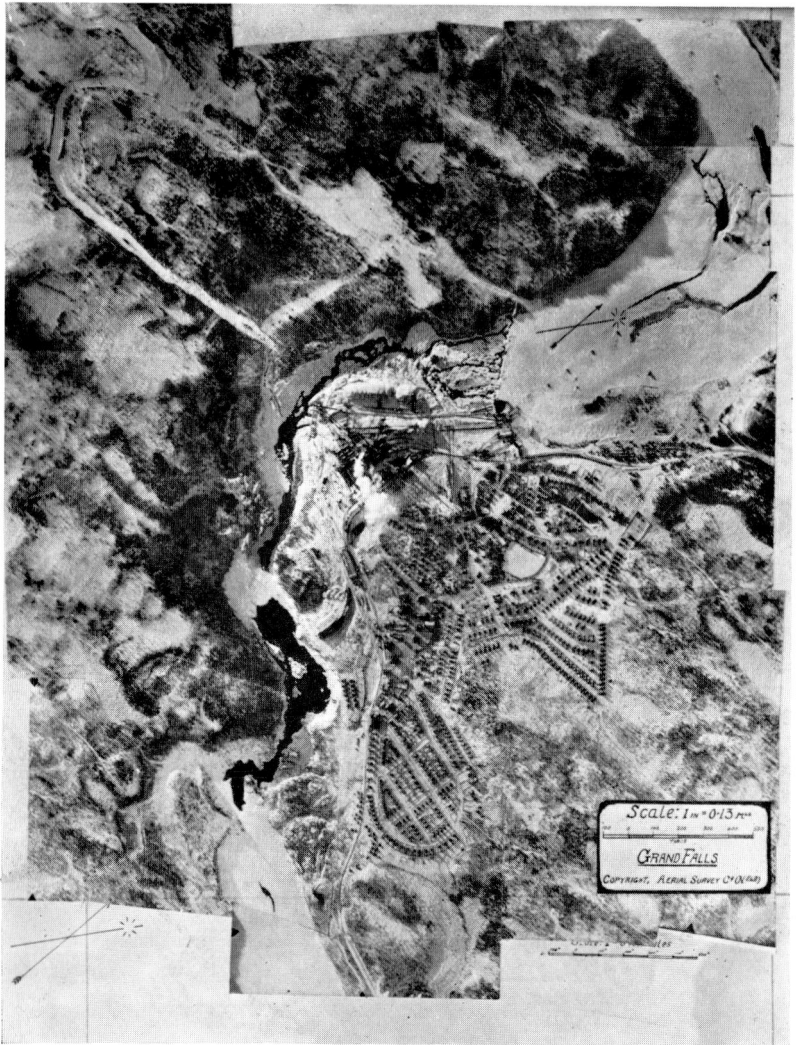

Scale: 1in = 0.13 mm

GRAND FALLS

COPYRIGHT, AERIAL SURVEY Cº (N.fld)

4. The 'mosaic' of Grand Falls, 1922

(*See page 61*)

9

The Courtauld Expedition

B ACK in London, I found myself with quite a nice profit on my patent introduction business and I took an office in Aldwych and began to study the stock market. This was something in which I had always taken an interest, and the only serious loss I had suffered – that of the Dunlop shares – had resulted from my being out of the country. Soon I had private lines installed to three different firms of brokers and my investments were not doing badly. I was ready to go for something rather bigger. I learned from friends that there were some shares available in a powdered fuel combustion company called Buell Combustion, of which I had heard good reports; a client of my friends had subscribed for the shares but he now wanted to sell. I was offered 25,000 shares at £1 apiece. If I decided to buy, the owner would come down from the Midlands to complete the deal. I didn't have £25,000, but my friends said they could arrange for me to pay £5,000 down and the rest over twelve months. I decided to buy.

I rang my brokers and asked them to make inquiries about Buell Combustion, and an hour or so later the owner of the shares arrived in my office. While we were working out the deal and drawing up the contract my brokers called back to say that Buell Combustion had gone up to 25s. It looked as though I was on to a good thing, but I rang off without any comment as I was afraid the owner might hear something and decide not to sell. In the next few minutes my brokers rang me twice, first to say that Buell were 30s. bid, then 35s. bid. I was sure the owner would guess what was happening and I kept trying to choke the brokers off. At last the agreement was signed and I gave the man his cheque for £5,000.

The shares went on going up steadily, and a few days later, much to my embarrassment, I saw the former owner in a restaurant, where we were both lunching. He came over to my table, and for a moment I feared there might be a scene. 'I thought I'd like to congratulate you,' he said, 'on buying those shares.' I said I was afraid he might be feeling angry with me. 'Not at all,' he said. 'I did very well out of them myself.

I paid 10s. a share and you gave me 20s., and I'm more than satisfied.'
Eventually the shares reached a market value of £80,000, so I sold
them, paid off the balance of the debt, and started investing in other
shares by way of the three magic telephones. It lasted for a while –
nearly two years, in fact. Then came 1929, and the market crashed.
By the time I had woken up to what was happening and given a panic
order to sell everything I was left with £10,000. Who had the rest I
didn't know. I got rid of my three telephones, seeing them at last for
the snare and delusion they were, and went on holiday to calm down.

I felt now that I must get into something entirely new. What, I
asked myself, was going to be the next big industrial development?
Eventually I decided on colour photography. I got myself an introduction to a clever little optical engineer named Chapman who was also
good at mechanics, and from our discussions I decided that the best
thing was to put the three colours on primary the lens of the camera so
that the spectrum would be split on the negative, subsequently being
brought together on the positive. We worked on this project for the
next two years and got some nice results before I discovered that this
was one of the oldest known ways of producing colour photographs and
that it didn't work commercially.

Early in March 1931, while I was still working on this project with
Chapman, I got a telephone call from Samuel Courtauld, chairman
of Courtauld's, the artificial silk firm, asking if I would be prepared
to organize an expedition to Greenland to search for his nephew,
Augustine Courtauld, who was stranded on the ice-cap. Augustine
Courtauld had been a member of the British Arctic Air Route Expedition, led by Gino Watkins and consisting of fourteen men, mostly
former Cambridge undergraduates with an average age of twenty-five,
whose prime object was to explore the possibilities of an air route to
Canada via the great circle. For this purpose they set up a meteorological station on the ice-cap about 120 miles north-west of Angmagsalik, on the Greenland coast opposite Iceland. Here the expedition
had arrived on 26th July 1930 and here it had set up its main base.
The meteorological station was established by the end of August, at a
height of 8,200 feet on the ice-cap, and a party of two left behind to man
it. The plan was to relieve the station monthly throughout the winter.

The first party was duly relieved on 2nd October. But Watkins had
been seriously misled about what he could expect from the weather.
Blizzards, which were supposed to be infrequent, blew at gale force
throughout October, and the second relief party arrived a month late.

It was clear that it might be impossible to send relief again until the winter was over. Meanwhile the support party had consumed supplies to such an extent that there wasn't enough left to support two men on the ice-cap through the winter. There might be enough for one.

Augustine Courtauld volunteered to remain on the ice-cap alone. He knew that this meant complete isolation in the most Spartan conditions for three to four months, possibly more, but he seems almost to have welcomed the prospect of such a test of character. The alternative was to abandon the station altogether, and with it the main object of the expedition; so Courtauld was allowed to stay.

During the winter the tent in which Courtauld was holding out and from which for a long time he managed to make daily observations on the weather, helped by various instruments, eventually became completely buried, until only the ventilator protruded through the snow. Meanwhile, as his supplies dwindled and he was finally trapped in complete darkness, his mental and physical condition deteriorated. An air search in February failed to locate the station, and a relief party that set out early in March was twice forced back by blizzards.

I was given a free hand and told to organize the expedition as I thought best and not to consider expense. An added poignancy was given to the situation by the fact that Augustine Courtauld, an only son, was the last of the male line of the Courtaulds and heir to the Courtauld fortune. (Samuel Courtauld had a daughter, married to R. A. Butler, now Lord Butler, Master of Trinity College, Cambridge, and William Courtauld, the third brother, had no children.)

Very little information was available from the base at Angmagsalik as their radio had broken down. I suggested that the first thing was to check the amount of food and supplies Courtauld had and estimate how long he could last. We finally decided that though his privations might be severe he ought to be able to hold out until the middle of May. This gave me time to organize the rescue properly, and my plan was that several separate rescue attempts would be converging on Courtauld so as to reach him not later than 10th May.

I sought advice first from Riiser Larsen, who had been Amundsen's pilot on his North Pole flight. I wanted a pilot with some knowledge of Greenland, and Larsen produced a Swedish pilot named Ahrenberg and a suitable plane for him, and I arranged for Ahrenberg to fly to Reykjavik in Iceland, fit skis on his plane and fly from there to the ice-cap, landing beside the station once he had located it and picking up Courtauld. Meanwhile Watkins was to start off independently with another relief party from Angmagsalik, and I would buy a second plane and fly to Reykjavik and stand by. If neither air nor ground search had found Courtauld by 10th May, or if either of them had been delayed for any reason, I would fly to the ice-cap myself and carry out a further search. Holding myself in reserve in this way left me free to organize the details.

I located a suitable plane, a Bellanca monoplane, in Italy, and I had it flown to London for inspection. The engine was a Wright Whirlwind, and I got the chief engineer of the Wright Engine Company's London office to inspect it. He pronounced it as in excellent condition and I bought the aircraft and flew it to Vickers at Weybridge to supervise the fitting of skis. I had these made on the same pattern as my New-foundland ski. Modifications were made to enable sledges and food supplies to be carried and dropped if necessary, and the R.A.F. pro-vided me with coloured parachutes for supply-dropping and offered me any help I required. I knew I would need pinpoint navigation to find the station and I asked for an expert navigator, and the R.A.F. said they had a pilot who was also one of the best navigators in the Air Force and they would grant him leave to accompany me. His name was Flt. Lt. L. K. Barnes.

Risseer Larsen found me a pair of man-hauled sleds as used by the Norwegians which came to pieces and could easily be transported by plane, and we packed each one separately and attached a parachute with instructions on how to erect it. Food supplies were also attached to coloured parachutes. Our own equipment included smoke flares and silk tents; I took these precautions in case we were unable to land alongside Courtauld's camp, and also to give us a means of survival if we were forced down; with luck we might still be able to get through to Courtauld or make our way back to the coast.

Towards the end of April the first relief party returned to Angmag-salik and a second party, under Gino Watkins, started out. A day or so later Captain Ahrenberg left Reykjavik for Angmagsalik, where he proposed changing floats as conditions had not been suitable for the use of skis at Reykjavik. Unfortunately he was forced back to Iceland by the weather. The Iceland Government, too, had been anxious to help, and they had put a small plane on their patrol ship *Odin*. The ship got to within sixty miles of Angmagsalik and on 2nd May the plane was put down on an ice-floe. It took off and headed for the ice-cap but developed engine trouble and had to return for repairs to Reykjavik.

On 5th May I left Hull by the Icelandic steamer *Dettifoss* with the dismantled Bellanca on deck, accompanied by my wife, Flt. Lt. Barnes, a wireless operator, and three engineers, among them J. R. Stannard, who had been with me fourteen years earlier at Bacton and again in Newfoundland. We arrived at Reykjavik early on 9th May and the engineers began to erect the plane on the dock-side, which I judged was long enough for take-off. Meanwhile I selected a site about twenty miles from Reykjavik for use as a base.

On 10th May we had the Bellanca ready for take-off. This was the day by which the relief party and Ahrenberg should have found Courtauld. I wondered what the day held for us and for Courtauld, and whether we should have to take off in the Bellanca. I was hoping to be in on the search, and yet I knew it would be a serious matter if Courtauld had not yet been located. I had heard nothing from Ahrenberg, nor was there any word from the ground party, but they had no radio and it might be several days before their news, if they had any, got through. In London Samuel Courtauld was keeping in touch with developments as far as he could, and he had promised to cable me if there was any news at his end, but he too was hampered by poor communications. I decided to stick to my schedule, and we were about to take off from the dock-side and fly down to the site I had chosen to refuel when I received a cable from Samuel Courtauld. Augustine Courtauld had been found.

It was a great moment for us, a triumph in which we felt we all shared. Although the actual rescue was made by the ground party, Ahrenberg was overhead and dropping supplies to them within forty-eight hours, and we had been ready with the Bellanca on schedule for a final effort if all else had failed.

We were naturally anxious to know details of the rescue, and how Courtauld had stood up to his ordeal. In fact, although he recovered quickly and made light of it afterwards, his diary revealed how near to the edge he had gone. Here are some extracts from entries made in the last fortnight before he was found.[1]

April 26th, Sunday. Just six months since we left Base and started living on sledge rations. Been here about twenty weeks. Everything running out. Using last candle. Very little paraffin. What I shall do for drinking water I don't know. Only two more biscuits. In four days I officially run out of food but have a reserve, thank God, a pemmican and marg.

[1] Quoted in Wilfrid Noyce, *They Survived, A Study of the Will to Live* (Heinemann, London, 1962).

May 1st, Friday. No sign of relief. Shall have to think of walking soon if I can get out. Biscuits finished, also candles. Am burning ski-wax for a light, but it mostly makes smoke. Have no sugar as the last tin is outside. Food has officially run out, but I still have a fair amount of essentials, though lemon juice is running low, which is pretty serious.

The main problems were the darkness and the lack of fuel, without which he could not melt down the snow to make the liquid he needed to live. His diary entries became increasingly despondent. He was entombed under the snow, and when Gino Watkins and his party first found the camp, all that was visible was the ventilator, sticking out no more than two feet above the snow, and a short mast at the top of which was a tattered Union Jack, almost ripped away by the gales. Some of the instruments, too, still showed through the surface. Watkins knelt in the snow and called down the ventilator, hardly expecting to get a reply. This is how Courtauld described this moment.

The primus gave its last gasp as I was melting water for the morning meal. I was lying in my bag after this so-called meal . . . when suddenly there was an appalling noise like a bus going by, followed by a confused yelling noise. I nearly jumped out of my skin. Was it the house falling in at last? A second later I realized the truth. It was somebody, some real human voice, calling down the ventilator. It was a wonderful moment. I could not think what to do or say. I yelled back some stuttering remarks that seemed quite futile for the occasion. . . . The whole world seemed turned inside out. At one moment I was lying in the dark wondering how ever I was going to see anybody again or ever get home, and the next, home was in sight . . .

Very soon Gino had smashed a hole in the roof and let in the blinding sunshine and blue sky, blinding even with dark snow-glasses on. The next moment they had dropped through the hole and we were grasping hands and thanking God that the job was done.

We dismantled and repacked the Bellanca and returned to Hull on the *Dettifoss*. The Courtauld incident was over—yet for me it had a sequel. After the Bellanca had been re-erected and test flown at Hanworth I was invited by the Reading Flying Club to take it over to

Woodley Aerodrome one Sunday afternoon. My wife went with me. There was much talk in the clubhouse at Woodley about the tremendous climbing performance of the Bellanca, so when I took off on a demonstration flight with a number of passengers, including Joan, I held the plane down to get up a good speed and then pulled up in a steep climb. At a height of 200 feet the engine suddenly packed up completely and black smoke poured from the nacelle.

I had always told Joan, who had meanwhile started learning to fly, never to turn back if she had an engine failure on take-off but to continue straight on no matter how bad the ground ahead. Although this might result in a serious crash it was better than trying to turn back for the aerodrome at a low height, which would almost certainly result in a stall and a dive straight into the ground. I had seen it happen so many times. Now straight ahead of me was a quarry, and instinctively I carried out a manoeuvre that I had practised many times in Sopwith one-and-a-half-strutters during the First World War. The Clerget engines in the Sopwith were not then as reliable as they might have been and they had a habit of cutting out after take-off, so to prepare myself for emergencies I used to practise taking off and then cutting the engine when I reached the edge of the field. I would then pull the plane up into a steep climb until just short of stalling point, then kick the left rudder hard. This reversed the flight direction without risking a stall and enabled a landing to be made back on the aerodrome. Without thinking about it I did much the same thing at Reading. While still in the climb and just before losing flying speed I kicked the left rudder hard and this brought the machine round in a quick flip to face the landing area.

I was too high to land inside the aerodrome, especially as I would be attempting to land downwind, so I dipped to the right and side-slipped still farther out until I was out of sight of the clubhouse. When I reached a point which I judged would enable me to turn back into the aerodrome without over-shooting I banked hard to the left and side-slipped until I was in position for a normal landing downwind. I had lost several hundred yards by these manoeuvres, but after touching down I could see that I would still overshoot the end of the field, where there was a fence and a six-foot drop to a road. The alternative was to ground-loop the machine. I gently pressed the left brake pedal and finding the machine was coming round nicely I put it on hard, ground-looped to the left and stopped with something to spare.

During my manoeuvres the chief instructor of the flying club had exclaimed 'My God, they haven't a chance,' upon which the mother of one of my passengers had fainted and several others had been greatly distressed, so when we landed safely a crowd of people ran over from the clubhouse to congratulate us. For long periods in my life I have used an aeroplane very much as the average person uses a car, so I hope I shall be forgiven for taking a pride in my flying and for quoting the following account of this incident which appeared in the *Aeroplane*, written by C. G. Grey:

The Exception that Proves the Rule

Last week a slight reference was made to an unusually able forced landing made by Mr Sidney Cotton with his Bellanca monoplane at Reading. The Wright Whirlwind engine cut out dead when he was at a height of between 150 and 200 feet over the aerodrome, and contrary to all the unwritten laws of the air he turned back into the aerodrome and brought off a perfect downwind landing in a 30-m.p.h. wind. The comment of the writer in the *Aeroplane* was that the execution of the manœuvre was as masterly as the example was bad.

This was not intended as an unkindly criticism of Mr Cotton but rather as a warning to young pilots that they must not try to emulate the performance of a master. . . .

The said circumstances were altogether unusual. . . . Mr Cotton found himself heading for a row of trees which at best he was bound to hit about half-way up their trunks. The only alternative was a landing in a sand-pit which meant turning upside down and possibly catching fire. As none of his passengers was strapped in, an upside-down landing would in any case have been rather serious. His only chance of getting the machine down undamaged was to turn and land downwind, which he did with a kind of Immelmann turn. . . .

Joan did not miss the opportunity of pointing out that I had done something against which I had warned her many times. As the plane swung round to a stop she leaned forward, touched me on the shoulder, and said: 'Practise what you preach.'

On examination of the disintegrated engine it was found that all the pistons had seized and all the connecting rods had broken; we then discovered that the pistons were of a type that had given trouble in

America and had been superseded by a new design. Since the engine had been passed as fit for use by the Wright representative in London, the company provided a new engine free of charge, but not until after the exchange of many letters. For my own part I could not help working out where we would have been on our rescue flight from Iceland to Greenland when the engine broke down – if Augustine Courtauld had not been found beforehand and if we had not received the cable on the morning of 10th May. We would have been somewhere on the 500-mile flight from Reykjavik to Angmagsalik, above the icy Denmark Strait. There would have been not the slightest chance for us there.

10

I Start in Colour Photography

'WHERE did you get this?'
    I was squinting through my microscope at a piece of film that had been brought to me by a man named Smith who had been an employee of Ilford for many years. A year had passed since the Courtauld rescue, and during that time I had come to the conclusion that a practical solution of the colour photography problem might be to find a way of putting dots of the three primary colours in a very fine pattern on the film base itself, then to cover the dye with a photographic emulsion to protect it. I had begun a long hunt to find someone who could do this and had visited Ilford, Kodak, Dupont, Agfa Ansco, Agfa in Germany and everyone I could think of in the photographic industry but they had all laughed at me. This man Smith, however, had apparently heard what I had been trying to do.

'I got that several years ago,' he told me. 'A Frenchman named Louis Dufay invented the process and offered it to Ilford's for £25,000, but they turned it down.'

Smith told me that a Madame Durand, an Englishwoman who had married a Frenchman and who lived in France, had made a deal with Dufay to finance him. She had secured substantial backing but she needed more. She heard that the firm of Spicer, the paper manufacturers, were making a transparent film for wrapping chocolate boxes, and she decided to investigate. She went to Spicer's and told them that she wanted large quantities of this film; she didn't mention colour photography at this stage. Then at a later meeting she asked Spicer's why they didn't produce a non-inflammable film for the motion-picture industry. Spicer's said that would be quite a different proposition. 'If I can show you a non-inflammable film suitable for the film industry which can be made on your machines,' she asked them, 'will you manufacture it?' Eventually a contract was drawn up under which Spicer's agreed that if Madame Durand could find the film they would manufacture it and give her the selling rights outside England. She thus became virtually a partner in their business–if she could find the film.

Madame Durand, shrewd woman that she was, had of course found the film already. After a suitable lapse of time she asked Spicer's to make her some more film for covering chocolate boxes but to make it a 32nd of an inch thick this time. When the film was delivered she took it to Pathé and got them to coat it with photographic emulsion. Pathé then slit the film and took some moving pictures with it, which Mrs Durand brought back to Spicer's, who agreed that the film, if she could get the exclusive rights on it, complied with the bargain. She then disclosed to them that it was their own film. This created a most amusing situation at Spicer's, but there was nothing they could do to get out of the agreement. Madame Durand had sold them their own film.

After hearing Smith's story I decided to go to Spicer's to see if we could work together. I'm afraid I didn't know what I was tackling. I was asked in haughty tones if I realized that the 'House of Spicer' never worked with anyone, and I was virtually shown the door. Smith suggested that I tackle the problem through Mrs Durand. 'She's a difficult person to deal with,' he said, 'but she's not satisfied with the progress Spicer's are making and she might well join forces with someone capable of handling them. If you could buy a part of her interests you could then talk to Spicer's from a different level.'

It took some time for Smith to persuade Mrs Durand to meet me, but eventually I lunched with her in Chartres, after which we visited the Cathedral. The sun was shining through the magnificent stained-glass windows, and when I remarked on them Mrs Durand assured me that the Dufay process could produce all these colours faithfully. My purpose was not to beat Mrs Durand down in any way but simply to acquire the Dufay patents and the Spicer contract, and I was able to agree to all Mrs Durand's demands. I was to pay her a total of £5,000, and in addition she would receive shares in the company I had already formed – Colortone Ltd. – representing a one-third interest. It was now time to tell Spicer's that they had a new partner.

I wrote to Sir Dykes Spicer, the partner dealing with the Dufay project, and told him the position, and this time Spicer's lost no time in fixing an appointment. I made it clear that I was fully aware of the importance of the agreement they had signed with Mrs Durand and said I wanted to take an active part in the development of the project. I suggested that a new company be formed called Dufaycolor Limited, into which they would put all their film interests, including the plant and machinery for making the film (located at Sawston, near

Cambridge), and I would put the shares in the Dufay process owned by Colortone. I suggested that Sir Dykes Spicer be chairman and that I should be managing director, and that I should be left to handle the financial side, bringing in what capital was necessary for development work. This appealed to Spicer's as the development costs were averaging £60,000 a year. My proposal assured my own company, Colortone, of a 52 per cent interest in the new company, thus giving me control. It was accepted by Spicer's, and Dufaycolor was registered as a limited company in January 1933.

The Dufaycolor system relied on the splitting of the spectrum into three parts, red, green and blue. When these three colours are projected together in the proper proportions they create white, and thus all the shades of the spectrum can be produced when they are projected back on the screen. The Dufaycolor process was a mosaic process which was designed so that dots of red, green and blue were regularly spaced alongside each other in such small size that when the light shone through them they looked as if they were joined together. It was an additive process; for instance, to make violet, minute dots of red and blue were placed side by side, and to make yellow, minute dots of red and green. Exposure on panchromatic film enabled the various gradations of colour to be projected on the screen, and if the film was held up to the light it reflected a colour image.

The film that Spicer's were making had 350,000 squares of colour to the square inch, equally divided between red, green and blue. A series of rollers, engraved with eleven lines to the millimetre, gave this number of squares. When the pictures were projected on to a screen the result was a sort of fish-net pattern, and it was obvious that the squares of colour, minute as they were, were too big. We would have to engrave a good many more than eleven lines to the millimetre to get a clear picture. A German firm in Kassel were making the rollers, and I went across to see them. They said that they were already engraving as many lines to the square inch as was technically feasible. I told them I wanted them to double the existing number of lines to the millimetre, but they said this was quite impossible. I knew they were the best firm in the world for this sort of job and that it was no good trying elsewhere, but I had been brought up to distrust that word 'impossible'. I told them I proposed to give them an order for thirty stainless steel rollers engraved with nineteen or twenty lines to the millimetre, the order to be confirmed on my return to London, and eventually they agreed to attempt what I asked. The price they quoted me was £100 a roller, making a total order of £3,000. They had no means of testing the rollers at Kassel so it was agreed that they would ship them to England and we would test them at Sawston. Any failures would have to go back to Germany to be skimmed and re-engraved.

I returned to London and reported to the Board, but I failed to get Spicer's support. They said they had been at the game too long and that it was impossible to do the engraving any finer. I pointed out that unless we could get lines on the rollers which would give us something approaching a million squares to the square inch the film would never be a success. I reminded them that the German firm was the only one capable of making these rollers and I urged them to order enough rollers to keep us going in case of another war with Germany. Hitler had now come to power, and I had seen enough in Germany to sense that trouble was coming. The representative of Spicer's who had accompanied me to Kassel, a man named Wycherley, gave me full and able support at this meeting but Spicer's refused to have anything to do with the proposed order. I therefore placed it on my own account.

As soon as the rollers started coming in I sent them to Sawston for testing. The German firm had succeeded in engraving nineteen lines to the millimetre and the naked eye could not detect any engraving, the rollers appearing to have a flat and highly polished surface. Of the thirty rollers delivered only five or six were perfect, but the rest went back for skimming and re-engraving and soon we had two complete sets of rollers. The film made with these rollers was an enormous advance on the old and really put us on the map for cinematograph and high-class lithographic work. When Spicer's saw it they were so pleased they agreed that Dufaycolor should take over the order.

I had gone into the colour film business with a realistic idea of what the film could and could not do. Dufaycolor was a negative that anyone could put into any camera and develop in the same way as black and white film, but there was one basic limitation: there was as yet no successful process for making colour prints. Many firms were developing processes, however, all of which could use the Dufaycolor negative, and I believed there would be a world-wide need for such a negative. I likened Dufaycolor to a cork which could float behind and be sucked along in the powerful wake of the big photographic companies; we had to persuade these companies to use our negative to produce their own colour results, drawing us forward rapidly and securely in the process. I therefore concentrated on developing alliances with the photographic companies and I spent a lot of time travelling backwards and forwards for meetings with Dupont, Agfa Ansco and Kodak in America, and with Agfa in Germany. My travels convinced me that 80 per cent of the world's photographic business was in America and I decided that ultimately I must form an American company. But first I had to see the British company safely launched, and I decided to try to get Ilford's to handle the British Empire Rights. If I could persuade them to come in, a big financial responsibility would be removed from my shoulders.

Ilford's, of course, had been offered the world rights in the Dufay process some years earlier and had turned them down. They had second thoughts when I showed them the results we were getting with our new rollers. I started negotiating with two of the directors, Colonel Ramsden, son-in-law of the chairman, Sir Ivor Phillips, and a man of impressive military bearing, and Major Mein, tall and thin and of agile mind. Ramsden and Mein agreed that our roll film and 35-millimetre cinematograph film were satisfactory, but they criticized the projection of our 16-millimetre cinematograph film because of a slight fish-net effect caused by the extra magnification necessary to project this smaller film. This 16-millimetre film was therefore left out of the deal – a point which assumed considerable importance later.

It was decided to form a new company to take over the British Empire Rights called Spicer–Dufay–British, in which Dufaycolor would have a 49 per cent interest and Ilford's, who would provide whatever finance was necessary, 51 per cent, giving them control. The new company had the exclusive manufacturing rights in the British Empire of Dufaycolor film, together with the corresponding sales rights provided that at the end of three years they were selling a minimum quantity of film. This minimum, amounting to 80,000 running feet of film per annum 16 inches wide, was a substantial one. There was also a protection clause which provided that if at any time Ilford's refused to put up more money Dufaycolor would be free to do so, thus regaining control. Ilford's showed every indication of being delighted with the deal and at their next annual meeting Sir Ivor Phillips proudly stated that his company had taken over the British Empire rights of the wonderful Dufaycolor process, putting this up as a bull-point for his shareholders.

Spicer–Dufay–British was formed in January 1934. A few weeks later Chapman, my optical engineer in Colortone, discovered that by inserting a thin diffusion glass in front of the lens of a 16-millimetre projector the fish-net effect disappeared from the screen. I arranged

THE DUFAYCOLOR COMPANIES

Date Formed	Name of Company	Function of Company	Share-holders	Company Officials
1932	COLORTONE LTD.	To acquire Mrs Durand's share of the rights in the Dufay colour process	Sidney Cotton 66⅔% Mrs Durand 33⅓%	Chairman and Managing Director– Sidney Cotton
Jan. 1933	DUFAYCOLOR LTD.	To link Colortone's share in the Dufay process to the share owned by Spicers	Colortone 52% Spicer's 48%	Chairman: Sir Dykes Spicer Managing Director: Sidney Cotton
Jan. 1934	SPICER– DUFAY– BRITISH LTD.	To bring in Ilford's to handle the British Empire Rights in the Dufay process – including manufacture and sales	Ilford's 51% Dufaycolor 49%	Chairman and Managing Director as for Dufaycolor Ltd.
May 1934	DUFAYCOLOR INC.	To handle all aspects of Dufaycolor film in America	Dufaycolor Ltd.	President and Managing Director: Sidney Cotton
Dec. 1935	DUFAY- CHROMEX LTD.	A merger of Dufaycolor and Chromex to provide finance for development work	Dufaycolor 51% Chromex 49% (but see p. 93 for proposals that left the new company independent)	Chairman: Lord Mottistone Joint Managing Directors: Demetre Daponte and Sidney Cotton

a demonstration for the directors of Dufaycolor and they agreed that this film was now ready for the market. We brought our new discovery to the notice of Ilford's and told them our intention was to put this film on the market ourselves in mid-July. They raised no objection and offered to order the developing tanks for us from an associate company.

Some weeks later I asked the Ilford directors what progress had been made in manufacturing the developing tanks and received a somewhat vague reply. At the next meeting I asked for the name of the firm who were making the tanks but Ilford's didn't seem to know it, so I made a mental note to order another set of tanks myself in case Ilford's let us down. I also asked the Board if I could rent an unused building in the Spicer–Dufay–British factory at Elstree to store some Dufaycolor equipment, and this was agreed; my intention was to fit my own developing tanks into this building. Later, in the middle of May, I engaged four technicians and sent them to the Spicer experimental plant at Wembley for training; I would want them to develop the film when the plant was ready.

When I brought up the question of the developing tanks with the Ilford directors at the next Board meeting of Spicer–Dufay–British on 9th July, they admitted that something had gone wrong. I asked them how they thought Dufaycolor was going to meet its target date of mid-July and they said that this of course was out of the question. The discussion became heated, and I told the chairman, Sir Dykes Spicer, that I had a report to make. 'It seems to me,' I said, 'that Ilford's are not keen to see the 16-millimetre film reach the market first, because it was not included in their deal. But as I felt that they were slow in ordering the equipment I have gone ahead on my own and completed plans to put this film on the market on 23rd July, two weeks from now.'

The meeting exploded at once into uproar. When the excitement had died down a little, Colonel Ramsden turned to the chairman. 'All this,' he said, 'only goes to show how totally unrealistic Cotton is and how little he knows about the film business. It would take at least six weeks to train technicians to develop this film, and in any case there are cartons to be made, printing and advertising to be decided upon and so on. It couldn't possibly be done in a fortnight.'

'Colonel Ramsden is right,' I said. 'It has taken six weeks to train the technicians. They are now in a laboratory which I have installed in the empty building at Elstree, which you may remember I rented. They have been developing films taken by my own men and the results are coming out well.'

'What about the cartons?' asked Ramsden.

I sent for my secretary and she brought in a selection of the cartons I had ordered. Ramsden and Mein then showed their hand. They said they could not possibly agree to this 16-millimetre film being put on the market before their own roll film was ready. I reminded them that they had no rights in the 16-millimetre film. 'I've already come to an agreement with Wallace Heaton to fill their window in Bond Street

with Dufaycolor film,' I said, 'and I've got several other agents lined
up. All our literature and Press publicity is ready and several thousand
rolls of film are available to start the sales campaign.' I suggested that
the meeting adjourn to Elstree to see the progress made; several dozen
films were shown to the Ilford directors and our results were obviously
good. They then asked for the meeting to be adjourned so that they
could consult their fellow directors.

When we resumed a few days later, Colonel Ramsden opened with
a brief statement of the Ilford position. 'Our directors take a very
serious view of this matter,' he said, 'and I am authorized to give you
formal notice that Ilford's will put up no further money for Spicer–
Dufay–British.' I asked the secretary to see that this statement was
recorded in the minutes, and soon afterwards the meeting broke up.
I could see that Sir Dykes Spicer was most upset; he knew as well as I
did that without Ilford's help things would be difficult for Dufaycolor.
But my own view was that Ilford's had put themselves in an impossible
position. Despite all the boasts of the Ilford chairman about securing
the Dufaycolor process, our film would be on the market in a week's
time without their name on it and their shareholders would be bound
to ask some awkward questions. I made a bet with Sir Dykes Spicer
that Ilford's would be back during the week to make a deal.

A few days later Colonel Ramsden phoned me and asked me out to
lunch. Major Mein was with him. We talked about everything in the
world except colour photography, and it was a long time before Major
Mein grinned at me and came to the point. 'Come on, Sidney,' he said,
'you know what we're here for.' At the end of half an hour's talk we
had agreed terms. Ilford's would provide any money necessary to
develop Spicer–Dufay–British, up to a quarter of a million pounds.
They further agreed to supply me with rolls of colour film base with
which to develop the American market, and I was to have the choice
of film, which meant that I could select the best. Ilford's would retain
control of the company, into which the 16-millimetre film rights would
now go. All this gratified me very much; Dufaycolor would have no
further financial problems, and I could now devote my time to the
American market and leave the British Empire Rights safely to
Ilford's. The deal was concluded in August 1934, and after a short
holiday I collected some film from Ilford's and began my drive to
break into the American market.

11

The Collapse of Dufaycolor

M Y work in America necessitated so much travelling that I decided to find myself a chauffeur-valet who could look after my car and my clothes on these trips and any other chores that needed to be attended to. I was fortunate in having a young cockney named Cyril Kelson recommended to me. He was only twenty-five and at first I was doubtful about his qualifications, but when I asked him for details he seemed a little upset. 'I've been in service since I was fourteen,' he told me, 'and my father and my grandfather were in service too. You'll find that I know all about the work of a gentleman's gentleman. I've got a Rolls-Royce certificate, I passed through their training school, and I'm well able to look after your cars.' I engaged Kelson and from then on he accompanied me wherever I went. He had a wonderful way of including himself in the conversation. 'Perhaps we should wear our brown suit today, sir,' he would say. It was always 'we', never 'you'; it was almost as though Kelson, too, was wearing the suit in his imagination. He insisted that I shouldn't wear the same suit more than once a fortnight; in that way, he said, my wardrobe would be kept in perfect condition. I had to buy a couple of dozen suits to satisfy him. He would only allow me to wear a pair of shoes once a week, so I had to find myself a dozen pairs – black, tan and sporting. He darned my socks, cooked my meals when necessary, and would have been the model for Wodehouse's Jeeves. In those days it used to cost me only £40 return to take Kelson and a Rolls-Royce to America. Kelson stayed with me until the end of 1938, when he decided it was his duty to go and help his father, who had been ill and who ran a pub in Leicestershire. When war was declared in 1939, however, I wrote to him, and he immediately came to London and rejoined me.

I had formed an American company to exploit Dufaycolor in May 1934 – Dufaycolor Incorporated, the shares being wholly owned by Dufaycolor Ltd., which remained the world parent company and in which I still held a controlling interest. My policy was just the same as it had been in England – to get the support of the big photographic companies—and one of my first visits was to George Eastman, president of Kodak and the man who invented photographic film, known everywhere as the 'father of photography'. Kodak's were producing their own colour film, called Kodachrome, but it was inferior at that time to Dufaycolor. George Eastman received me most cordially and asked what sort of proposition I had in mind, and I suggested the formation of a separate company to handle the world rights of Dufaycolor outside the British Empire on a fifty-fifty basis. Eastman said this sounded all right but he would have to put it to his firm. 'It may take a couple of weeks to convince them,' he said, 'they think I'm getting old, you know.' He had just recovered from a serious illness but he seemed far from senile. I knew that a tie-up with Kodak's was the biggest thing I could possibly hope for and I was quite prepared to wait around for a time, but Eastman suggested that I pay a visit to Florida and come back a fortnight later. He recommended an hotel and promised to arrange the booking. As Joan was with me I thought this would be a wonderful idea and I accepted. We drove down in a Delage sports car lent to me by an old friend named A. J. Miranda, and we covered the 1,250 miles in under twenty hours' driving, an average of 64 m.p.h. But when I got there I was in low spirits. On the way down, as we were passing through Raleigh in North Carolina, we heard a newsboy shouting something about a photographer. Then we read on a newsboard the headline 'Photographer Shoots Self'. Something made me stop and buy a paper, and it was a terrible shock to read that George Eastman, whom I had seen only forty-eight hours earlier, had had another attack of his illness and had shot himself rather than become a burden to his family. He had left a note to say that he felt his life's work was done.

I now had to start all over again with Kodak's. Sir Dykes Spicer came over from London to meet the new president of the company, a man named Lovejoy, and we seemed at first to be making progress, but then Lovejoy told me that although his directors believed the Dufay process to be a good one they thought there was still some work to be done to perfect it and they could not agree to partnership on a fifty-fifty basis. They still wouldn't make up their minds to a firm proposition, so I decided to present them with some competition. I organized a big sales campaign in Florida, where I got three photographic agents to put on a window show of Dufaycolor film, and within a few days each agent was visited by a high-pressure salesman from Kodak's demanding a similar display for Kodachrome. I then carried out similar 'spot' sales campaigns in different parts of America, until, after five or six of these campaigns, Kodak's decided to join in and help me to market Dufaycolor film. They said this was cheaper than sending out salesmen to offset my 'spot' campaigns. They even sold Dufaycolor in their store in Madison Avenue, New York – the first time that Kodak had ever marketed a competitor's product – and a few weeks later Dufaycolor actually outsold Kodachrome in Kodak's own store.

Returning to England, where my wife had gone some weeks earlier for a holiday, I was faced with a calamity which was inexplicable to me. Since the birth of our daughter Jill in 1930, Joan had not been so fit as earlier, but she had continued to accompany me everywhere and had often expressed her preference for this sort of life, rather than staying at home while I travelled. Now Joan's doctor, who was a woman, asked to see me. She was sympathetic but blunt. 'I'm only telling you this,' she said, 'because I know you'll decide to do the right thing for Joan's sake.' She then disclosed powerful therapeutic reasons why I should give Joan her freedom.

I was shocked and distressed, too upset to think rationally, and although I believe I murmured something non-committal in reply I have little recollection of what I did in the next few hours. My reaction was to run away, to disappear as quickly as I could, to give myself time to think. I just couldn't face things for the moment. I went home and packed a bag, told Joan that something urgent had cropped up in America, and left next morning on the *Bremen* for New York. I was travelling to and fro so often at that time that my abrupt departure was no surprise to Joan.

I had known Joan since she was fifteen, when she had been such a fascinating companion up at Hawkes Bay; she was now twenty-seven, we had been everywhere together, and she had shared every facet of my life. Now, after nearly ten years of marriage, we drifted apart. I was forty-one, and I was quite certain I would never marry again. Joan, I am glad to say, was later fully restored to health.

About this time I heard that a company called Chromex Ltd., financed by Sir Malcolm Stewart, the brick and cement millionaire, was developing a new colour system under the direction of a Roumanian named Daponte. On investigation I found that they were using the age-old prism system, the one I had wasted so much time on, as others had done before me. Here was a chance to join forces to our mutual advantage; Dufaycolor Limited needed money for development work, and we had a proved system to offer. The result was that Sir Malcolm Stewart agreed to a merger between Chromex and Dufaycolor, the effect of which was that he would provide finance when it was wanted. The new company, called Dufay–Chromex, acquired the assets of Chromex and Dufaycolor but left Dufaycolor in control. Since my own company, Colortone Ltd., controlled Dufaycolor, I would retain effective personal control of the new company. However, at a dinner given in December 1935 to celebrate the launching of the company, it was put to me that my responsibilities were excessively heavy. We now had a million-pound company, I was often out of the country, flying off on some risky venture, and if anything happened to me my estate would be left in control. Would it not be more prudent for control to be shared?

It was therefore suggested to me that instead of Dufay–Chromex acquiring the assets of Dufaycolor under the merger, the shares themselves should be taken over. This would leave me with only a 25 per cent shareholding in the new company and I would lose control.

All the partners gave me their personal assurance that this manœuvre was inspired by prudence and not by any other motive; they expressed the view that I was almost entirely responsible for bringing the business to its present stage, and they assured me that I would be allowed to carry on the management and development at my own discretion. Perhaps a good dinner and the belief that I was amongst friends influenced me unduly. Anyway my memory of the many battles I had fought to carry my policies through was dimmed and I accepted their assurances and their proposal.

Back in America I made good progress with Dufaycolor Inc. Whereas all exposed Kodachrome film had to be mailed to Kodak's in Rochester from all over the world to be developed, the Dufaycolor negative could be developed on the spot in ordinary developer and the photographer could see his results straight away. This led to the introduction of Dufaycolor in the National Geographic Magazine, and for several years after this the majority of their colour photographs were made on Dufaycolor film. This in turn stimulated further successes, more than a score of American newspapers using Dufaycolor in their Sunday colour supplements. Interest spread to most of the big photographic and film companies – Agfa Ansco, Dupont, Kodak, 20th Century-Fox, Technicolor and so on – and the necessary finance to meet the enormous development that we had in prospect was promised by a leading American finance house. Yet in spite of all this, and of the assurances I had been given of support and a free hand in developing the American side of the business, I was having difficulty with my colleagues in London. They believed that the American photographic companies could only be interested in signing agreements with Dufaycolor in order to get the company thoroughly tied up and then eliminate it as a competitor. This was absurd, but throughout 1936, during which I must have crossed the Atlantic twenty times, there was a standing battle between myself and my colleagues in London on this point. Sooner or later, I knew, it would come to a head.

In December 1936, while I was in New York finalizing the negotiations for financing Dufaycolor Inc., I got a demand from the Official Receiver for the payment of £13,800 on account of Messrs Hamilton, Mackay, brokers, now in bankruptcy. This referred to the loss sustained by the firm in 1927 in buying Dunlop shares contrary to my cabled instructions. Now, nine years later, I was faced with a claim that I thought was dead. I wrote at once to my solicitor in London enclosing a copy of the Hamilton, Mackay letter in which they agreed never to make any claim against me, and I received a disturbing reply. The Official Receiver would not be obliged to recognize the Hamilton, Mackay letter and I would be well advised, he said, to let him try to arrange a settlement.

My negotiations with the New York financiers were going well and I did not feel I ought to leave New York until they were completed, so I authorized my solicitor to make the best settlement he could with the Receiver and then to arrange with Dufay–Chromex, who owed me a substantial sum in back salary and expenses, to advance the necessary payment. My solicitor cabled back that the Receiver had agreed to settle for £5,000. This was well within the sum owed to me by Dufay–Chromex, and at the next Board meeting the directors agreed to pay it into court on 15th January 1937, when the case was due to be heard. They said they preferred to do this themselves rather than hand the money over to my solicitor.

Had I not been so deeply involved in America I might have seen the danger I was in. The Official Receiver could not have taken action against me for the £5,000 unaided; someone must have backed it. And why weren't Dufay–Chromex prepared to hand over my own money to my own solicitor? Anyway, on the appointed day there was no one present to pay the money into court, which meant that a receiving order was automatically made against me. Under English law the issue of a receiving order automatically cancels all directorships. So as a direct result of the omission I forfeited my position on the boards of all the companies I had formed and helped to form. If someone had been setting out to eliminate me from the entire Dufaycolor picture they could not have acted in a more Machiavellian way.

I concluded the negotiations in New York as quickly as I could and returned to London, where my fellow directors in Spicer–Dufay–British and Dufay–Chromex, ignoring my demand to know why they had not paid the money into court as agreed, did not conceal their satisfaction at my elimination as a director. It was clear that during my long and frequent absences in America, the feeling that had built up against the policies I had always laid down for the advance of Dufaycolor had become intense.

I went to the Official Receiver and told him the whole story, and he accepted the justice of my case and gave me written permission to be reappointed a director of all the companies; but getting myself reappointed was quite another matter. My own examination, too, had to take its normal course. The Inland Revenue had taken the opportunity to slap in a demand for £18,000 in back taxes, which I did not owe, but before I could get the receiving order rescinded I either had to pay up or fight and win the case, which following counsel's advice I was confident of doing. My position, in fact, was quite fluid, but it was nearly a year before the case could be brought and won. The receiving order was then rescinded.

The Directors of Dufay–Chromex were 'too busy' to see me for several weeks after my return from America. When at last I did hear from them, it was only to learn that they had signed a contract with an American whereby they sold him the American rights for £12,000 in cash and a minority interest in the American company. I was dismissed from the presidency of Dufaycolor Incorporated, and shortly afterwards the American companies broke the bonds I had been forging with them.

The years of frustration, and the treatment I had received at the hands of the Board of the company I had founded, finally brought me to a state of nervous collapse, and meanwhile I had to stand by and watch the policies I had been pursuing to build up Dufaycolor being reversed on both sides of the Atlantic. In England, the British Empire Rights were bought back from Ilford's in a piece of extraordinary folly, £25,000 being paid for them when they would shortly have lapsed anyway; and in America, the situation deteriorated so quickly that in a short time Dufaycolor Inc. had ceased to operate. To raise capital in England, Dufay–Chromex made a large issue of shares to the public, then put on a costly sales campaign to encourage the purchase of Dufaycolor film at 3s. 6d. a roll, apparently unaware that it was costing more than that to produce. When, as was inevitable, funds ran short, Spicer's, Ilford's and Chromex made loans, and further public issues were made. Each time funds ran short the shares fell, and I then bought as many as I could lay my hands on, hoping one day to regain a decisive voice in the running of the company.

Meanwhile I was preparing my case against Dufay–Chromex; but in 1939 before I was able to start proceedings, I was drawn into a project for clandestine photographic air reconnaissance, after which all thoughts of legal action were swamped by the work I took on in the first months of the war. There was, however, a postscript to the Dufaycolor story; it did not occur until 1943, but for the sake of continuity I will relate it now.

A friend of mine named Leon Lewitt came to see me in January 1943. He was managing director of Polyphoto (England), the multi-position photographers, and he knew all about my interest in Dufaycolor. He told me he had decided to sell Polyphoto; the firm's profits were £133,000 a year but all but £5,000 of that was going to the Government in Excess Profits Tax. 'With all your development losses in Dufay-color,' he said, 'you should be able to absorb most of the Polyphoto profits and avoid paying such heavy E.P.T.' The sum he was asking was £125,000.

I immediately grasped the importance of what he had said. Lewitt gave me an option for thirty days to buy Polyphoto, and while I was mulling over the best way of handling the deal I had a telephone call from Daponte, the Rumanian who had run Chromex for Sir Malcolm Stewart and who had succeeded me as managing director of Dufay–Chromex. He told me a depressing story of how the company was still losing money and how Spicer's had now told him to put it into liquidation. He wanted to know if there was anything I could do to help.

It was an extraordinary coincidence that he should come to me at

that moment, and I was greatly struck too by the irony of the situation
–that Dufay–Chromex, after all that had happened, should come to
me in their hour of need. But the company was my creation and I
still remained one of the biggest shareholders. If they bought Polyphoto they would be back on their feet.

I telephoned my brokers and told them to buy all the Dufay–
Chromex shares they could lay their hands on. The shares were quoted
nominally, and it was elementary that as soon as it became known that
Dufay–Chromex had bought Polyphoto they would have a substantial
asset value. But I wasn't prepared just to hand over the deal. My idea
was that I would take up the option on Polyphoto myself and then
sell a 75 per cent interest in it to Dufay–Chromex for £125,000, retain-
ing a 25 per cent interest in Polyphoto as my profit on the deal.

Next there was the question of raising the £125,000. Spicer's,
Ilford's, Chromex and Colortone each owned approximately 25 per
cent of Dufay–Chromex, and by selling a proportion of these shares
to a finance house for cash, we could lend that cash back to Dufay–
Chromex to buy Polyphoto. With the prospect of a big rise in asset
value we would have no difficulty in getting a finance house to buy
at a reasonable figure. Daponte saw that we had a sound proposition
and he got the agreement of Spicer's, Ilford's and Chromex. A contract
was drawn up between Dufay–Chromex and myself under which they
agreed to buy 75 per cent of Polyphoto for £125,000.

At this point, because of my preoccupation with the war effort, I
was obliged to be out of London for a time, and I appointed a Trust
Company to act as my Trustee. They insisted on a clause in our agreement enabling them to use their discretion in my absence to make any
minor modifications to the deal that they might consider necessary,
and when I returned to London I found that the deal had gone through
but that they had felt it desirable to let Dufay–Chromex have my 25
per cent of Polyphoto as well as the 75 per cent agreed, without any
increase in price. When I protested that they couldn't do this without
consulting me they invoked the discretion clause. I consulted counsel
and they confirmed that the Trust Company had the legal right to do
what they had done.

Although I lost my 25 per cent interest in Polyphoto I still came
extremely well out of the deal. I had been buying Dufay–Chromex
shares at or near rock bottom for some time and my brokers continued
to buy all the shares I could finance before the deal was completed.
The shares rocketed when the merger became known and I was able

to sell at a substantial profit. Being a capital gain no tax was payable.

I now felt I had been rewarded to some extent for all the work I had put into the building up of Dufaycolor over the years. But no financial gain could ever compensate me for the collapse of the structure I had tried to create, and despite the money that I made out of Dufaycolor I look upon my ten years in colour photography as a failure.

After the war the directors of Dufay–Chromex failed to get further backing in England, but an Italian company agreed to finance them provided the plant was moved to Elba. Eventually the Italian company, too, was reported to have gone into liquidation, and as far as I know the plant still lies rotting in Elba. Today the Dufaycolor film, which still gives a more faithful reproduction of colour than any other process, is a thing of the past. Yet I remain convinced that if the four big original partner–shareholders had allowed me to follow my policy of allying Dufaycolor to the big photographic companies, instead of attempting to compete with them, Dufaycolor today would be a household word. Major Adrian Klein, in his book *Colour Cinematography*,[1] has this to say about Dufaycolor:

> No colour process can claim all qualities and Dufaycolor has many points in its favour. It is a single film printed from a single original, both of which bear the whole image; thus the analysis and the synthesis is reduced to a purely photographic operation with a minimum chance for defects to arise during a series of difficult transformations. The colour range is all that could be desired, delicate tones being rendered with great beauty. As a technical achievement nothing more remarkable has been done in the history of photography, gigantic difficulties had to be surmounted at every step. Dufaycolor is one of those instances in applied science in which had the whole project been put before experienced photographic manufacturers in the first place, it would probably have been rejected as chimerical. It could only have reached the present state of practicability by the untiring belief and support of private individuals unacquainted with the prodigious problems involved.

[1] Chapman and Hall, London, 1939.

12

The Secret Flights

THERE are people whom we rarely see, sometimes for years on end, whose friendship nevertheless means a lot to us. For me, A. J. (Alfred) Miranda, whom I had first met at the New York Motor Show in 1927, was one of these. The arrival of a telegram from him on 14th September 1938 brought me out of a deep trough of depression following the failure of my plans for Dufaycolor. The telegram was to say that A.J., as I always called him, was to arrive in London next day. It was A. J. Miranda who had lent me the Delage sports car in which I had driven from Washington to Miami in 1934. I had not seen him since.

A.J. told me when he arrived that he had to go straight on to Paris on business, and he insisted that I go with him. Waiting to meet us in Paris was Miranda's European agent, Paul Koster, a man of over seventy, but sprightly and animated and full of amusing talk; we got on very well together. Next day, after spending the morning with Koster, A.J. came back to our hotel for lunch and told me that he had had a long talk with Koster about me. He lowered his voice. 'Paul has asked me,' he said, 'to sound you out on whether you would be willing to co-operate in certain work.'

I felt certain from A.J.'s tone and manner that the work they had been talking about was connected with the intense military activity that was going on at that time in Germany, and A.J. confirmed that this was so. This was the month of the Munich agreement, and the relevant intelligence departments in Paris and London, I was told, believed that war could not be avoided much longer; therefore it was vitally important to get as much information as possible about fortifications, airfields and military establishments in Germany and Italy while there was still time. Unfortunately the Nazi and Fascist security services had been so drastically reorganized in recent months that information of this kind was becoming much harder to get. The idea therefore was to supplement existing sources of information by means of clandestine aerial photography.

To avoid suspicion, the help of a private owner well known in European aviation circles was to be enlisted. A British aircraft would have to be the medium as French aircraft were too closely watched. Koster, it seemed, had been asked to look out for an owner who might be prepared to co-operate, and I had been approached because I had been in the habit of flying my own plane round the European capitals for years. I told A.J. that I would have no objection provided the British Government agreed, and I was then taken to see Paul Koster. Koster told me that someone would get in touch with me as soon as I got back to London. He couldn't tell me who it would be, but I would know when the time came. The day after I returned to London I received a phone call.

'Major Cotton?'

'Speaking.' I had long since been dubbed 'major', a rank to which I was not entitled, but it was the equivalent of my retiring Royal Naval Air Service rank and I had got used to answering to it.

'I understand that you have just returned from Paris, where you met my friend Paul.'

'Yes,' I said, 'that is so.' This, clearly, was the man I was to look out for. The voice was superbly anonymous.

'I'd like to come and see you right away if I may.'

'Certainly.'

A few minutes later a Major Winterbotham was announced, and I looked up to see a man of about my own age, dressed in a grey lounge suit which toned perfectly with his grey eyes and greying hair. There was a quiet look of discretion about him. We shook hands. 'I am Paul's friend,' he said. He talked of the importance of getting as much information as possible while there was still time. He said that I only had to play the part of the well-known aeroplane owner; another crew would fly the plane on the actual missions, so it was best that I should know as little as possible of what these missions were.

I was not quite so happy about this. If I was to lend my name to the project I felt that I ought to know more about it. However, in view of the urgency of the situation I agreed to co-operate. Once I was in there might be a chance of doing more.

Major Winterbotham said that all expenses would be paid by the intelligence department concerned. He asked what sort of remuneration I would require, and I replied that as long as my out-of-pocket expenses were met I should be content.

We met several times in the next few days, dining at Arlington

House, where I was now living. It was convenient to dine in the restaurant and then have coffee afterwards in my flat, where we could talk freely. It emerged that the venture was to be a combined Anglo–French one, the French having put up most of the cash. They had already done some aerial photography in short-range aircraft over the Rhineland and the Siegfried Line, but they now wanted to operate a faster and more modern aircraft on longer trips into Germany and Italy. Winterbotham was not convinced that the idea was practicable, but his department had agreed to try it out. I was to use the aircraft fairly frequently myself to substantiate the story of a privately-owned British plane.

I suggested that we use a Lockheed 12A. Winterbotham agreed, and I phoned A. J. Miranda in New York and asked him to get me one. He did so, and it arrived at Southampton towards the end of January 1939. I had it erected and flown to Heston, and a pilot from the Lockheed firm made a test flight with me before giving me some dual, explaining all the instruments and the cockpit drill. I then made a couple of solo flights and packed up for the day, feeling very pleased with myself. I had not flown for nearly two years. I dined with Winterbotham that night and reported that everything was ready for the flights.

Two days later several French officers and a French pilot arrived at Heston from Paris. Winterbotham and I met them, and I took them for a flight in the Lockheed. At 10,000 feet I handed over to the French pilot, but he proved very ham-fisted on the controls, and after half an hour I took over again and landed back at Heston. I was then asked to take the French pilot up with me on my own and let him do a few landings. On his first three attempts he got progressively worse, and on the fourth attempt I was forced to take over and land the plane myself. By this time I had had enough for one day, and my temper wasn't improved when, on my way across to the restaurant to rejoin the others, I was asked by the chief instructor of the local flying club whether I was feeling all right. He had noticed, he said, that my landings were not up to my usual standard. I flushed and said something about everyone having their off days.

Winterbotham urged me to persevere, but next day the result was the same, and to complicate matters several people began to show an interest in my new French friends and to ask why I was giving them dual. To allay suspicion I put out the story that the French were buying a Lockheed and as there were no demonstrators available I had agreed to demonstrate mine; but that night I told Winterbotham that I was afraid the idea of a French crew wouldn't work out. I had always flown my own plane; the introduction of a French crew would get more and more difficult to account for. The best thing, I said, was to let me do the flying myself. The French then suggested a compromise under which I would fly the Lockheed to a little-known airfield outside Paris, where the French would take over. The airfield chosen was Toussous-le-Noble, a small grass field fifteen miles south-west of Paris that was just about long enough for a fully-loaded take-off.

When I got there I was asked to give some more tuition to my friend Monsieur 'X', the French pilot. As my French is not worth mentioning and the Frenchman knew no English, another man accompanied us as interpreter. Unfortunately he wasn't a pilot. He stood just behind the front compartment, translating for us as best he could, but referring continually to a large French–English dictionary whenever he was stumped by some technical word or phrase. It was not the best means of communication, for instructor or pupil.

Monsieur 'X' made three unsuccessful approaches, all in the wrong direction, so I took over and demonstrated what I felt to be a reasonable landing. We took off again, and this time he made his approach correctly but overshot and touched down heavily about half-way across the field, bouncing high into the air. I took over the controls, opened the throttles, and just managed to get away safely by flying between two hangars. I then flew on to Le Bourget, deciding that it was useless to persevere any further with Monsieur 'X'. In any case I was not prepared to fly again with him at the controls. The *Deuxième Bureau* then accepted my proposal that I do the flying myself.

I asked Winterbotham if he could find me a good engineer-pilot who would be prepared to fly with me on these missions and at the same time maintain and service the plane. I asked for an Australian or a Canadian for preference, as I wanted someone with initiative who wouldn't mind roughing it if that should be necessary. Winterbotham soon produced a Canadian named Bob Niven, whose short-service commission in the R.A.F. was about to expire, and I liked the look of him. When I told him that I did a lot of flying to various places and that the flights were not altogether devoid of risk his interest grew.

Bob Niven, tall, zestful and enthusiastic, came from Calgary, in the great open spaces of Alberta, where he had once been a bus-driver. It had been his ambition since childhood to fly, and his opportunity came in 1935 when he was offered a short-service commission in the R.A.F. He was just coming to the end of his engagement so I was able to get him released to fly with me. We did several flights together to Aero Club meetings in France and he proved a good mixer. Winterbotham agreed that I should warn him discreetly of what we were planning to do, to give him a chance to pull out, but Bob of course was keener than ever. We were ready to fly our first mission towards the end of February 1939.

We flew over from Heston to Toussous-le-Noble, where we were met by a burly and jovial Irishman named Tom Green who was a liaison officer with the *Deuxième Bureau*. That evening at Green's flat a Captain Pépin of the *Bureau* came in to go over our plans for the following day. Short and compactly built, with the physique of a boxer, Pépin had been trained as a fighter pilot in the French Air Force, and it was soon apparent that he felt that no one but the French knew much about this sort of work. His manner was that of the lecturer, precise and pedantic, without a glimmer of humour.

'We have arranged for one of our best photographers to accompany you tomorrow,' he said. 'He is a French-Canadian named Bois who has already operated several times on short missions over the frontier. He will join you with his equipment at Toussous tomorrow morning. All you have to do is to go where he tells you.'

'I shall want to know where the places are that we have to photograph,' I said. 'I shall want to plan the flight most carefully.'

'That, I'm afraid,' said Pépin, 'is impossible. It is most secret. Bois will bring a map and full instructions.'

I said nothing more in front of Pépin; but when he'd gone I protested to Green. 'Success is going to depend on careful planning,' I said. 'If they think I'm going to risk my neck on blind missions they're crazy. I don't mind what risks I take so long as I do my own planning.'

'Do a flight or two first,' urged Green. 'The French have been doing this sort of thing for years and they think they're good at it.'

Early next morning we joined up with Bois at Toussous. I was glad to find that he was ready to explain our mission in some detail. There had been reports of new airfields and arms factories on the outskirts of Mannheim, seventy miles north-east of Strasbourg, and we were to get photographs of the town and its surroundings. Our take-off was timed for eleven o'clock, to arrive over Mannheim about the same time as the morning passenger plane from Strasbourg, and we were to approach from the same direction. This, it was hoped, might help us to avoid detection. It sounded a reasonable plan. If we were spotted by an unfriendly aircraft outside French territory and forced down, we were to jettison our cameras and all incriminating evidence over water or failing that into a forest. A large aperture had been cut in the floor of the cabin through which the lens of the camera could get an unobstructed view and through which we could jettison everything in an emergency. We knew, of course, that to be forced down meant almost certainly to be arrested as spies, with all that that meant, but we could not complain at that.

Bois said it was absolutely necessary to get the camera into the Lockheed without being seen. Someone might be watching. The Lockheed was parked in a hangar and the camera was in the boot of Bois's car. Having satisfied himself that there was no one lurking about in the hangar, Bois got his driver to back the car up to the hangar door. They then proceeded to wrestle with the camera. Niven and I watched all this highly suspicious behaviour with some amusement. The camera proved to be a bulky piece of machinery about five feet long, and although it was encased in a linen bag it was not difficult to guess what it was. Bois and his driver had just lifted it out of the car and set it down on the ground for a moment when someone came out of the hangar.

Bois and his driver now enacted a strange pantomime. They put on an air of exaggerated innocence and began walking away from the camera in opposite directions. The little French mechanic who had been concealed in the hangar watched their antics in astonishment. Then he saw Niven and me. We tried to compose our features, but it was too late, and the little French mechanic joined in the laughter.

As soon as he had gone, Bois and his driver rushed back to the camera and lifted it into the Lockheed. When they had fitted it into place we pushed the plane out of the hangar, warmed up the engines, and took off on our baptism of cloak-and-dagger flying.

We followed the normal air transport route from Paris due east as far as Strasbourg, climbing steadily. When we reached 15,000 feet, however, the windscreen became completely covered with hoar frost and we couldn't see out at all. I tried to slide the window back on my side with the idea of chipping at the front with a screw-driver, but I couldn't move it. Eventually I got it open about a quarter of an inch, but it wouldn't come any farther. In less than a minute, however, the frost disappeared.

After a while I began to get cold, so I closed the window. Almost at once the windscreen frosted over again. I forced the pane open and the frost disappeared as before, so I kept the pane slightly open from then on. I concluded that when the pane was open the warm air in the cock-

5(a). Shackleton's
Baby Avro

5(b). Pulling the D.H. 9 into a hangar in a blizzard

). Four of our
es outside the
hangar at
Botwood

6(a). The *Sagona* in the ice-floes, taken from the Westland

6(b). After a successful hunt – a "pan" of seals

pit was sucked out past the windscreen by the airstream, the difference in temperature preventing the air from condensing and freezing. I put this lesson to good effect later.

We approached Mannheim from the south-south-west at 20,000 feet, altering course continually to follow the curve of the Rhine as it meandered northwards. Conditions were good and I hoped Bois was getting his pictures. Even at that height we could sometimes pick out the vast concrete structures of the Siegfried Line. My alterations of course were dictated by Bois. He was out of sight and earshot back in the fuselage, but he had attached a long string lead to each of my elbows, and he kept pulling one and then the other depending on which way he wanted me to turn to get his pictures. We were just finishing our run, about three miles north of Mannheim and deep into Germany, when Bois suddenly burst into the front compartment. 'There's a small fighter plane,' he shouted, 'climbing very fast towards us.' He said he'd been watching it for some time but had lost it in the sun. He was certain it was about to attack us.

I turned at once for the French border, south-west, straight into the sun. We saw nothing more of the fighter, and we crossed the frontier with some relief a few minutes later. Bois felt we must have aroused suspicion, and he believed that on future missions we might be attacked, but we completed several more flights with him in the next few days, over the Siegfried Line, along the Swiss border and to the north of Lake Constance, all without incident. One thing that disturbed me, however, was that the *Deuxième Bureau* refused to let me see our photographs, on security grounds, so I had no means of judging how well we were doing the job.

After pointing out the stupidity of this on several occasions, I was at last allowed to see the photographs, also a map on which were plotted the exact areas covered by our pictures. The results were most disappointing. The Mannheim pictures, for instance, disclosed many gaps, although we had believed at the time that we were covering the area thoroughly. Some of the most important targets had been missed altogether. We would have to improve our methods, which were crude in the extreme. Another thing that worried me was that anyone catching a glimpse of the erratic course we were obliged to steer to get our pictures would surely guess what we were doing.

In the following month, March 1939, Hitler committed a flagrant breach of the Munich agreement by marching his troops into Prague. Chamberlain promised full military support for Poland – the next

E

country, it was clear, on Hitler's list – and war looked inevitable. It was vital to get as much work done in the next few months as possible, and that meant devising a means of covering a much greater area per exposure. I knew that one of the new cameras specially designed for the R.A.F., the F.24, would take pictures which from 20,000 feet would cover several miles on each exposure, but the definition with ordinary Air Force film was not very good. However, I believed that if I used Leica film and a fine-grain developer I would get better results. The F.24 camera was only about 10 inches high by 6 inches square, in comparison to the 5 feet by 15 inches of the clumsy French camera, and it was small and light enough to go into a suitcase, which would cut out the elaborate pantomime we had to endure at present.

I made up a frame to carry three F.24 cameras, mounted lengthwise down the fuselage, one behind the other, the front camera tilted to the right, the rear one to the left, and the centre one pointing straight down, set at such an angle that the pictures overlapped slightly. The photographs we took at our maximum height of 20,000 feet would then cover a strip of country ten miles wide, enabling us to maintain a straight course, greatly reducing the risk of arousing suspicion.

I returned to France in high spirits, but to my disgust the *Deuxième Bureau* would have nothing to do with my scheme. They said they'd been doing this sort of work for years and I could teach them nothing. I was so upset that I went straight back to London and advised Winterbotham to hand over the Lockheed to the French. I was not prepared to continue with these missions, with their obvious dangers, unless I could plan and carry them out in an efficient manner. Winterbotham supported me, and the French agreed to take over, but they asked me to carry out one more urgent flight, this time to Sicily and North Africa, as they couldn't get another crew ready in time. On condition that I was allowed to do my own flight planning I eventually agreed.

We arrived in Paris on 17th April and were due to take off for Tunis next morning. After dinner at Tom Green's flat, our old friend Captain Pépin came in to brief us. The briefing went on for hours and was full of the kind of detail that a pilot normally decides for himself. Pépin would take us on a flight of fancy from Paris to Orange, south of Lyons, where we were to refuel, then say 'résumé' and go over that particular leg all over again. The same thing happened with the next leg, and the next, by which time we had dubbed him 'Résumé' for good. He had absolutely no idea how a private owner behaved or operated, but he went on in this strain until 2 a.m., and the only way I could stop him in the finish was to get up off the floor, which was by this time littered with maps, yawn with a note of finality, and announce that with an early start to face in the morning I was off to bed. Even then he insisted on giving me my cover story. 'You are to be a rich English milord,' he said, 'a close friend of the King, passionately interested in ruins, flying down to Tunis for a holiday. As befits your rank and title, a car will be placed at your disposal.' I thought this might have complications, but I was too tired to argue.

We took off early next morning and arrived at Orange on schedule, refuelled and went on to Bastia in Corsica. We intended to fly straight through to Tunis in one day, but the weather beyond Bastia was so bad that we stayed there the night. So much for the plans of 'Résumé'. At Tunis we were met by the Dunlop and Shell representative, a man named Dupont, who proved to be 'in the know' and who told us he was to be our line of communication with Paris. Our first task was to be the photographing of an Italian air base near Tripoli, amongst other things, but we were not to take off until he told us the weather was suitable. My cover story had been leaked discreetly, and we had no trouble with Customs. Dupont said there was a car waiting for me, and he gave me the name of my hotel.

'Is that the best hotel?'

'Yes,' he said, a little uncertainly I thought. 'It is the best.'

'That's funny, Thomas Cook's recommended another one.' I told him its name.

'That's an Italian hotel.'

'Is it the best one?'

'Well, yes, but the French don't use it because it's wired with dictaphones and full of Italians.'

I told Dupont that as a close friend of the King I must stay at the best hotel, and that in any case I preferred to stay at an Italian hotel as this would make it quite evident that I was not working with the French. Dupont was horrified, but he said no more and led me to my car. He pointed proudly to a dilapidated little French car, rather like an ancient Baby Austin. 'That is your car, sir,' he said.

The time had come to live up to the cover story the French had concocted for me. The nobility were expected to be eccentric, so it didn't matter if I caused a scene. 'I didn't expect you to provide my engineer with a car as well,' I said, deliberately misunderstanding Dupont, 'but thank you all the same. Now, where is *my* car?' Dupont was speechless, so I carried straight on. 'I want you to get me a large Fiat, and a chauffeur to go with it.' My friend the King, I felt, would hardly have approved of anything less. In an astonishingly short space of time, Fiat and chauffeur appeared.

Day after day Dupont told us that the weather was unsuitable, although it looked all right to us, so we spent our time amongst the Roman ruins in the Tunis area. We wasted ten days like this, and then Pépin arrived from Paris to see what was causing the delay. When I told him of the orders we'd had from Dupont he seemed puzzled, but said nothing. We then discussed the plans I had made for the trip.

I told Pépin that I proposed taking off from Tunis just after the Italian civil plane bound for Tripoli, and following it across the Bay of Tunis direct to Tripoli, where I would turn south for the new aerodrome at Castel Benito, then return along the coast. This, I felt, would confuse any Italian detectors. Pépin did not like the plan and insisted that we fly due south down the Tunisian coast to Ben Gardene, then east along the coast to a point twenty miles beyond Tripoli, then south towards Castel Benito. We would then fly north to Tripoli, and follow the coast back to Tunis. This route certainly gave us more changes of course. but I couldn't see who was going to be confused by this. At 20,000 feet in that clear atmosphere we could easily be seen, and I still thought our best chance of avoiding detection on the way in was to cut straight across the Bay behind the Italian civil plane. If we were spotted after that it wouldn't matter so much, as it wouldn't be so obvious where we'd come from. But Pépin persisted and to save any more argument I agreed to do it his way.

According to the Civil Air Code we had to declare our destination, but I didn't have one, not in that sense. I could hardly say I was going on a joy-ride round Tunisia, but any airfield for which I cleared would be alerted to expect us, and would report our non-arrival. I stressed this to Pépin and asked if he could name a small French airfield in the desert which we could clear for but which he could warn not to report our non-arrival. He named an obscure landing-ground and promised to make the necessary arrangements.

We took off next morning and carried out the flight according to Pépin's plan in perfect weather, except that I varied the plan slightly by keeping fifteen miles out to sea down the Tunisian coast. There was much to be seen and photographed both on Castel Benito airfield and along the coast, and it was seven hours before we landed back at Tunis. Ten minutes later the controller told us that a high-flying aircraft had been seen near Ben Gardene and asked if we had been in that direction.

This was many miles away from our declared flight plan, so I was forced to say no. But a few moments later he returned with another signal: the landing-ground we had cleared for had reported our non-arrival, and not surprisingly he wanted an explanation. Since there wasn't one I sent for Dupont and told him to get hold of Pépin, who must untangle what was his own mess as best he could. I was very upset at this shocking inefficiency, and I feared that our flight plan and purpose would be known in a matter of hours. But I heard nothing more.

When I saw Pépin later that day I told him that I proposed to photograph the coastline of Sicily, which was to be our next task, in three stages, using Malta as an intermediate stop. Pépin wanted me to do the whole mission in one flight, but this time I refused to give way. Pépin, too, was adamant, so I phoned London for instructions, while Pépin promised to contact both Paris and London. Next day a telegram arrived telling me to return at once by Air France and to hand over the Lockheed to Bob Niven, who was to carry out Pépin's instructions.

I couldn't understand London acting in this way. Neither could I forget Pépin's failure to warn the French landing-ground. He had offered no explanation. I had a heated meeting with Pépin amongst the Roman ruins of Carthage, and I got out of him that he had told London I had a business appointment and was anxious to get back. That explained the London telegram. I had lost whatever confidence I had in Pépin, and it was time to pull out. We flew back to Toussous-le-Noble next morning and left the Lockheed there, returning to London by Air France.

It was clear that further co-operation with the *Deuxième Bureau* on this project was impossible. If worthwhile results were to be obtained I must have my own aircraft and operate in my own way.

13

Cameras Over the Red Sea

M Y proposals for operating independently of the French were accepted and the next thing to do was to get another Lockheed. Once again I contacted A. J. Miranda, he found one for me that had just been thoroughly overhauled by Lockheed's, and it arrived at Southampton in the first week of May 1939. The firm of Cunliffe-Owen assembled it for me at Eastleigh, and I flew it to Heston on 11th May. Fred Winterbotham told me that our first task would be a series of long flights in the Middle East, so I decided to have some additional petrol tanks fitted, aiming at a range in still air of not less than 1,600 miles. The normal range of a Lockheed 12A was 700 miles.

Cunliffe-Owen's agreed to make two 70-gallon tanks and fit them in the fuselage immediately behind the pilot's compartment, so I flew the plane back to Eastleigh. I told them I needed the plane urgently for a flight to Africa on business, and they promised to complete the work within ten days. But when at the end of May the work was still not completed I flew the plane, together with the unfinished tanks, back to Heston and got Airwork to finish the job. Time was short and a promise was a promise. Letters of protest from Cunliffe-Owen Ltd. followed me for many a day.

Airwork also cut a hole in the entrance door and two holes in the floor of the cabin, one on each side, to enable cameras to be installed and operated easily. Neat little metal panels, almost impossible to detect, covered the holes when the cameras were not in use. I made up some simple fittings to take the three F.24 cameras in line ahead, similar to those I had used in the French Lockheed, and I had three long leads fitted to the electric control boxes so that I could operate the cameras from the cockpit.

In order to see downwards from the cockpit when nearing the target I devised a Perspex pear-shaped window which protruded into the slipstream and enabled me to put my head out and see straight down. It also greatly improved my vision immediately forward and to the rear. I patented the tear-drop and licensed it to Triplex, and it became a feature of many British aircraft, over 100,000 of them being made during the war. I had a contract with Triplex that would have brought me 10s. for each tear-drop fitted, over £50,000 in all, but as only war-time aircraft were involved I made no claim.

One day at Heston I was watching the Maharajah of Jodhpur take off in his private plane, and very soon after it left the ground I lost sight of it. Soon I realized that it had disappeared altogether. It was painted a pale, duck-egg green, and I was convinced that this was why I had lost sight of it; it had simply merged into the background. I got the Titanine Dope Company to make up a similar paint, slightly lighter in hue, and I registered it as 'Camotint' (although I took out no patents), and had the Lockheed painted with it. It was nothing unusual for a private owner to paint his aeroplane in some gay colour, and I felt that now, when flying at height, I would be practically invisible from below.

I fitted all our operational equipment, cameras, spares and so on, into ordinary suitcases, which I covered with old travel labels to make them look like innocent luggage. Once we were in the air it was a simple matter to unpack them and set up the cameras, and when we had finished taking pictures the cameras and film were just as easily dismantled, packed and stowed before landing.

By 12th June the tanks were fitted and all our equipment was collected and tested. But the new tanks and the extra petrol, together with the cameras, had given us a considerable overload, so much so that the Air Registration Board in London refused me a certificate of airworthiness. I had already cabled Lockheed's about this overload and they had assured me that, although the plane was only approved for an all-up weight of 9,200 lb., our new all-up weight of 11,300 lb. was perfectly safe. Eventually I was granted a temporary permit by the A.R.B. provided the extra petrol tanks were not used. This seemed to put us back where we started, but I decided that I could hardly be blamed if someone filled the extra tanks 'in error'. Honour would thus be satisfied on both sides.

We were due to take off for Malta on the first leg of our flight to the Middle East on 14th June. I drove out to Heston early that morning with one suitcase containing my personal kit together with three more suitcases containing the cameras and portable oxygen gear. We had decided not to fit permanent oxygen equipment as we thought it might be imprudent to advertise the height at which we intended to fly. Our additional tanks, of course, had been filled, and it was a popular

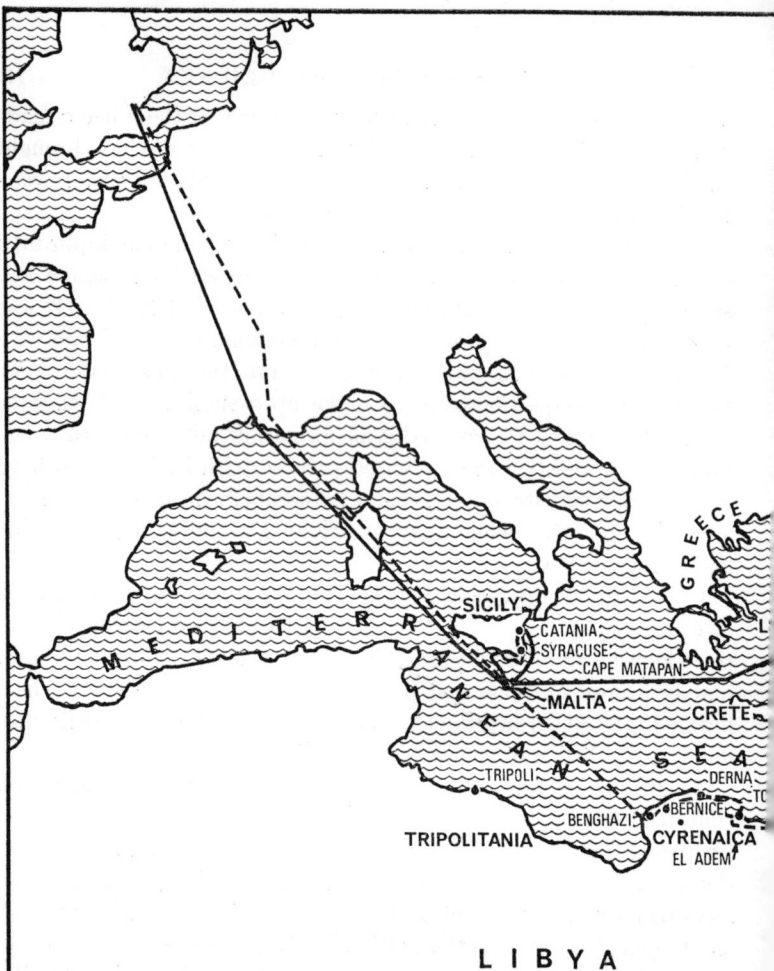

Outward journey
Homeward journey

MY AIR TOUR OF THE MIDDLE EAST,
JUNE 1939

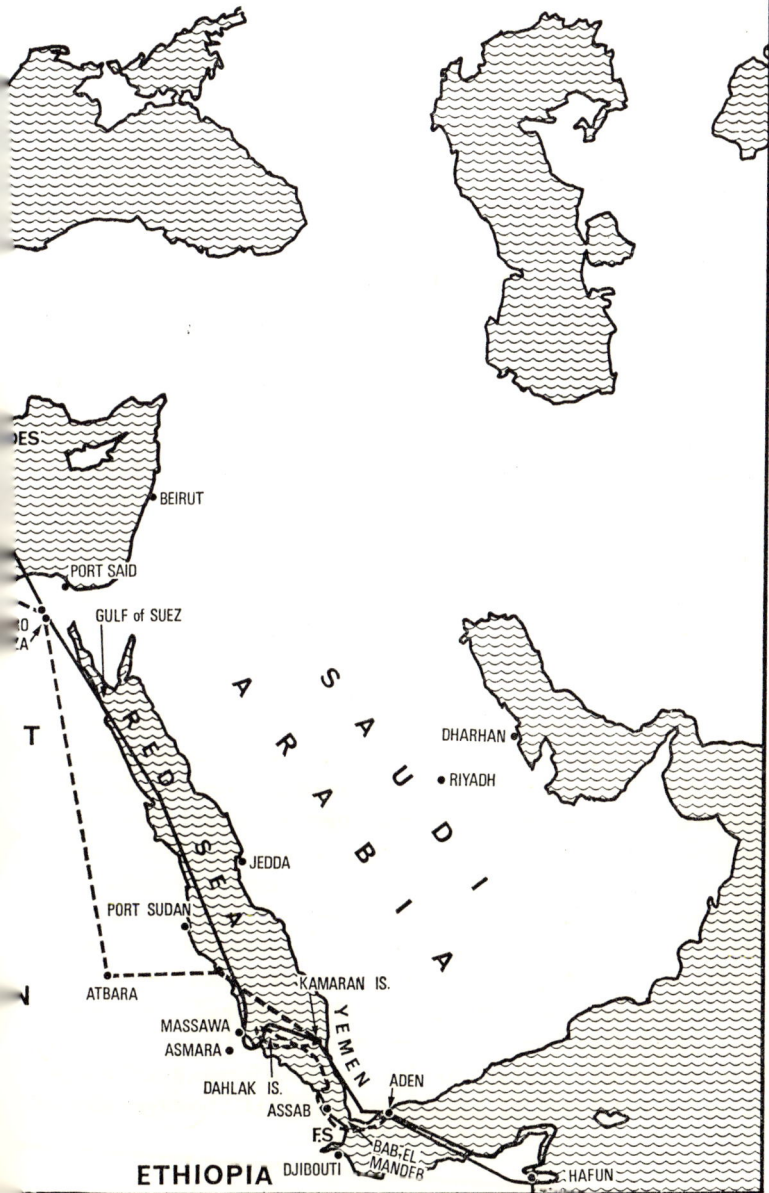

BEIRUT

PORT SAID

GULF of SUEZ

DES

O
A

T

N

ATBARA

PORT SUDAN

MASSAWA
ASMARA

DAHLAK IS.

ASSAB

F.S

DJIBOUTI

ETHIOPIA

BAB EL
MANDEB

R
E
D

S
E
A

A
R
A
B
I
A

S
A
U
D
I

JEDDA

DHARHAN

RIYADH

KAMARAN IS.

Y
E
M
E
N

ADEN

HAFUN

rumour amongst the regulars at Heston that we were overloaded and would never get off.

Bob Niven was to fly with me, in the second pilot's seat. We were taking a V.I.P. and another passenger to Malta, and while we break-fasted with them in the airport restaurant we could see the fire wagon and an ambulance moving into position in anticipation of our take-off run. The emergency services meant to be ready for us. Our passengers, though, had no inkling of all this and we didn't spoil their breakfast by mentioning it.

We climbed aboard at 08.45 and taxied to the north-east corner of the airfield. There was a very light wind from the west. I opened the throttles at 08.57 and we were airborne in 300 yards, which pleased me very much. I had felt completely confident, but I had thought we might take the full length of the field, about 600 yards, to get off. I retracted the undercarriage and we had reached a speed of 130 m.p.h. as we passed the control tower. We were then on a level with the con-troller's window, so in view of the uneasiness shown by our friends before take-off I could not resist the temptation to pull the Lockheed into a climbing left-hand turn round the control tower, grinning and waving to the controller to assure him that the plane was behaving well. We continued in a climbing turn until we reached 1,000 feet, turned back for a run across the airfield, and then set course.

For the next twelve months we flew almost daily in all kinds of weather and climate with an overload of up to 3,000 lb. without ex-periencing any trouble, even when taking off from small airfields or landing under difficult conditions.

I had tried to get approval to take a photographer with me on this trip, someone who could take charge of the cameras, check them over after we landed, have the films developed at each stopping point, and so on, but this had been refused on economy grounds, although it seemed to me that compared with the outlay for the Lockheed and its equipment, and in proportion to the value of the photographs we were after, the cost would be infinitesimal. When we got to Malta I was introduced to an R.A.F. pilot named 'Shorty' Longbottom, a young man with a slide-rule mind who was keenly interested in aerial photo-graphy. Shorty had earned his nickname as much from his height – he was 5 feet 4 inches – as from his name. Here it seemed was an oppor-tunity to get what I wanted at no extra cost, and I asked the A.O.C. Malta if he would let Longbottom accompany us for the next fortnight on our trip to the Red Sea and beyond. The A.O.C., however, seemed piqued because he hadn't been warned of our mission and hadn't apparently been allowed to let his own crews try for the photographs we were after, and he wouldn't help, either by releasing Shorty or by discussing targets with us. No doubt he was worried, too, about what would happen to Shorty if we were forced down; our cameras would give us away. So I continued to be photographer-in-chief. The A.O.C. did, however, relent to the extent of giving Shorty twenty-four hours leave so that he could accompany us on a flight over Sicily next day.

We flew high over Sicily and photographed Comiso, Augusta, Catania and Syracuse. I was very glad to have Shorty with me as he checked over the working of the cameras and gave me many useful tips on their operation. We got some excellent photographs, and I hoped they might soften the A.O.C.'s heart, but he still wouldn't release Shorty. Bob Niven and I took off at daybreak next day, 16th June, for the long flight to Cairo via Leros and Rhodes.

It was a beautiful day and from 10,000 feet we could see Crete and Cape Matapan ahead of us at a distance of 150 miles. After first sighting the Cape, at the southern extremity of Greece, it took us nearly an hour to reach and pass it to the south. Then between Cape Matapan and Crete we got a magnificent panoramic view of almost the whole spread of the Aegean. How peaceful it all seemed, the many small boats looking like tiny specks on the water. Crete was floating on a cobalt sea to our right, and the mountainous hinterland of Greece to our left looked bare and forbidding. Ahead of us the islands of the Aegean were scattered across the sea like confetti, their shapes haphazard as a jigsaw. We steered east-north-east across the islands, climbing steadily, and when we reached Leros in the Dodecanese I started the cameras working.

There was a lot of work going on in the harbour and the surrounding fortifications at Leros, and we spotted numerous gun emplacements in the hills. There was a large floating dock, and several big flying-boats were moored off what looked like a new seaplane station. We were now flying at 22,000 feet, and we turned south-east for Cos and Rhodes, where we photographed the main airfield and half a dozen warships, and looked for another airfield which it was thought was being built. We didn't see it, but we kept our cameras running, and when our pictures were developed they showed the new airfield in the course of construction. We then headed south-west for Scarpanto, on the southern tip of Rhodes, but it was covered in cloud, so we flew on south and then set course for Cairo. We landed at Almaza at 3.30 that afternoon after a flight of seven and a half hours.

Although there were several R.A.F. airfields in Egypt, my role as a private-owner-on-holiday obliged me to head for the civil airport at Almaza, so we were faced with the problem of getting our special cases through the Customs when we got there. We had, however, worked out a plan. The manager of Airwork at Heston had told me before we left that the Chief Customs Officer at Almaza was very fond of giving tea-parties, and that one particular brand of tea was his special favourite, so I had taken several pounds of this tea with me as a gift, which I presented to him soon after we landed. This made us popular at once, and we were invited into the Chief's office for tea. Meanwhile the R.A.F. officer who met us was collecting our suitcases. Our little gift was also to produce valuable results when we took off for Malta on the return flight.

We spent the next two days at the R.A.F. headquarters in Cairo, collecting and analysing the information we needed for the next stage of our flight, down the Red Sea to Aden. Our brief was to photograph areas in Eritrea and Italian Somaliland where it was thought fortifications might exist, and the success of the flight, we were told, depended on our remaining undetected. So far, we learned, there had been no complaints of high-flying aircraft over any of the places we had photographed, which showed that our flight planning had been successful.

I decided to take a direct route to Aden, cutting across the desert to just north of Port Sudan, then keeping to the middle of the Red Sea, out of sight of land, until we were opposite Massawa; at that point we turned in towards the Eritrean coast. We had been asked to photograph the area around Massawa in detail, and we covered the off-shore islands and the entrance to Massawa successfully enough; but when we flew inland to photograph the new Caproni Aeroplane Works at Asmara, which was another of our targets, a tablecloth of cloud lay on the hills and we turned about and made for Kamaran Island, half-way down the Red Sea, to refuel. Here we were met by the British Resident. The weather to the south looked murky, and I always made it a rule to have plenty of fuel on board for emergencies.

After leaving Kamaran we ran into thunderstorms with torrential rain and I abandoned my plan to take a short cut across the mountains of the Yemen. I was glad I had stopped to refuel. We were flying now at about 500 feet, and the heat and humidity were appalling. We came out of the storm at Cape Bab el Mandeb, where the Red Sea runs into the Gulf of Aden, and we noticed many rivers newly formed by the storm cascading down the hills into the sea. The picture of the sun throwing splashes of colour into the falling water and glistening on the wet surface of the barren land is one I shall always remember. We landed at Aden late that afternoon after eleven and a half hours airborne time.

I had dinner that evening with the C.-in-C., who arranged for me to meet the heads of the various intelligence departments later that night. I was shown several reports which indicated where military works were believed to be under construction in Italian Somaliland. The R.A.F. had not been able to check their information as they were not allowed to fly close enough to Italian territory to get pictures. I was finally passed on to the Resident Naval Officer at eleven o'clock that night, and over a much-needed cup of coffee I was told of his anxiety to check a report that the Italians had built or were building a submarine base on the peninsula of Hafun, which juts out into the Indian Ocean southeast of Aden. He also asked me to look out for signs of a road from Hafun to the west, along the southern borders of British Somaliland, its probable object being to provide overland communications with Eritrea, avoiding the Red Sea. It was axiomatic that in the event of war with Italy, Britain would close the Suez Canal and the Red Sea, thus cutting Italy off from Eritrea and Abyssinia unless another means of access could be found.

I finally got back to the Crescent Hotel, where we were staying, about midnight. What a stifling night it was. We got very little sleep, and we were up again at four o'clock for an early take-off; it is best in that heat to get off the ground early, before the sun comes up. We flew south across the Gulf of Aden and crossed the coastline of Italian Somaliland at Gourgi Nour, then covered the area inland of the Hafun peninsula, looking for signs of a road. All we could see were camel tracks, although these stood out quite clearly. We set the cameras going just in case. When we reached the peninsula itself we noticed buildings and then what appeared to be a jetty, with a large blob on the end. We covered the peninsula thoroughly, making two separate runs, and we saw what appeared to be an underwater pipeline, which confirmed what the Navy had suspected – that Mussolini was indeed planning to refuel his submarines outside the Red Sea.

Next morning, 21st June, the weather was bad so we stayed in Aden and went shopping. Much to my surprise I noticed Dufaycolor film on sale at one of the shops. The owner told me that he sold it to people off the P. & O. steamers and also used it himself, doing his own developing. It was a gratifying moment. After all my years of effort in Dufaycolor, it was heartening to know that the film was being bought by tourists as far afield as Aden.

We eventually took off at 3.15 that afternoon, but the weather was still disappointing. The area we were interested in, between Djibouti and Assab at the entrance to the Red Sea, was hidden by cloud. Visibility, too, was bad, so we returned to Aden. I decided that as I could cover this area on my way back to Cairo, we would aim at an early take-off on the following day, landing at Kamaran again to refuel.

When I went to the desk at the Crescent Hotel next morning to pay my bill, the manager rather transparently engaged me in conversation. He knew, he said, that we could hardly be visiting Aden for pleasure. Was it true that we were surveying a new route for Imperial Airways? I said I was very unhappy that this had leaked out and asked him not to mention it to anyone. That, I felt, was the best way of perpetuating the rumour. Next morning as we were leaving the hotel, someone stopped me in the foyer.

'When's this new route going to open?'

'What route?' I asked. I had completely forgotten about my subterfuge of the previous night.

'The route for Imperial Airways.'

'I can't comment on that,' I said, and walked on, thankful that the real object of our visit was apparently not suspected. We got off at 9.30 and headed for French Somaliland, turning north-east for Assab before we hit the coast, and getting photographs of several coastal airfields and gun emplacements along the coastline of Eritrea. After passing Assab we eased out into the middle of the Red Sea and landed at Kamaran in mid-afternoon.

Major Thompson, the British Resident, met us at the airfield and took us on a tour of the island. It is as flat as a pancake, and the surface is so hard and even that there is no need for made roads, but this had not deterred Major Thompson, a keen motorist and a lifelong member of the A.A., from erecting all manner of A.A. road signs. Having acquired these signs, he had set about making a track to fit them. One sign that must have presented him with a problem was 'Dangerous Steep Hill. Descend in low gear', but he had overcome it by building a false rise in the ground. Between Mecca seasons, he said, his natives had nothing else to do.

We took off early next morning and headed west across the Red Sea to the Dahlak Islands, off Massawa, parts of which we had missed on our run of a few days earlier. We also had another try for the Caproni Works at Asmara but again it was covered in cloud. We then set course for Atbara in the Sudan, where an R.A.F. Blenheim was due to meet us and collect our special suitcases. The plan was that the Blenheim would land back at the R.A.F. airfield at Heliopolis, just outside Cairo, while we would go on to Almaza to clear Customs. I was hoping the Blenheim wouldn't be late, as I didn't have long to spare on the ground at Atbara if I was to get back to Cairo before dark. There were no night-flying facilities *en route* or at Almaza. Thus I was relieved to see the Blenheim landing just ahead of us as we descended into Atbara.

We had to wait half an hour at Atbara for the Sudan Railway Company's representatives to arrive from the town; they had charge of the petrol. They arrived in a ramshackle old car, bringing some labourers with them; and then all the petrol, which was in four-gallon tins, had to be carried from a near-by store. While the labourers carried and opened the tins we poured the petrol into the tanks. Sand was blowing in all directions and it would certainly have got into our tanks if we hadn't carried our own protective funnel.

It was slow and unpleasant work, I was worried about the blowing sand, and time was getting on. I began to realize that if I was to get to Cairo before dark I would have to cut down on my fuel load: the method of refuelling was so laborious. There was a following wind, which would help a little, and I decided that I would make do with a 25 per cent margin – a total load of one and a quarter times what I would actually need. When I was satisfied that I had this margin I signalled to the labourers to stop, but they misunderstood me, and opened four more tins. We couldn't leave the tins there in the open, and we could hardly pour them into the sand, so although it involved further delay I allowed them to be put in the tank.

I was departing from a lifelong rule of always allowing myself very much more petrol, at least 50 per cent more, than I could possibly need. And when, two hours after leaving Atbara, we ran into a headwind, I really began to worry. The desert below us looked a most inhospitable place for a forced landing, and I cursed myself for my stupidity. We cruised with the engines at about one-third power and I asked Niven to stay up front with me so as to get the centre of gravity as far forward as possible: we had found that a forward centre of gravity added some speed. It may not have helped much but we felt that every hundred yards saved might mean all the difference. We worked the petrol taps and checked and re-checked the gauges, but we still didn't give ourselves much chance of reaching Cairo.

The gauges were showing empty when we finally reached Almaza, but we got down safely. A check revealed that the tanks were almost dry. The extra few gallons that the labourers at Atbara had opened by mistake had saved us a forced landing in the desert.

The cup of tea we were invited to share with our friend the Chief Customs Officer was welcome indeed. We told him what a wonderful trip we had had, and we explained that on the way back we had run short of petrol and been forced to land at Atbara. I then asked permission to take the Lockheed over to Heliopolis straight away so that the R.A.F. mechanics could inspect the engines for me, and he agreed readily. It was only a few minutes' flight. We put about 50 gallons of petrol in the tank and flew across to Heliopolis, landing almost in darkness, and we were quite exhausted when we got there. Since leaving Kamaran that morning we had been airborne for over eleven hours.

Next morning, after helping to service the Lockheed, I began to worry about our final Customs clearance from Almaza. We would need our cameras to photograph targets in Libya and Cyrenaica on the way home, and regulations obliged us to clear through Almaza, where an examination of our suitcases would be disastrous. I ordered all the petrol tanks of the Lockheed to be filled, and I then drove over to Almaza to see the Chief Customs Officer. I chose to arrive about tea-time, and the usual tea ceremony was put into operation. I told him of the stupidity of the English mechanics at Heliopolis, who had filled all the petrol tanks to the brim; they would now have to be emptied again, as I could not land in the space available at Almaza with a full load of petrol. I painted a dramatic picture of the Lockheed over-running the landing-ground, hitting the hangar and bursting into flames. Would it, I asked, be taking advantage of his great kindness if I suggested that in the circumstances one of his men might come over and clear me from Heliopolis? I added that I was due to leave next morning at 4 a.m.

The Chief Customs Officer said that he could not delegate his authority. He would have to clear us himself. But he didn't like rising that early. He had a better idea. If only I had brought my log-books with me he could have stamped them there and then, and I could have taken off when I liked. I found, of course, that I had brought them with me, so all was well.

On the first leg of the flight back to Malta we flew along the Egyptian coast about fifteen miles out to sea so as not to be seen from the shore, then turned in towards land opposite Bardia, put our oxygen masks on, and climbed to 18,500 feet. I set the cameras running, and we got pictures of Bardia and the Gulf of Sollum, then El Adem, Tobruk, Derna, Bernice and Benghazi. We had been warned to look out for a big petrol and ammunition dump in this area whose existence was suspected but whose location was not known, and following the railway line south of Bernice we saw what appeared to be a fort at the end of a spur of the railway, so we made several runs over it. When our films were developed back in London it was evident that we had found the dump; it was reputed to hold two years' supplies for the Italian Army in North Africa.

We flew over Benghazi during the midday siesta and were glad no one seemed alert enough to fly the many fighters we saw on the airfield. Then, just in case we had been seen, we headed for Tripoli, holding this course until we were out of sight of land, when we turned northwest for Malta. After night-stopping at Malta we covered the rest of our journey in one day, refuelling at Lyons and landing back at Heston at 7.30 that night, 25th June 1939. Our friends at Heston thought we had been to an air rally in Hungary, and we did not enlighten them.

Our Middle East tour had lasted only eleven days, of which three had been spent on the ground, and we had spent seventy-six hours in the air, an average of nine and a half hours per flying day. The flight had been a great success, and the interested departments in Whitehall were delighted with the photographs. But for my part I was impatient to tackle the main objective, Germany. Obviously this would be a much more difficult proposition, but there was plenty of evidence that Hitler was preparing to strike and that time was short. If a quick series of missions could be flown, the latest information on airfields, military installations, factories and shipyards could be obtained. I had a useful business cover for such missions as I had recently acquired the exclusive sales rights of Dufaycolor cinefilm throughout Europe.

14

A Last Look at Nazi Germany

'I wAS trying to get you all last week.' The speaker was the Ruman-
ian Daponte, now managing director of Dufay–Chromex. I, of
course, had been away in the Middle East. 'I wanted you to meet a
German who is interested in developing a market for Dufaycolor in
Germany. His name is Schoene and he was in the Richthofen circus
during the war. I told him you had the sales rights for Europe.'
  'Where is he now?'
  'He's gone back to Germany.'
  It was extraordinarily fortuitous that the Germans should have
come to me in this way, infinitely preferable to my starting off by
having to go to them. The opportunity that I sought was clearly at
hand. But I decided to be careful not to rush my fences, and I began by
inviting Schoene over to London to discuss the possibilities for Dufaycolor in Germany.
  Within a few days Schoene came over. He had been a test pilot for
Heinkel, I learned, also a flying instructor in Brazil, but then he had
lost a leg in an air crash. Now his interest was in the film business, and
he had some very high connections in Germany, or so he told me. He
was friendly with Goering, with whom he had served in the Richthofen circus, and with Herr Traeder, the man who looked after
Goering's personal affairs and who had also been a member of the
famous circus. Goering, according to Schoene, was virtually the boss
of all industry in Germany, and his blessing for any project connected
with Dufaycolor in Germany would be essential. Schoene, tall and
jovial, and claiming to be anti-Nazi in spite of his friendship with
Goering, made a good impression on me and I decided to make him
my agent in Germany.
  Within a week Schoene telegraphed to say that he was making
excellent progress and would I come over to Berlin. This was the
invitation I wanted, but again I didn't want to appear too eager, so
I asked Schoene to visit me again first, stressing that I wanted to be
satisfied, before going any further, that progress had been firm and

on the right basis. He came over at once and explained that Tobis, the big German film combine, were willing to buy Dufaycolor film provided we put the colour on to Agfa base and let Agfa apply the emulsion coating; it could then be presented as mainly a German product, and Goering would enforce its use.

I told Schoene that I would put this to my directors, and he returned to Germany. I then paid a call on Fred Winterbotham at his 'cover' address in south-west London. My suggestion was that I should visit Germany at once in the Lockheed, but Winterbotham shook his head. His department feared that our earlier missions might have made us suspect and that the whole project – the inquiry by Schoene and his invitation to me – could be a trap. This was certainly a point to be considered, but although we had had one or two narrow escapes while I was working with the French I was fairly confident that no one had guessed what we were doing. In any case it was a risk that I felt we would have to accept. I pressed this point at the highest level in the intelligence service to which I had access, and eventually I was given a free hand to carry on as I thought best. If anything went wrong, of course, it would be no good asking for help.

I flew from Heston to Berlin with Bob Niven on 26th July 1939. I went simply as a businessman interested in selling Dufaycolor film, and we took no cameras, although I had had special modifications made so that we could carry two Leicas, mounted in the wings and covered by sliding panels cut along the seams, hidden, or almost hidden, by rivets. It would be asking for trouble to take our normal 'luggage' of F.24s on short trips to Berlin. We landed at Tempelhof, and as I switched off the engines I saw about a dozen jack-booted Nazi soldiers doubling towards us. 'Look what's coming!' said Bob. It certainly looked as though Winterbotham's fears were about to be realized. There was nothing we could do but stick to our story, however, so we opened the doors of the Lockheed and started to climb out. As we did so the soldiers lined up in front of us, not to make an arrest, as we expected, but to form a guard of honour, and when we started to walk down the avenue they had formed, Schoene appeared and greeted us. 'You see how close I am to Goering,' he said proudly. 'This is a special guard of honour sent by him.'

'Heil Hitler!'

This sudden salute, given by the guard of honour, took me so completely by surprise, and Schoene's salute in reaction to it was so immediate, that involuntarily I found myself giving the salute in turn.

I couldn't fail to notice that my action went down very well with Schoene and his friends, and from this point on I always responded on these occasions. We were not at war with the Germans, Hitler was their leader, and I was prepared for the moment to pay him whatever respect the Germans felt should be accorded to him. It was, after all, of vital importance that I be looked upon as a friend.

Schoene and I went into the restaurant while Bob Niven taxied the Lockheed into a special hangar. We realized how special it was when we learned that it was the Gestapo hangar. We knew our plane would be thoroughly searched, and we were glad we hadn't brought our cameras. But would the Gestapo discover the sliding panels in the wings, suitably camouflaged but clearly meant to accommodate two Leicas? Would they discover any other tell-tale fittings? All we could do was keep our fingers crossed.

Schoene and I had some coffee, and then I mentioned Customs. 'No,' said Schoene, 'all that is arranged.' We were escorted to a couple of large Mercedes saloons which were flying the Nazi flag on each wing, and we were then driven at great speed to the Adlon Hotel. 'I hope that the welcome you've received, from Goering's personal bodyguard,' said Schoene, 'will satisfy you about my friendship with Goering and convince you that all I told you about Goering's interest in Tobis and Dufaycolor is true.' I said that we couldn't have had a nicer welcome. No Customs examination, a jack-booted escort, and the special suite at the Adlon – Schoene certainly knew the right people.

We dined that evening with Schoene and Traeder, Goering's business manager, and next morning Schoene drove us out to the Tobis studios to plan the tests they were to make on Dufaycolor film. Then we had lunch, and as we relaxed from business the talk inevitably turned to the prospects of war. I took the line that as an Australian I didn't follow British politics very closely, but said I felt that although the British people didn't want war they would fight if Poland was invaded because they would feel their honour was at stake. This seemed to have a slightly depressing effect on Schoene and Traeder, which was what I had intended.

We flew back to Heston that afternoon, 27th July, with some of the film exposed in the Tobis tests, to have it developed and printed at the Dufaycolor Laboratories in London. Schoene was anxious that we return with the prints as soon as possible, and we also had an invitation from the Commandant of Tempelhof Airport, Herr Böttger, to attend an international air meeting for sports pilots at Frankfurt, which had actually started that day but which was to last for the next four days, so we had good legitimate reasons for getting back to Germany at once. There was still the possibility that we were hurrying into a trap, especially if the Gestapo had found anything suspicious in the Lockheed, but I was sure I would have detected something in the manner of Schoene and the others if this had been so. I therefore had the two Leicas mounted in the wings. They were operated by a tiny button hidden under my seat, connected to the motor of an ordinary car windscreen-wiper, which was powerful enough to open and close the secret panels. This button also set the cameras working, using rolls of film of 250 exposures each. In addition I had two loose Leicas hidden where they could be reached from the cabin but where they were almost impossible to find unless one knew exactly where to look for them.

We left Heston soon after midday next day, 28th July, bound for Frankfurt via Brussels, where I had promised to pick up Margaret Gilruth ('Gillie') of the Australian Press. Another of my passengers was Charles Grey of the *Aeroplane*, also bound for Frankfurt. I welcomed the stop at Brussels as I hoped it would enable me to cover a more extensive area of the Siegfried Line without arousing suspicion, but when we got to Brussels we were given strict instructions about the route we were to follow into Frankfurt, a route which avoided the Siegfried Line altogether. I departed from it as much as I dared, resolving to cover what I missed on the return journey.

When we reached Frankfurt the rally had been in progress for two days and there were long rows of private aeroplanes of all sizes and markings parked side by side, but Schoene, who was expecting me, recognized the Lockheed and as we taxied in he drove across to meet us and took us to our hotel. The hotel seemed to be full of *Luftwaffe* uniforms, and Schoene explained that *Luftwaffe* officers had been ordered to attend the meeting in force as a demonstration of Germany's great friendship for England. It might also, of course, have been intended to intimidate us. 'Even Milch is going to be present,' said Schoene.[1] He seemed to be *persona grata* with all the brass-hats and I was introduced to many of them. The invariable topic was my 'Kolossal Lockheed', and the Commandant of Tempelhof, who had also been there to meet me, asked if I would take him up for a flight.

The opportunity of doing some authorized local flying and taking some photographs at the same time seemed too good to miss, and there

[1] General, later Field Marshal Ernest Milch, was deputy head of the Luftwaffe under Goering.

was one area that I was particularly anxious to cover. 'I had a favourite aunt who always raved about the beautiful Rhine at Mannheim,' I said, remembering what a high priority the French had put on Mannheim as a target and how we had missed covering it properly on an earlier flight. 'I should love to fly you down to Mannheim if it could be permitted.' It was not more than about fifty miles south of Frankfurt, just about right for a short pleasure trip. Schoene spoke to one of the brass-hats and returned beaming. 'You have permission to fly to Mannheim tomorrow,' he said.

Next day, 29th July, I flew again over the terrain which I had tried so unsuccessfully to photograph with Bois from Toussous-le-Noble three months earlier. We flew over many new airfields and buildings and from 2,000 feet I saw all I wanted to see, duly recording it by pressing the button under my seat and setting the cameras in motion, while the unsuspecting Commandant of Tempelhof sat next to me admiring the view. I blessed my non-existent favourite aunt. On passing over a particularly conspicuous military-looking installation I blushingly hid my face in my hands. 'I'm sure I'm not supposed to see that,' I said. The Commandant laughed heartily at my joke.

After the international meeting we were again ordered to fly out on a specified route, avoiding all military strongpoints, and I had no doubt that all observation posts would be alerted. With so many aircraft leaving Frankfurt at about the same time I had intended to divert as much as possible from the authorized course and hope not to be identified, but the silhouette of my 'Kolossal Lockheed' had now become well known. When we took off, however, there was a lot of cloud about, and I decided that here was my opportunity. Making use of the cloud to deliberately lose my way, I flew south-west to the Siegfried Line and then followed it northwards, keeping inside the German border all the way to Aachen before turning west for Brussels. I finished the flight without incident but with much new information in the Leicas, which worked without a hitch throughout. They were, of course, German-made.

I had given Schoene the Dufaycolor prints for Tobis while I was at Frankfurt, and there was little I could do now but wait for further word from him. He had, however, asked me if I could arrange, in the course of one of my visits, for some Dufaycolor photographs to be taken of Karin Hall, Goering's palatial home near Berlin; he said this

might help him to get the deal through with Goering. So when a fortnight went by and I heard nothing more from Schoene about the Tobis
deal, I cabled him to say that I was sending two Dufaycolor men over
to take the Karin Hall photographs and that I would come over myself in the Lockheed to see what further progress could be made. In
the meantime I had made several trips to other parts of the Continent
to fortify my image as a private-owner-on-business.

I took off from Heston at three o'clock on the afternoon of 17th
August, reaching Berlin after a three hours forty minutes flight. I had
been asked to photograph some airfield targets to the north of Berlin,
and this had taken me forty miles north of my normal track. Schoene
was there to meet me when I landed at Tempelhof, and he looked
worried. 'Security would like to see you,' he said. 'They want to know
why you were flying so far north.'

'I always fly a great circle course,' I said.

'Oh,' beamed Schoene, his face an amusing mixture of understand-
ing and incomprehension, 'like Lindbergh.' He must have dealt with
the Security people himself, because I heard no more about it.

The Dufaycolor men got a good series of stills of Karin Hall, but
there was one significant incident. They were allowed to take as many
pictures as they liked of the front and sides of the house, but they were
forbidden to go round to the back. This so aroused their curiosity that
one of them kept a look-out while the other wandered round to the
back on some pretext. He soon came upon the secret. Behind the
beautiful façade there were huge mounds of earth, piles of cement and
a maze of scaffolding and steel girders. The construction of Goering's
private air-raid shelter was well under way.

'Goering is wavering,' Schoene told me when I sounded him out on
the prospects of war. 'He used to think that England would not fight
over Poland, but now he's not so sure.'

I had made my own views abundantly clear on this subject, and I
repeated them now. Then, on the spur of the moment, I found myself
making a strange invitation. I suggested to Schoene that he ask
Goering to make a flying trip to England with me as my guest. I
assured Schoene and his party that Goering would be well received.
My idea was that if Goering could be finally convinced that England
would fight he might in turn convince Hitler. This seemed the best
remaining hope of averting war. To my surprise the idea was taken up
at once, and the invitation was passed on to Goering. Next day I was
told that my invitation had been accepted and that Goering would

Dear Mr Cotton

I write this note to say that
if your friend comes over soon,
the Prime Minister and I,
who have both already met
him, shall be very glad to see
him, and will arrange a
meeting under suitable conditions.

Halifax.

Aug 21. 1939.

fly to England with me in one week's time, on Thursday 24th August.
I now began to wonder if I had gone too far, and I flew back to England
next day, 19th August, and reported on what I had done.

I told the chief of intelligence that my impression was that Goering
had more influence with Hitler than anyone. If we could convince him
of our determination to fight, anything might follow. 'Well done,' I
was told, 'this might change everything.' A telephone call was made
in my presence to the Prime Minister, Neville Chamberlain, and within
a minute or so Lord Halifax came on the line. 'The Prime Minister has
agreed to your proposal,' I was told when the call was over, 'and you
will receive a letter from Lord Halifax saying your friend will be welcome. When are you going back to Berlin?' I said I would be going
on the 22nd at the latest, and that I was due to bring Goering back
on the 24th.

Next day, 21st August, the letter from Lord Halifax arrived. 'The
Prime Minister and I,' he wrote, 'who have both already met him
[Goering], shall be very glad to see him.' A facsimile of this letter is
reproduced opposite.

I was given details of an agreed plan. The Prime Minister, I was
told, would like me to arrive at White Waltham aerodrome at noon on
the 24th. An official car would be waiting to take Goering to lunch at
Chequers. The Foreign Secretary would be there and talks would start
immediately after lunch. I was to be ready to take Goering back to
Germany that evening, or possibly next day.

All this was totally foreign to my own ideas of the meeting. I thought
it sounded much too formal and might put Goering off. I asked if I
could make a suggestion. 'Goering has accepted an invitation to come
over on a private visit as my guest,' I said. 'In the first place, he may
not relish an early start. Wouldn't it be better if we took off at a respectable hour, so as to arrive in the afternoon? And I'm not sure that
we should use an official car. He's coming over in my aeroplane, so he
should be met by my car. He could then be driven to Chequers to
arrive in time for tea. In the evening I suggest there should be an in-
formal dinner, with attractive ladies and good company, not a battery
of impeccable politicians and civil servants with black coats, striped
trousers and long faces, all sitting round ready to pounce. Out of the
atmosphere of a pleasant evening, with perhaps some shooting and
other relaxations over the next day or so, something really positive
might emerge, and the truth about the real intentions of the British
if Hitler marches into Poland might be impressed on Goering's mind.'

My point was taken, and it was agreed that an attempt would be made to arrange something on these lines with the Prime Minister. 'In the meantime,' I was told, 'get back to Berlin and bring your friend over.' He was not, of course, my friend, but this was how they talked in the intelligence service.

That evening, after flying down to White Waltham to arrange the details there, I called in to see Fred Winterbotham. He was not at all happy about my plan. 'Take care,' he said, 'the outlook is getting worse every day. The latest bombshell is that Ribbentrop is in Moscow. We've been trying to line the Russians up on our side, but we can't seem to get anywhere with them. I don't want you to get caught out in Berlin when the balloon goes up. If the situation looks really desperate I'll cable you saying "Mother is ill." I'll sign it "Mary". If you get a cable like that, come back at once. Otherwise at the very least you'll be interned. If they find out what you've been doing you'll be shot.' I told him to keep his fingers crossed, and I reminded him that he'd started me off in this intelligence business anyway. 'I know,' he said, 'that's what worries me.'

Leaving the wing Leicas behind, and taking only the two loose cameras secreted in the cabin, I flew back to Berlin with Bob Niven on 22nd August and produced the Halifax letter to Goering's entourage. Traeder asked me to lend it to him so that he could show it to Bodenschatz, Goering's chief of staff, and soon afterwards another high party official appeared and was introduced to me. I have forgotten his name. Everyone stood up and heiled Hitler, but this time I did not feel obliged to follow suit. 'Everything has been arranged,' I was told, 'you are to meet the Field-Marshal at Munich at 10 o'clock on Thursday morning. The Führer has given special permission for you to land at his private aerodrome near Munich, and his own personal pilot will fly to Berlin beforehand so as to accompany you to Munich and guide you to the airfield. Heil Hitler.'

Meanwhile the atmosphere in Berlin was becoming more and more oppressive as the tension mounted hourly. The fabricated case against Poland on the Danzig issue was being whipped up into an excuse for war. Poland was being isolated by various astute political moves, and a non-aggression pact with Russia, unknown to us, was being negotiated by Ribbentrop, after which Poland was to be carved up and Britain presented with a *fait accompli*. Troops marched through Berlin all that day, and I have never heard a more ominous sound than the tramping of their feet. Staff cars carrying the Nazi emblem dashed to and fro, and black-out exercises were held that evening. I felt as though a volcano was about to erupt underneath me, but I pretended not to take the situation too seriously, maintaining stolidly that neither the British nor the Germans wanted war and that some solution must be found.

During the evening of the 23rd the German leaders received news of the signing in Moscow of the Russo–German non-aggression pact, and I must have been one of the first foreigners to be told. Schoene and Traeder came round to the Adlon, where I was staying, in great agitation. The flight to Munich, they said, had been postponed. They were afraid that the pact with Russia might alter everything. How right they were. Word came through soon afterwards that Goering's trip to England was off.

'Ribbentrop is certain that England will not help Poland,' said Schoene.

'England will honour her pledge,' I said stiffly.

'Goering and his staff think so too,' said Schoene, 'but Ribbentrop has convinced the Führer that she won't.'

At eight o'clock next morning, 24th August, Schoene came and told me that Baron Wiedsacker, second secretary at the German Foreign Office, would like to see me before I left. He suggested that this might be a useful opportunity of making my views known. But when I got there Wiedsacker had literally flown: he had received an urgent call from Ribbentrop to take some papers to Moscow and had rushed off to Tempelhof. Herr Wormann, the third secretary, was deputed to see me instead. I was pleased enough to meet Wormann, who, I happened to know, was married to a cousin of mine. But Wormann sneered at me in a most unpleasant manner. 'So you're the person who is trying to convince us that the British will fight?' he said.

'That is my opinion, Herr Wormann,' I said. 'I'm sorry to have missed Herr Wiedsacker, but I'm glad of the chance of meeting you, as we happen to be related by marriage.' Wormann raised his eyebrows at this, but said nothing. 'You married the daughter of the Lomans who used to control the Nord Deutscher Lloyd Shipping Line, did you not?'

'That is so.'

'She is a cousin of mine. I am a descendent through my mother of the Baron de Bode.'

Wormann thawed a little at this and we talked for the next half-hour. He seemed interested in what I had to say about the English

determination to fight over Poland, and he promised to convey my
views to the right quarter without delay. 'I'm afraid, though,' he
said, 'that it won't be believed in view of the opinion Herr Ribbentrop
has given the Führer.'

I took my leave of Wormann and rejoined Schoene and Traeder at
the Adlon. There a cable was awaiting me from Fred Winterbotham,
signed 'Mary' and telling me that Mother was ill. This was my signal
to go. Schoene and Traeder, too, tried to persuade me to leave Berlin
at once, but I told them I could not think of deserting my friends at
such a time. I was determined not to leave until I had done everything
I could to convince the Germans that Britain would fight. Schoene and
Traeder got very panicky at this and implored me to leave, and when
I still refused they excused themselves for a few minutes, presumably
to confer with Goering or the German Foreign Office. When they came
back they said they had been authorized to tell me the reason why I
must leave, but first I must give my word of honour as a pilot not to
repeat it to anyone. I gave my promise, and they told me that Hitler
had already prepared the orders and named the date for the march into
Poland, that it was due to take place within forty-eight hours, and that
confirmation was expected at any moment.[1] When that confirmation
came, it was quite certain that I would not be allowed to leave.

While we were talking another cable reached me from 'Mary'. The
text this time was: 'Mother very low and asking for you.' I admired
Winterbotham's phraseology; undoubtedly it was time to go. I was
an Australian and Bob Niven was a Canadian, but if England went
to war I had no doubt that our two countries would follow suit at
once and we would both be interned. To Schoene's obvious relief I
agreed to be driven out to Tempelhof. It was still quite early – about
9.45 a.m.

Now that we had decided to go, however, no one could be found
capable of giving the authority for us to do so. The V.I.P. treatment
was wearing thin. Schoene, looking more worried than ever, apologized
for the delay and said that Traeder was trying to get special permission
from Goering. As he was presumably still in Munich, I could see that
we might be held up for some time. Meanwhile war might be declared.
I began to think about making a dash for it, and I got into the Lockheed with Niven and taxied slowly out to the bottom of the runway.

---

[1] The order to attack was to be given next day, 25th August. This order was
in fact given, then withdrawn as a result of the signing of an alliance between
Britain and Poland and the temporary defection of Mussolini.

No one stopped us, but when I turned into wind I got a prolonged red light from the control tower. What would happen if I defied it?

All round us on the airfield were brand-new fighter planes, including what we later realized was a Messerschmitt 110, very sleek and fast in appearance, which came in to land right in front of us. We scrutinized it through binoculars and made notes of its main points of recognition.

Looking at the map, I realized that the shortest route out of Germany would be east into Poland and then north to Sweden, but with Hitler's troops massing to the east of Berlin and conditions in Poland uncertain, this route seemed to offer too many hazards. We thought of taking off and heading for London for a few minutes as a feint, then changing course and heading at treetop height for Italy or Roumania or Yugoslavia, but all these courses presented the same risk—the preliminary dash to get clear of Germany. There was hardly any cloud about and long before we could reach a height at which our camouflage would be effective the fighters would catch up with us.

I decided to give myself a deadline. If there was no sign of permission being given by 11.15, or if there was any attempt to recall us to the parking area before then, I would take off and fly at zero height to the south-east into the sun, changing course continually so that fighter airfields ahead couldn't easily be warned of our approach. Once clear of German territory we would land to refuel, probably in Italy, and then head for home.

After nearly an hour of waiting we saw two figures leave the control tower and get into a car and drive across the airfield towards us. My hands moved towards the throttles, but I decided to wait. The car proved to contain Schoene and an airport official. 'All flying is banned,' said Schoene. 'We're still trying to get special permission for you to take off.' Schoene was deathly pale and his hands were shaking. We had some brandy on board and we invited him to have a drink, and he gulped it down. 'Be patient,' he said. 'Try not to appear too nervous.' Bob and I had to laugh at this. We were scared enough but I don't think we were half as nervous as Schoene.

The two men went back to the control tower, and there followed another long wait. The time was approaching 11.15. Then Schoene appeared again, this time with Traeder and my old friend the Airport Commandant. 'We've had one hell of a job,' said Schoene, 'but Traeder went to see Goering's chief of staff personally and thanks to him and our friend here all is now in order.' The anti-aircraft batteries, said Schoene, had been advised of our route; we were to fly at a height of exactly 300 metres, and provided we obeyed our instructions we would be allowed to pass. Schoene then gave me a slip of paper with our instructions clearly marked, and he begged us to keep to the exact courses shown. Otherwise, he said, we would certainly be shot down.

Poor Schoene, he seemed so afraid for us. I tried to cheer him up, and perhaps myself as well. 'Don't worry,' I said, 'if you've ever been on a pheasant shoot you'll know what a lot of birds get away.' Bob and I then shook hands warmly with each man. These three at least had shown genuine friendship and had seemed to hate the idea of war. I knew how they felt, caught up in a deception on behalf of their country, forced to tell lies to people they genuinely liked. I pushed open the throttles rather miserably and we became airborne at 11.15 precisely. In spite of the warmth of our handshakes, tomorrow we would be at war.

For the next few minutes I was absorbed with my thoughts and with flying the Lockheed. It was some time, too, before Bob spoke. 'That was a close one,' he said at length. 'Too close,' I said. 'What if they hadn't cleared us?' Bob was anxious that we shouldn't count our chickens. 'It's still 250 miles to the border,' he reminded me. The direction we had been given was west-north-west towards Bremen, and the pinpoints we were to fly over included Rathenow, Salzwedal, Soltau and Oldenburg, hitting the German–Dutch border due west of Oldenburg. We kept rigidly to our route, and although we saw numerous bombers flying to and fro we saw no fighters and nothing molested us. The bombers, we realized, were hurrying to their rendezvous for the invasion of Poland. Their camouflage was much darker than that in use in the R.A.F. and several times when we were flying above forest areas we almost missed seeing them.

When we had recovered our poise, out came the two Leicas and we looked for possible targets. We saw little of interest, however, until we crossed the Dutch border approaching Groningen. Then, looking back over our right shoulders towards Wilhelmshaven, we saw an astonishing sight, a freak of light and distance that no one could possibly have foreseen. Fifty miles to the north-east of us, anchored in the Schillig roads outside Wilhelmshaven, glinting in the sun, was a line of silver pencils which we realized must be major units of the German fleet, perhaps about to put to sea. We photographed them excitedly. Here was something that would certainly interest the Admiralty.

When at last we got back to Heston, after a flight lasting nearly four hours, the Customs officer greeted us laconically. 'Where from?' he asked.

'Berlin.'

'Left it a bit late, haven't you?'

Hitler postponed his march into Poland for exactly a week, but the Lockheed, which in the last month of peace had helped us to get hundreds of valuable photographs of war preparations in Nazi Germany, was the last civilian plane out of Berlin.

15

The German Fleet

Two days after our return from Berlin, on 26th August, Fred Winterbotham told me that the Admiralty were very pleased with our pictures of Wilhelmshaven. There were, as shown by our photographs, six big ships in the roads, plus Hitler's yacht *Grille*. It was this white-painted yacht which had first caught our eye looking back from the Dutch border. Now, said Winterbotham, the Admiralty would like to know what warships if any were at Heligoland. The Air Ministry, too, were interested in this area and wanted pictures of airfields on the Frisian Islands and Sylt if we could get them. All these targets were on the periphery of Germany and I thought we ought to be able to photograph them without too great a risk of being intercepted.

When we had planned our trip to the Middle East and Aden in June of that year we had thought it might help to give the impression of a holiday atmosphere if we took a girl along. We had had a volunteer in Pat Martin, a twenty-two-year-old girl who lacked neither courage nor looks and was an expert photographer. The decision had finally gone against her, but not before she had familiarized herself with our camera equipment, and ever since then she had pestered us to take her along. On this particular evening she called in at my flat at Arlington House for dinner. We were sprawled out on the floor studying maps and we told her rather brusquely that dinner was off.

'I'll cook the dinner,' she said.

'Fine.'

'On one condition.'

Bob and I looked at each other. We knew what was coming and we both answered together. 'Quite impossible.'

In the cinema the next shot generally shows the girl in the plane. I'm afraid that for once real life was just like the movies. We knew Pat was a good cook, we were hungry, and more important, we needed an

7(a). Searching for Nungesser and Coli – the Fokker seaplane

7(b). Gino Watkins shouts down the ventilator to Augustine Courtauld

(*See page 82*)

8(a). Photographic Reconnaissance – the Wilhelmshaven Naval Base
2nd March 1940

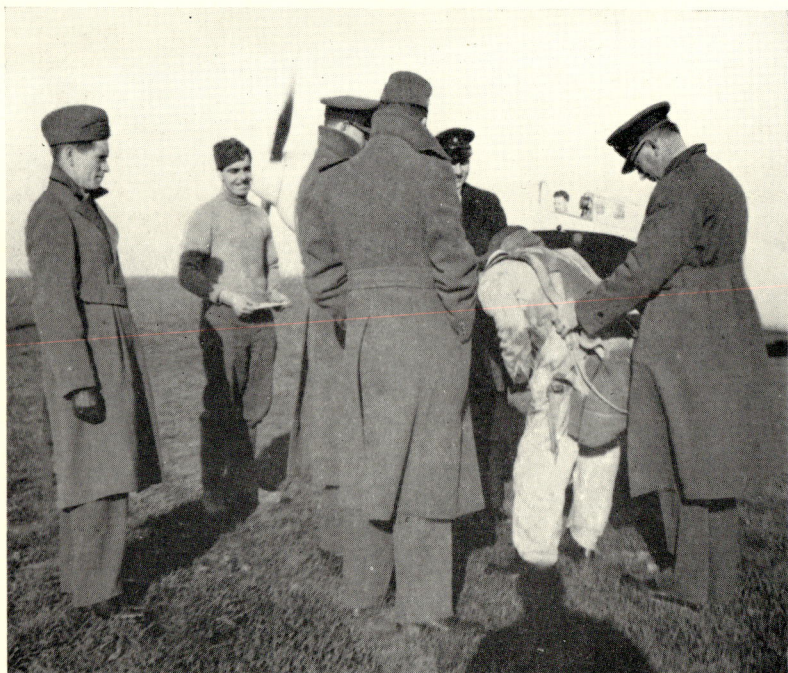

8(b). I adjust Shorty Longbottom's parachute harness for the first Spitfire
P.R. sortie

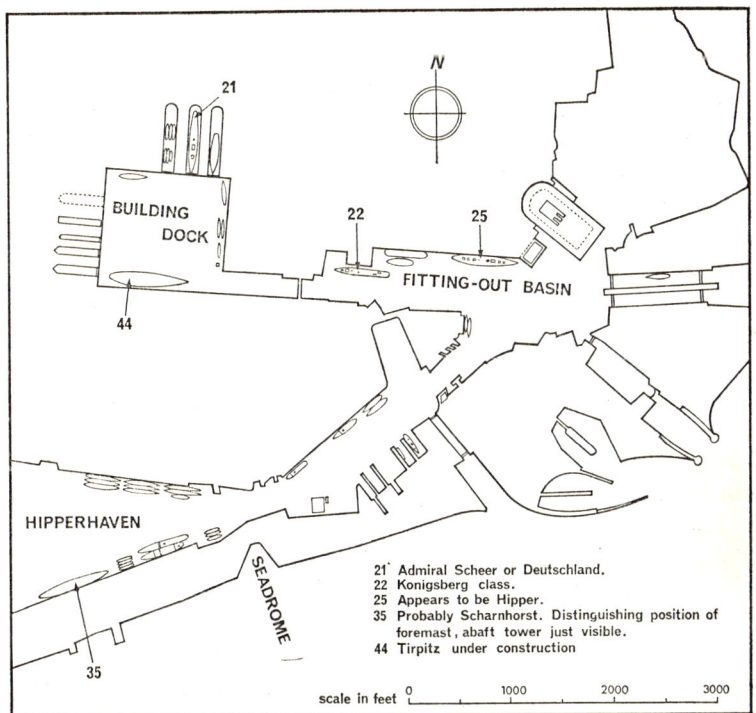

21' Admiral Scheer or Deutschland.
22 Konigsberg class.
25 Appears to be Hipper.
35 Probably Scharnhorst. Distinguishing position of foremast, abaft tower just visible.
44 Tirpitz under construction

A plot annotated by naval interpreters of a section of the
photograph opposite

expert to work the Leicas while Bob worked the obliques from the cabin and I worked the verticals from the pilot's seat. I was putting every available camera aboard.

We took off from Heston on the morning of 27th August and headed for Rotterdam, where we turned north-east across the Zuider Zee for the Frisian Islands. Our cover story, if we were forced down, was that we were on a civil flight to Copenhagen, where I was developing my Dufaycolor interests. A destination in Denmark agreed with our route.

After crossing Holland we fitted our F.24s into position in the fuselage and were ready to start taking pictures as we approached Borkum, the first of the German-held islands of the Frisian group. We got some good pictures there, and we then headed east for Nordeney, the second of the main islands in this group. As we approached Nordeney I told Pat, who was sitting on my right in the second pilot's seat, operating a Leica, to keep a sharp look-out towards the mainland for fighter

F

patrols. I had hardly spoken when she tapped my arm and pointed out of her window. There, not 300 yards ahead and to starboard, flying on an opposite course, was a German fighter.

I started the cameras straight away, motioning to the others to get what pictures they could, and as the fighter flashed by I began a gentle turn northwards towards Heligoland. I dared not manœuvre to see if the fighter was on our tail in case this made us conspicuous, but we did not see him again. I think he couldn't have seen us, or he would have come in for a closer look. I am sure it was our greeny-white 'Camotint' that saved us that day; the German pilot simply didn't see us against the background of sea and sky.

We continued northwards towards Heligoland and Sylt. Heligoland, unfortunately, was shrouded in fog, but we got some lovely shots of Sylt. We got back to Heston safely after a six-hour flight and I went along to Fred's office and gave him the film. It was the same story – stacks of military aircraft everywhere.

Early on the morning of Friday, 1st September, Hitler marched into Poland. Hostilities had started, yet there was still no formal declaration of war. During the morning I received a call from Fred Winterbotham; I was to go to the Admiralty to see Commander Charles Drake of the Naval Intelligence Division. I had first met Drake some two months earlier, when he had briefed me on naval intelligence matters prior to my tour of the Middle East, and I had seen him once or twice since then.

Drake explained to me that the delay in declaring war was presenting the Navy with an almost insoluble problem. They were afraid that major German naval units, taking advantage of the hiatus, would break out into the Atlantic so as to be at their war stations astride our communications when war was declared; we would then be too late to intercept them or head them off. To counteract this threat, virtually the entire Home Fleet had already sailed from its bases and was now careering about north of the Shetlands, trying to block the exit of the German ships into the Atlantic. The trouble was that no one really knew where the major German ships were. The Admiralty had had good intelligence on them up to 25th August, of which my own photographs on the way out of Berlin had been a part, but since then unconfirmed reports from secret intelligence sources indicated that two of the heavier ships, the battle-cruiser *Gneisenau* and the battleship *Deutschland*, possibly accompanied by others, had left the Schillig roads for northern waters. At first the Admiralty had treated these

reports with reserve, but at the end of August the Home Fleet had
sailed. So far they had seen nothing, and some of the smaller vessels
would soon be running short of fuel. It seemed that the secret service
report must have been false. In any case it was bad strategy to have the
Fleet stretched out like this on doubtful intelligence when another
threat might develop elsewhere.

What was urgently wanted, Drake stressed, was up-to-date cover
of the north German ports, and especially of Wilhelmshaven. It was
quite possible that the German ships were still in the Schillig roads,
in which case the Fleet could be recalled. The R.A.F. were no doubt
capable of getting the required cover, and an R.A.F. Blenheim was in
fact standing by to take off directly war was declared; but it was not
possible to send a military aircraft over foreign territory in peacetime.
Such action might trigger off the war that everyone on our side was
still desperately striving to avoid.

I said that I could see no difficulty in getting the required pictures
provided the weather was favourable. I added that I would be quite
ready to do it. Drake then took me in to see Admiral Godfrey, chief
of N.I.D. 'We want a photograph of the Wilhelmshaven roads,' said
Admiral Godfrey. 'We think the German ships may still be there, and
if so there's no point in the Battle Fleet stooging around north of
the Shetlands.' It was agreed that I should try to get the pictures next
day.

Some time earlier I had bought a Beechcraft, a light, single-engined,
four-seater cabin monoplane which I had also had painted duck-egg
green and which I thought would be less likely to be spotted than the
Lockheed. It had a ceiling of more than 20,000 feet. Bob Niven was
very fond of flying it, and when I got back to Heston and Bob heard
about my plans for the flight, he pressed to be allowed to go. Bob's
main argument was that he was small and light, some four or five stone
lighter than me (my weight was fifteen stone), and that this would
give him possibly another two or three thousand feet of height, which
might well be decisive in avoiding German patrols. The weight
factor was of special importance as the Beechcraft had no automatic
pilot and no fitted cameras, so a photographer would have to be
carried to get the pictures. Niven backed this up with another
argument. 'I think,' he said, 'that in any case I've earned this
flight.'

There was no doubt that he had. I had become very fond of Bob
Niven, looking upon him almost as a son, and I was reluctant to let

him go, but there was good sense in what he said, and I agreed. We worked out the flight plan together. My idea was that he should simply repeat the manœuvre that we had carried out so fortuitously on our last flight out of Berlin–namely, to fly to the Dutch border east of Groningen and time his arrival to coincide with the moment when we had taken our earlier photographs, about 1.15 p.m., taking advantage of the remarkable trick of light and sun that we had benefited from then. The weather was good, and we hoped that conditions in north Germany would be the same. I had no doubt that the Wilhelmshaven area would be under surveillance by German fighters, and I impressed upon Niven that he must take no chances, other than those inherent in our plan.

While Bob was away on this flight I kept kicking myself for letting him go, but my fears were unfounded. He returned with some lovely negatives, and I rang Drake straight away to tell him that I'd got his pictures. The prints, greatly enlarged, gave a grainy silhouette of the ships in the roads which the Admiralty were able to interpret with certainty. I took the photographs to Drake later that day, made up into an album, and after showing them to Admiral Godfrey he took them into the First Sea Lord, Admiral Sir Dudley Pound. The date and time of the photography were overprinted on the photographs. 'Where did you get these?' asked Pound.

'From a friend of mine,' said Drake.

'In the Air Force?'

'No–in an unarmed aircraft, wearing a civilian suit.'

'How do you know they were taken today?'

'I've only got his word for that. But there's not a shadow of doubt that they were.'

From these photographs the Admiralty were able to confirm that the ships previously sighted by us in the Schillig roads a week earlier were still there. As a result of this intelligence, obtained by a private aircraft, the Battle Fleet was eventually recalled, arriving back at its bases on 5th September. This, unfortunately, did not mean that none of the German ships had got out: we now know that the *Graf Spee*, for instance, got away from Germany and through the Denmark Strait into the Atlantic in the latter part of August, some days before war was declared. But it did impress upon the Naval Intelligence Division how absolutely essential good air photographs, backed up by continual air cover, were to the Navy. The information that could be gleaned from a single group of photographs was always limited by the extent and regularity of previous cover; unless one had past intelligence to refer to, much of the meaning was gone.

I was looking at prints of some of these pictures in Fred Winterbotham's office on the following morning, Sunday 3rd September, when Chamberlain's voice came on the radio; we were expecting it, and some fifteen or twenty people were in Fred's office to hear it, but there was no excitement, just a rather set calm. After Chamberlain had finished there was silence for a few moments, and then someone said, 'So that's that.' I think that was the mood everywhere. Very few of us in that office could take any immediate action, and when the sirens went a few minutes later most of us went underground. But personally I couldn't bring myself to hide in cellars, and I escaped into a near-by park to see what was happening. It was the first of many false alarms.

The most important immediate war plan of the R.A.F. was a bombing attack on the German fleet in its North Sea bases directly war was declared. Swift action by a powerful strike force could have had a decisive influence on the war at sea for many months to come – as the Japanese showed later at Pearl Harbour. But instead of mounting an attack on the basis of Niven's photographs, taken less than twenty-four hours earlier, of which they had copies, the R.A.F. preferred to await the result of their own reconnaissance. Forty-eight minutes after war was declared, an R.A.F. Blenheim with a naval observer on board took off for Wilhelmshaven. The plan was that the pilot, Flying Officer A. McPherson, besides taking photographs, should radio a report back to base with the help of his naval observer, on the basis of which the strike force of Blenheims and Wellingtons would take off.

From 24,000 feet McPherson and his observer saw and identified many ships, but the intense cold had frozen their wireless (as well as their cameras), and they were unable to pass on their information until after they landed. Meanwhile the weather was deteriorating. The strike force did in fact take off before McPherson landed, 'only to be baulked', says the *Official History*, 'by thunderstorms and darkness'.

The opportunity for a successful strike on the first day of hostilities, for which all the necessary information had been readily available, had been lost. However, there was another day tomorrow. McPherson went again on 4th September, but low cloud forced him down to 300 feet, and although he saw and photographed warships in Brunsbüttel, Wilhelmshaven and the Schillig roads, the strike force was delayed through another wireless failure, and also through having to change its armament from semi-armour-piercing bombs to general purpose bombs fused to eleven seconds delay, so that they wouldn't blow themselves up when they dropped them. The attack was eventually made from 500 feet, which was the height of the cloud-base, under intense defensive fire. One section made a determined attack on the *Admiral Scheer*, straddling it with bombs and scoring several hits, but the bombs failed to explode. Being fused for eleven seconds delay, says the *Official History*, they probably bounced overboard from the armoured decks. The main damage seems to have been done by a Blenheim which crashed into the fo'c'sle of the *Emden*, killing and injuring many of the cruiser's crew.

Of the twenty-nine aircraft that took part in these attacks, seven failed to return. No one in any case could have had much hope of success against capital ships with this type of bomb. A full-scale attack from high-level in the good conditions of the previous day might have had significant results, but the chance had been lost.

Like many others, from an early stage I was constantly finding myself extremely critical of the general handling of the war. On 4th September, for instance, Fred Winterbotham had some matters to discuss with the *Deuxième Bureau* in Paris so I offered to fly him over. We found that civil aircraft were now routed via Haslemere in Sussex to Shoreham, where they had to land for overseas clearance before crossing the Channel. We then had to over-fly Dieppe before heading for Paris. The whole performance had to be repeated on the return journey. The routeing added at least an hour to both the outward and inward flights, for no good reason that I could see. Bureaucracy had already begun to slow down the tempo.

16

I Form a Special Unit

A WEEK after the outbreak of war, on 10th or 11th September, Ian Fleming, later to become famous as the creator of James Bond, visited my flat from the Naval Intelligence Division, where he was then personal assistant to the D.N.I. His restless, fantastic mind had hit upon a possible weakness in our plans for combating the German U-boat menace. Our best chance of sinking U-boats was in port or along the routes they had to traverse to reach the shipping lanes. But what if the Nazis were able to arrange for refuelling bases in remote parts of neutral Southern Ireland? The length of submarine cruises could then be considerably extended and the time spent in the danger zones greatly reduced. The Admiralty as a whole were not inclined to take this threat too seriously, and it was difficult to see what we could do about it in any case; but Fleming wanted to know if it might be possible to get some sort of check on the situation from air photographs. I said that I could certainly photograph the bays on the Irish coast and that any pipelines, barrels, beach installations or storage tanks would show up.

Bob Niven and I took off next morning, 12th September, for a preliminary reconnaissance. We refuelled at Speke, then set course for the west coast of Ireland, flying at 10,000 feet. We took a great many photographs, and when the Admiralty saw them next day they asked us to take them down to the C.-in-C. Plymouth for his comments. This we did on 14th September. The C.-in-C., Admiral Sir Martin Dunbar-Nasmith, V.C., was interested in our pictures but wanted them taken from a much lower height, about 2,000 feet, to get better definition, and this we agreed to consider. The only doubt in my mind was whether Irish coastal batteries might fire on us at this height.

It happened that A. J. Miranda had recently sold the Irish a single American anti-aircraft gun. So far as we knew, this was the only modern anti-aircraft gun they had. Miranda conducted all his European business through my office in St. James's Square, so I knew all about this gun, its performance and where it was likely to be sited. My friends told me that after my flight of 12th September the Irish had mounted the gun on a railway carriage and were running it up and down the west coast in readiness for me, but I suspect that they were pulling my leg. We did in fact photograph the entire Irish Atlantic coast in the course of the next few weeks, proving beyond doubt that no refuelling facilities existed there.

Before I could get any further with the Irish photographs, however, I got a phone call from Fred Winterbotham asking me to come to his office as soon as possible: the Air Ministry wanted to see me. I had already experienced some hostility when landing at Air Force stations, due to my inability to disclose my destination and purpose, and I naturally wondered if this was why I had been sent for. The R.A.F. authorities at station level were peeved at the way I flew in and out of the country without, as it seemed to them, any special clearance, although Winterbotham had arranged with the Air Ministry that all I had to do before a flight was to phone Fighter Command and say 'White Flight taking off', which would protect me from interception by R.A.F. fighters. It is true that I was never intercepted or 'buzzed', but I had my own ideas at that time about the efficiency of the early warning system.

'The Air Ministry want to see your special equipment,' Fred Winterbotham told me when I got to his office. It seemed that the quality of the photographs I had taken on my previous flights had surprised them. I was relieved to know that my fears of some sort of showdown were unwarranted, but puzzled nevertheless. 'What do they mean by special equipment?' I asked Winterbotham. 'I use standard R.A.F. cameras, which they lent me themselves, with Leica film, developed in fine grain developer. What's the flap?'

'The R.A.F. are having camera trouble,' said Winterbotham. 'They can't get any photographs over enemy territory because their cameras keep freezing up. The First Sea Lord wants some photos of foreign ports, the R.A.F. can't get them, and everyone from the Prime Minister down is raising hell.'

Next morning I went along to the Air Ministry, where I had an appointment with the Director General of Operations, Air Vice-Marshal Richard Peck, at eleven o'clock. I was introduced to a slightish man of medium height who looked and talked like an accountant. He had a most pleasing voice, an easy, direct manner, and considerable charm. He came straight to the point.

'Winterbotham has told me that you have no special equipment. Is that right?'

'Yes.'

'I'm very disappointed to hear it. We're having great difficulty with our photographic equipment. It's letting us down badly. We hoped very much that you'd be able to suggest something.'

'What's the trouble?'

'Every time we try to photograph an important target – which we have to do from high level to avoid enemy defences – the cameras freeze.'

I told Peck that it wasn't the cameras that froze but the condensation. I said I had had the same trouble in my Lockheed, and explained how I had overcome it. We talked for some time about various problems of aerial photography, and eventually Peck asked me if I was prepared to give the R.A.F. the benefit of my knowledge and experience in an effort to find out what was wrong with their methods and try to put them right. I said I would be ready to do anything, but added that I doubted if it would be possible for anyone to re-organize the whole R.A.F. photographic system in a matter of days or even weeks. Peck asked me to come and see him again at ten o'clock next day.

I couldn't see that I would be likely to achieve much by joining or working with the R.A.F. Photographic Section; they could not be expected to be very receptive to the ideas of an outsider, and I might waste a lot of time trying to convince them. The more I thought about it the more certain I was that the best answer, both for getting immediate results and for the future development of R.A.F. photography, was for the nucleus already in being at Heston to be expanded on a war footing, proving the system by taking whatever pictures were wanted. When the unit and its methods had become properly established, the R.A.F. could take it over.

I didn't know it at the time, but this was exactly the attitude of the Admiralty. When they asked the R.A.F. for photographs they couldn't get a single picture. When they asked me for photographs I brought them an album. It was the R.A.F.'s job to get air photographs, so the R.A.F. were under pressure to take over what the Admiralty were pleased to call 'Cotton's unit'. If they didn't, the Admiralty threatened to take it over themselves. This broadside had originated from Churchill himself, and it opened up all the old arguments about responsibility for land-based aircraft.

Next morning in Peck's office I found myself surrounded by officers of varying ranks, some very senior and some quite junior, all on the defensive, all stubbornly insisting that the R.A.F. knew best and all out to prove – or so it seemed to me – that this man Cotton didn't know what he was talking about. When the senior officers spoke there was a general murmur of concurrence. When the juniors spoke they were listened to indulgently. When I spoke there was scepticism and even hostility. The R.A.F. believed that intelligence had to be fought for; my conception of a fast, unarmed aircraft covering large areas of enemy territory from high level almost at will was one they were not yet adjusted to. In the end I made an appeal to their reason. 'Surely,' I said, 'I've been sent for because somebody thinks I can take pictures. Yesterday I was asked if I was ready to help, and I said I was. Wouldn't it be better to let me have a try?'

At that point an officer came in with a signal for Peck. Peck read it and then got up hurriedly and went into the next office. I had noticed as I came through the corridor that the adjacent office housed the Vice-Chief of the Air Staff, Air Marshal Sir Richard Peirse. I was curious to know what was in that signal, and my curiosity was soon satisfied. It must have been another broadside from the First Lord. Peck came back after a minute or so accompanied by Air Marshal Peirse, virtually No. 2 at the Air Ministry at that time. Peirse was tall and with a proud carriage, hair greying at the temples but well brilliantined. His manner seemed to dare anyone to oppose his ideas. Peck began by addressing me, and I noticed at once his complete change of tone.

'Cotton, we're all in this together now, so we propose to let you into our confidence, relying on your discretion.' After many hours of talk we had got as far as this! 'German naval movements have been reported and there are two places on the Dutch coast which it is imperative that we photograph without delay. The first is Flushing, and the second is Ymuiden. Our crews have tried again and again in the last few days without success, and the First Lord is very disturbed about it. Can you suggest anything?'

'Lend me a Blenheim,' I said, 'and I'll get the pictures right away.'

This wasn't the answer they wanted. They couldn't possibly have a civilian flying about in military aircraft. If I got shot down I'd be shot as a spy. I said there was a war on and I was prepared to take the risk, but Peck said it was out of the question. They had their own aircraft and crews, but they would be grateful for any suggestions I could make. I said that when I wanted something done I generally went to a specialist of some kind or other, whether it was a cobbler to mend my shoes or a surgeon to operate. Presumably they had sent for me now as a photographic specialist. Couldn't they just let me get on with the job of taking the pictures, especially as they were so urgently required? It would save a great deal of time in discussion, and have the further virtue of showing whether I could do it or not.

It was decided to get hold of the squadron pilots who had been trying to take the pictures, plus a technical man whom Peck wanted to bring up from Farnborough, and hold another meeting next day. 'Until tomorrow morning, then,' said Peck, and soon after midday we broke up. I discovered afterwards that the expert from Farnborough was being called to disprove my condensation theory; Farnborough had scoffed at the idea, and Peck was beginning to suspect that I was a charlatan.

I went back to my office high above St James's Square and stared dejectedly out of the window, over the hills to the twin towers of the old Crystal Palace and beyond. The morning mist had cleared and it was a lovely warm September day. I watched the fleecy clouds floating idly by as I pondered on a means of breaking the deadlock. One thing seemed certain – they would never let me try to get the pictures on my own. I saw ahead of me nothing but endless conferences and talk, with the weight of opinion always against me, and I found the prospect intolerably frustrating. Then I looked again at the blue sky and the clouds. It was one of those days when anyone who loves flying longs to get airborne. Why not? Why not take the Lockheed and go and get the pictures now?

I rang Bob Niven at Heston and asked him to get me a weather report for Holland. He rang back almost at once to say that the weather there was much the same as here. This was just what I wanted. The big woolpacks of cloud would give us the cover we needed. I told Bob to get the Lockheed out and to warm the engines up ready for take-off, and as neither of us had had lunch I asked him to get the airport restaurant to pack us a hamper. I rang Winterbotham and asked him if he knew of any German fighter patrols operating along the Dutch coast, and he said it was quite possible if German naval movements were in progress. I was more thankful than ever for the cloud conditions. We had no photographic processing facilities at Heston, so I asked Winterbotham if he could arrange for Farnborough to be ready to develop and print some pictures for me later in the day, warning them that it was a rush job and I might want them to work through the night. I told my secretary to tell callers that I would be out for the afternoon, and then Kelson drove me to Heston. There was little traffic on the roads, my telephone calls had taken only a few minutes, and when I got to Heston the Lockheed was only just ready. We actually took off at one o'clock, less than an hour after I had left Peck's office.

I asked Heston Control as soon as we had taken off to tell Fighter Command that White Flight was proceeding out over the sea off the Kent coast on a test flight, returning later to Farnborough, and we climbed to 11,000 feet. We couldn't go any higher as I wanted to keep fairly near the woolpacks. We crossed the Kent coast at Ramsgate, then set course for Flushing, at the entrance to the Scheldt. The weather was ideal at both Flushing and Ymuiden, with plenty of gaps in the cloud for photography, and we flew right across both targets with our cameras running. We saw no other aircraft, and we headed back across the North Sea to Farnborough to deliver our pictures for processing. The photographic section entered into the spirit of the thing and worked all night developing the film and printing enlargements to about 12 inches by 12 inches, and the enlarged prints were mounted in an album with a Kodatrace leaf of transparent paper over each print, on which we noted the interpretation of significant points on each picture. Kelson drove me back to London in the early morning and I snatched a couple of hours sleep at my flat, leaving Niven to fly the Lockheed back to Heston during the day. At ten o'clock next morning I was in Peck's office with the album of enlargements in my brief-case. Peck opened the meeting and the talk proceeded much as it had done the day before. After half an hour I produced the album. 'Is this the sort of thing you want?' I asked.

Peck examined each print critically and was full of praise for the photography. The prints were clearly marked with the respective place-names, but it was taken for granted that they were of pre-war origin. Peck asked me again what special equipment I had used, and I answered as before. 'These are first-class,' said Peck, handing the album round, 'but we wouldn't expect this sort of quality in war-time.' I fixed my eye on the middle-distance and said nothing. Then someone asked when the pictures were taken, and I pulled the pin.

'At three-fifteen yesterday.'

The room was suddenly full of incredulous noises, which quickly turned to indignation as the truth went home. The commotion rose to such a pitch that I wondered what crime I could have committed. 'You had no right to do such a thing . . . flaunting authority . . . what would happen if everyone behaved like that . . .?' These and other angry phrases were detectable above the hubbub. The value of the pictures was lost for the moment in a fog of aggrieved bureaucracy. Someone even said I ought to be arrested. I could stand such nonsense no longer, and I decided to get out of the room before I told them what I thought of them. I'm told that I walked slowly to the door and slammed it as I went out.

Next morning Peck telephoned to say that the Chief of the Air Staff would like to come and see me. I said I couldn't possibly put him to that trouble and that I would come to see him, calling first at Peck's office. When I arrived Peck was alone. 'The Royal Air Force will never live down what you did yesterday,' he said, 'but between ourselves I congratulate you on your audacity.' Then he disappeared into the next office. Presently he emerged with a tall, ascetic-looking Air Chief Marshal whom I recognized as Sir Cyril Newall, the Chief of the Air Staff.

'So you're the man who's giving us all this trouble,' said Newall.

'No, sir – his name is Hitler.'

He laughed, and we shook hands. 'In spite of your unorthodox behaviour,' said Newall, 'I want to congratulate you on those pictures. They were badly wanted and we've been quite unable to get them ourselves. You'll be glad to know that they served their purpose.' He then asked me what I thought was wrong with the R.A.F.'s photographic section.

I asked him if he wanted the truth, reminding him that I was an Australian and that someone had once said that while Englishmen called a spade a spade, Australians were apt to call it a bloody shovel, and he smiled again and asked if I was free for lunch. He took me to the United Service Club in Pall Mall, and as soon as we sat down he asked me to tell him why the R.A.F.'s photography had failed. He stressed that it had failed completely, that most of the time the cameras froze, and that even when they didn't the pictures just didn't seem to be there. I said that condensation was the main trouble and that breakdowns or failures of the photographic equipment itself seldom occurred. I told him how I had quite accidentally discovered how to eliminate condensation, and said that once this was done there was nothing to freeze, since the oil used in the camera mechanism was specially selected to withstand low temperatures. The film itself might become stiff and the camera might slow down at very low temperatures, but the film-holder could easily be warmed. My good-quality prints, I explained, came from using Leica film and developing it with a fine-grain developer. It was all perfectly simple and anybody could do it. I added that the R.A.F.'s technical side was poor for two reasons: first, because of Lord Trenchard's insistence that there should be no specialists, and secondly because the photographic side had been neglected as unadventurous and shied away from by the men who might have fostered its development.

'Would you be prepared to help?' he asked.

'Of course I would.'

'Then I want you to take charge of the R.A.F.'s photographic section.'

'I'm afraid that wouldn't work, sir. It wouldn't get results quickly enough.'

'Why?'

'Because all the regular officers in the R.A.F. would resent my intrusion. They've done so already. I can only help if I'm allowed to form a special unit and given *carte blanche* in the choice of men, machines and equipment. On that basis I'm prepared to take it on.'

'Cotton,' he said, 'I'm afraid you're right. I agree to your proposal. You'll have *carte blanche* and you'll report to me. I'll arrange that Peck acts as liaison between us, and if you can't get what you want from him, come direct to me.' He then said that the unit must be designated top secret and must work from a secret aerodrome, and he asked me if I had any ideas about location.

'Yes, sir, I would like Heston.'

'But that's a civil airport.'

'Yes – nobody would suspect that secret work would be done from there.'

'You've got something there, Cotton. Heston it is.'

All this was too good to be true, and since I had spoken plainly and won my point I felt it was now time to soft-pedal a bit. So I said that I would do my best to keep within the red tape and general organization of the Air Force. 'For God's sake don't do that, Cotton!' said Newall. 'Your value to me lies in your continuing to do things in your own unorthodox way. I want results.'

When I saw Peck next day he said that everything would be set in motion and that I would be offered the rank of wing commander. I was to work directly under Peck, with Fred Winterbotham acting as liaison between us. I wrote to Peck the same day accepting the proposal that I form a special flight and welcoming the assurance that I was to have *carte blanche* in carrying out this work. The decision was ratified at a special meeting in the Department of the Directorate of Operations at which Peck presided on 22nd September, when 'it was decided to form an experimental unit for the purpose of testing, and if found to be successful, developing certain novel methods for making photographic reconnaissances over enemy territory. . . . In order to make the new unit productive from its inception, machines from other units are to be treated, to produce improved performance and camouflage'. Air Force planes and personnel could hardly be handed over to me as a civilian, so a week later I was somewhat reluctantly commissioned as a squadron leader, with the acting rank of wing commander. I wasn't much interested in rank anyway, and I shut my eyes to the fact that Peck hadn't quite kept his promise.

The difficulty of a civilian in uniform trying to deal with a maze of departments on a matter that had been designated 'Top Secret' soon became evident, and I spent many weary hours tramping from department to department and back to Peck, wasting valuable time. I suggested that an officer be attached to my unit who knew the names and locations of the various departments I had to deal with and their function in the scheme of things, but Peck wouldn't agree on security grounds. Eventually he called a conference to enable me to put my requirements forward, and at that conference I met a most helpful and energetic officer named Lionel Stubbs, a squadron leader in the Royal Air Force Volunteer Reserve who was head of a section of one of the most important departments with which I had to deal – Establishments. Stubbs took me by the hand after that first meeting and for the next few months was my most valuable friend at court. He explained to me that under the Air Force system my unit must be part of a larger establishment for administration, and he suggested it would be best to be attached to Fighter Command, who would not be a client for photographs and would therefore leave us alone. This was soon effected. Once I had selected the pilots I wanted, he helped me to get them. Niven, of course, stayed with me, taking the rank of flight lieutenant, and to complete a trio which would comprise the planning team of the unit I asked for Shorty Longbottom, who had just come back from Malta, and Stubbs got him for me. The nucleus of my special flight was to be five officers, not including myself, and seventeen other ranks. For the accommodation we took over the hangar and offices of Airwork Ltd. at Heston, also the flying club premises and part of the Airport Hotel. For the moment we would continue to use the processing facilities at Farnborough, but a photographic section was scheduled to be built at Heston. I concentrated my own efforts at this time on the aircraft and equipment side.

I had already been given a letter of introduction to Air Chief Marshal Sir Wilfred Freeman, the man who was responsible for the development and production of R.A.F. aircraft, and on 18th September I had been to Harrogate to see him; his department had been evacuated from London. Freeman was busy when I arrived but he delegated the task of looking after me to a quiet, almost meek, but charming and efficient air commodore named Tedder, then Director General of Research and Development. I spent an hour with Tedder explaining why it was that, although the Spitfire was the one aircraft everyone said I couldn't have, it was the one aircraft I wanted. In fact, I wanted two. I told Tedder that photographic intelligence would play one of the most important roles in the war and that to be fully effective it must have maximum freedom of action while keeping losses to a minimum. I said I based my policy on two factors, speed and ceiling. If we used the fastest aeroplanes in the world, flying at the highest altitude, they could not be intercepted. Any fighter aircraft cleaned up, with the guns eliminated, must be faster than the same plane as a fighter, and so long as such aircraft operated at their maximum altitude nothing could catch them. Such aircraft would have no use for radio or armour plating, leaving room for the carrying of extra fuel to give increased range.

Tedder passed me on to two of his technical experts, and these two men spent the rest of the day explaining to me, patiently but with long-suffering looks on their faces, that it would be technically impossible to equip Spitfires with cameras, and that in any case the absolute maximum range of the Spitfire in such a role would be 800 miles. They kept on trotting out the Blenheim as the answer to my problem, and finally they said that in any case that was all I could have. I went back to Tedder and reported the gist of what had been said, and he advised me to take the Blenheim and prove that it wouldn't do the job and then have another shot at getting the Spit-fires. I protested that this would be a criminal waste of time; there was ample evidence that the Blenheim was unsuitable.

'Cotton,' he said, 'I'm used to Service methods. Take my advice and you'll save time in the long run. I'll arrange for Farnborough to carry out any modifications you want to the Blenheims, and you'll have a free hand; but don't forget that you can't do much without Farnborough's approval. It's just as well to keep on the right side of them.'

I thanked him for his advice and said I would accept the Blenheim for the time being, but I flew back to Heston that night with a feeling of deep frustration. I appreciated that I had to be realistic about the choice of planes, but I knew the Blenheim wouldn't do.

Three days after my meeting with Tedder, on 21st September, two Mark IV long-nosed Blenheims arrived at Heston. I flew one down to Farnborough and met the Chief Superintendent, Mr A. H. Hall, who showed great interest in my ideas about streamlining and polishing to increase speed. I found over the next few months that Hall was always ready to try out new ideas, carrying out the most exhaustive calculations and tests to prove or disprove their soundness. We didn't always agree, but it was refreshing to meet a man so lacking in prejudice.

In cleaning up the Blenheim to get more speed we had all the thick dope taken off and replaced by a hard, semi-glossy dope with a very smooth surface. All holes were blocked up and all projections smoothed or streamlined, and we fitted a spinner to the propeller which helped to cool the engines and made it unnecessary to open the gills. Teardrop windows and Perspex front panels improved vision, and a retractable tail-wheel and retracting dump valves under the petrol tank gave further streamlining. The result was a speed increase of 18 m.p.h. This was a useful increase, but it did not make the Blenheim suitable for a photographic role. We needed at least another 100 miles an hour. The Blenheim was thus a disappointment, but it served its purpose as a flying laboratory, and we imagined that we had no choice anyway but to make the best of it. As it happened, however, the streamlined Blenheim was instrumental, in a most unexpected way, in my getting hold of the Spitfires I coveted.

Air Chief Marshal Sir Hugh Dowding, C.-in-C. Fighter Command, was fitting out Blenheims as long-range fighters, although they were really much too slow for this role. The rumour soon got about that I had done something to a Blenheim to increase its speed, and Dowding turned up at Heston one day and asked me if I could really make the Blenheim go faster. We arranged that one of his pilots should test a Blenheim and note its performance and then bring it over to Heston. After we had cleaned it up the pilot said it was fully 20 m.p.h. faster. Dowding was delighted, and he appealed to the Air Ministry to 'Cottonize' all his Blenheims, as he called my process. The Air Ministry were sceptical about any real increase in speed, and they told Dowding that in any case they had no facilities available for carrying out such a task, so Dowding came back to me. I told him that if he would requisition another hangar for me at Heston I would do the job. We 'Cottonized' eight Blenheims in a week, and in addition to the speeding-up process we fitted my patent tear-drop windows which enabled the pilot to see downwards and to the rear. We painted the Blenheims the same pale green as my Lockheed, and this later became standard camouflage for all R.A.F. fighter aircraft.

Some days later Dowding invited me to tea at Stanmore. He told me how pleased he was with the Blenheims, and he asked if there was anything he could do for me, so I decided to take the plunge. 'There is one thing, sir,' I said, fully realizing what I was asking and fully expecting a shocked refusal. 'Could you lend me a couple of Spitfires?'

Dowding's face remained for the moment inscrutable. 'What for?'

I expounded my views on the requirements of photographic reconnaissance, and Dowding listened politely enough – even perhaps attentively, I could not tell which. There was a pause when I had finished, and then Dowding spoke.

'When would you like them?'

'Yesterday!'

'Would nine o'clock tomorrow morning do?'

I accepted gratefully, and at nine o'clock next morning two Spitfires landed at Heston. We took out the guns and gun fittings and got rid of all excess weight, we filled in the gun holes with metal plates, we stopped up all cracks with plaster of Paris and we polished the external surfaces into a hard, sleek gloss. In this way we increased the speed of these two Spitfires from 360 to 396 m.p.h. But knowledge that Heston had two Spitfires soon got about, and it brought all sorts of trouble on Dowding's head (so he told me later) as well as on mine. Peck had me on the mat and asked what I meant by getting new aircraft without reference to the Air Ministry: did I know that Fighter

Command were desperately short of these planes? How was I going to service and fly them without additional trained staff? Did I intend to pinch these as well? I pointed out that my unit was established on and administered by Fighter Command and that the attachment of these aircraft to my unit was a domestic affair – thanking God as I did so for the foresight of Lionel Stubbs. Peck didn't like it but there was nothing he could do about it. With the help of Lionel Stubbs I soon acquired expert Rolls-Royce engineers to service these two planes.

Having increased the speed of the Spitfires I now had to increase their range. I wanted to put a 30-gallon petrol tank under the pilot's seat which would increase the range to 1,250 miles at 30,000 feet, but the R.A.E. wouldn't approve it because they said it would shift the centre of gravity too far back. I wanted to put a 64-lb. camera just behind the pilot's seat as well, but they rejected this out of hand for the same reason, so I decided to take one thing at a time. First, the petrol tank. I refused to accept the R.A.E.'s figures as my own calculations indicated that we could quite safely install both the tank and the camera, and eventually the R.A.E. approved the installation of a 29-gallon tank. I let them get away with the odd gallon as a compromise. Now for the rather more complex matter of the camera.

I went over my calculations and flew the machine again to be quite sure I was right. Then I decided on a little subterfuge. My Spitfires were fitted with three-bladed steel airscrews, which were heavier than the original wooden airscrews. Spitfires with steel airscrews had to have lead weights totalling 32 lb. fitted in the tail to compensate for the additional weight up front, and a set of these weights was fitted in the tail of my Spitfire. One of the Farnborough pilots air-tested the machine and reported himself satisfied with its handling. One of my pilots also tested it and approved. I then called for a screwdriver and unscrewed the inspection panel in the rear of the fuselage and revealed the lead weights. This showed what the makers thought of the centre of gravity problem. There were some red faces at Farnborough, but they now agreed to the camera fitment. The loading worked most satisfactorily and we never had any trouble.

Getting the men, converting the Blenheims, modifying the Spitfires – all this took some time, but by the end of October I had two aircraft capable of a cruising speed of close on 400 m.p.h. with a range of 1,250 miles at 30,000 feet, fitted with the best photographic equipment I could get. With the help of Lionel Stubbs I had gathered a first-class team around me, a team that would expand rapidly, as it was clearly intended that the unit should grow. The Heston Flight, or No. 2 Camouflage Unit as it was soon to be cryptically designated, was ready to start operations.

17

Quarrels with the Air Staff

THE pre-war concept of air reconnaissance was that the Westland Lysander, a small single-engined Army Co-operation aircraft, would look after the short-range work at low level in close support of the Army while longer-range cover would be supplied by the Blenheims, flying at 10,000 to 12,000 feet, the maximum height at which the cameras then in use were reckoned to give acceptable definition. Good results could only be obtained in clear weather, and it had always been my view that at these heights the Blenheim, which was not a fast aircraft, would become an ideal target for enemy fighters. I was upset to have confirmation from Peck, towards the end of 1939, that very heavy losses were in fact being suffered by the Blenheim reconnaissance squadrons in France.

From the strategic standpoint, the Ruhr was obviously destined to be one of the main targets for our bombers and we badly needed comprehensive air photography of the area for intelligence purposes and for the preparation of target maps and plans. Following attack we must also be able to re-photograph the area so that by comparison with earlier cover we could assess the damage. Tactically, we needed to mount regular surveillance sorties over enemy movements and communications. These requirements were incapable of fulfilment by the Blenheims, although they were still being persisted with, and I suggested to Peck that I go over and see Air Marshal Arthur Barratt, C.-in-C. British Air Forces France, and discuss his requirements with him. Peck agreed, but he gave me a letter for Barratt in which he stressed that my unit was still in the development stage, that its work was top secret, and that it must remain for the present based at Heston and could not be absorbed into B.A.F.F.

Barratt told me that he was being pressed by General Gort, C.-in-C. of the British Expeditionary Force, for aerial photography of Belgium. The French High Command, certain that the Maginot Line and the Ardennes Forest adjacent to it presented an impassable barrier to tanks and armoured forces, concluded that the main German effort would fall in the north, across the Belgian plain between Namur and Antwerp. The aim would be to outflank the Maginot Line and race across Belgium to the Channel ports before swinging left to encircle Paris. This was in fact the basis of the German plan at that time. The Allied response would be to throw a defensive line across the Franco–Belgian frontier and swing it northwards on its axis to meet the German advance, joining up with the Belgian and Dutch armies and preserving as much of their territory as possible from which to mount a counter-offensive later on. Unfortunately neither the Dutch nor the Belgians would concert their plans with the Allies for fear of offering Hitler a pretext for invasion. Thus Gort lacked much basic information without which he might be unable to play an effective part if the Germans invaded Belgium. More than anything else he needed to correct his maps.

I expressed surprise that we were unable to get this sort of information from the Belgians, but Barratt reiterated how touchy they were about their neutrality. Flying over neutral countries, he reminded me, was forbidden; but did I think that my high-flying Spitfires might be able to photograph Belgium without being intercepted, supposing we could get permission to do it? I said that without doubt they could, but that due to range limitations they would have to be based in France to carry out such a task. That would need the concurrence of the Air Ministry.

I flew back to London and told Peck what Barratt had asked. Peck said that we could certainly detach aircraft for short periods to France, but the orders were quite definite about Allied aircraft not flying over neutral territory. 'The Belgian Government have been particularly insistent on this,' he said. 'They're afraid of some incident which might precipitate an attack on their country.'

'Surely the Germans will have made their plans, irrespective of the flights of one or two reconnaissance aircraft?'

'I entirely agree,' said Peck, 'but those are the orders and there's nothing we can do about it.'

I went back to see Barratt and told him of my talk with Peck. I then mentioned an idea that was forming in my mind. 'If we were to detach a mobile unit with a Spitfire to an advanced base in France,' I said, 'preferably near the Belgian border, we could probably do several useful jobs for you, and while we were there it is possible that the pilots might have compass trouble and occasionally find them-

selves over Belgium.' Barratt opened his eyes a little wider, but his
expression did not change. 'Let's go and see Gort,' he said. Thus it was
that on 5th November I set out with Barratt and Air Vice-Marshal
Charles Blount, A.O.C. of the Air Component in France, to select a
suitable advanced base. We chose an airfield at Seclin, near Lille,
less than ten miles from the Belgian border, and we took over a
hangar to establish an 'advanced training school' – or so we told the
other R.A.F. occupants of the airfield. Secrecy, I believed, remained
essential, and I insisted that the two pilots I detached to Seclin should
not mix with other units but should be kept to themselves at a local
hotel. This also applied to the six mechanics and two photographers
who completed the detachment. It was always my view that our
work would prove of such value that the Germans would be forced
to seek us out and try to destroy us, and this view was later vindicated.

The first sortie from Lille–Seclin, and the first photographic sortie
of any kind in a Spitfire, was flown by Shorty Longbottom on 18th
November; he took off at one o'clock that afternoon, bound for the
German border, intending to fly north as far as Aachen. The weather
prevented him from photographing his targets, but he did get some
wonderful pictures from 33,000 feet of the country just west of the
frontier. 'It was a historic occasion,' wrote Constance Babington
Smith many years later: 'for the first time successful exposures had
been made at high altitude under war conditions by cameras mounted in a Spitfire.[1]

Lille–Seclin, while ideal for the 'X' series of sorties, was a long
way from the German border, and to give Longbottom more time
in the target area on his next sortie I resolved to refuel the Spitfire
at some intermediate airfield in eastern France. We chose Challerange, thirty miles from the Luxembourg border, and two days later,
on 20th November, I flew there in the Lockheed to make the refuelling arrangements while Shorty followed in the Spitfire. We made
an early start, and Shorty was able to take off for the German
border soon after 10.30 that morning. The weather was good and I
was hopeful that we would get the pictures we wanted this time.

I had such confidence in my theories and methods that I had
hardly considered the possibility that the Spitfire might be intercepted; it never really occurred to me that Shorty might be shot

---

[1] In *Evidence in Camera* (Chatto & Windus, London, 1958).

down. Yet, as one o'clock approached and there was no sign of him, I began to feel anxious. His range of 1,250 miles gave him a safe endurance of little more than three hours, so that by 1.30 I would have to consider him overdue. One-thirty came, and then 1.45, and still he did not return.

Most of the men who worked for me became my personal friends, and my regard for Shorty Longbottom was deep; but I knew it was no good brooding if in fact he was missing. The men of the servicing team whom I took down with me in the Lockheed have since told me that all I said was: 'We must get another Spitfire.' My faith in high-speed high-altitude aerial reconnaissance was unshaken. I took off with them in the Lockheed, flew towards the border to see if we could see any sign of the missing Spitfire on the ground, and then headed for Coulommiers, thirty-seven miles east of Paris, where Barratt had his headquarters. The other Spitfire that Dowding had lent me was still at Heston, where it was in daily use for training purposes, but I hoped that with Barratt's help I might get another.

As I was circling Coulommiers, something caught my eye on the ground and I shouted to the crew. 'There's Shorty! Look!' Parked near a hangar was a highly-polished Spitfire, unmistakable in its camouflage of duck-egg green. Shorty must have missed Challerange and put down here. We landed and found Shorty in high spirits. Large areas of German territory had been photographed for the first time since the war. I had been told all along the line that this sort of work in unarmed aircraft was impossible in wartime, and I shared Shorty's sense of achievement. Cameras could not be fitted into Spitfires, everyone had said; they did not have the range, and in any case I couldn't have any. In exactly two months all these strictures had been proved wrong.

Until photographic trailers, which I was asking for, could be made available for developing and printing on the spot, the film was rushed back to Heston for processing, one set of prints then being flown to Gort's headquarters at Arras or to Barratt's headquarters at Coulommiers as appropriate, sometimes to both. For these communication flights we made use of the Blenheims at first, but they were not really suitable, and I asked for two Hudsons, to enable mobile units to move easily from one airfield to another. Later these aircraft were duly delivered.

The small processing section at Heston, not yet expanded as planned, soon found itself unable to cope with the volume of work, and as I could not use Farnborough other than temporarily I was forced to look for new capacity elsewhere. A further complication was that no specialist organization existed to interpret our photographs and to extract intelligence from them. The neglect in laying the foundations of such an organization is astonishing when one considers that by the end of the war the Allied Central Interpretation Unit employed about 550 officers and 2,000 other ranks, providing about 80 per cent of our high-grade intelligence on the enemy. On the outbreak of war our total interpretation capacity consisted of two R.A.F. officers at the Air Ministry, recruited from civilian ranks and with virtually no experience, two Army officers who were soon moved to France to join the B.E.F., and a small nucleus at the Admiralty. Unless some organization could be provided quickly our work was going to be wasted.

Another source of exasperation was that the photographs we were taking in the Spitfire evoked little interest at the Air Ministry. We were using the same cameras as the Blenheims were using, and as we were flying at heights of up to 36,000 feet the scale was so minute that the Air Ministry regarded them as useless for the purposes of interpretation. I felt that this wasn't good enough, and I became involved in a series of disagreements with the Air Ministry on this and related matters. I knew well enough the importance of resolution in photographic film, but I did not agree that the scale and quality of our photographs from 36,000 feet rendered them useless for interpretation; my use of Leica film and fine-grain developer, for instance, brought a great improvement. In any case, the task of maintaining a reconnaissance watch on the whole of Germany from 10,000 feet was clearly impossible, and the position was that only from a height of 30,000 feet or above could we get any reliable cover without prohibitive losses. The answer was to improve our interpretation methods, and ultimately to acquire or develop a more suitable camera.

I soon thought of an ideal solution to the interpretation problem, and through it we took our first steps towards improved equipment. An old friend of mine who had run my aerial survey department in Newfoundland nearly twenty years earlier, 'Lemnos' Hemming, was running an aerial survey business at Wembley called the Aircraft Operating Company, with modern photogrammetric equipment and trained interpreters. Since the outbreak of war his business had inevitably declined and he was anxious for his firm, which had much to offer, to be requisitioned, but the Air Ministry had turned him down.

Having no idea of the value of his equipment and staff, they took the view that his company was losing money and that he was simply trying to cut his losses. I took this up with Peck at once, but could not at first convince anyone that a mistake had been made. Meanwhile the backlog of film was building up so seriously that I began to make unofficial use of Hemming's facilities, which were quite unobtainable elsewhere, swearing him and his staff to secrecy and personally guaranteeing his account. I justified my action by a phrase much in use at that time, but understood by very few in those 'phoney' days – 'There's a war on'.

Hemming's organization knew nothing of military intelligence, but they knew what non-military detail looked like, which put them ahead of the official interpreters, and they soon learned the rest. Their early reports may have been crude and wordy, but they served their purpose as they at least showed that something could be seen. On later flights, after the official interpreters had reported that there was little of value to be seen in our photographs, Hemming's men were able to show that a great deal of detail on German defences, down to such things as anti-tank obstructions, was positively identifiable to anyone used to examining air photographs stereoscopically.

Hemming told me he had a camera with a 20-inch focal length; the focal length of the R.A.F. camera installed in the Spitfire was only 5 inches. It occurred to me that we might supplement the coverage we were getting with the 5-inch camera by using the 20-inch, which gave a scale of 1/18,000 at 30,000 feet against 1/72,000 for the 5-inch. The 5-inch covered much more territory, but the combination of the two proved most useful. The success we got with this camera finally stirred the Air Ministry into action and resulted in the development in 1940 of the F.52 camera, which gave a scale of 1/10,000 from 30,000 feet and became the standard reconnaissance camera from 1941 on.

I was continually flying to and from France at this time, and Barratt agreed that I ought to have a forward headquarters there, not too far from his own, and that I must be ready to form other mobile units as required, using Heston as a rear headquarters. Peck, too, agreed, and I found an old mill-house in the peaceful village of Tigeaux which was ideal for my purpose: it was unobtrusive, and within a few miles of Barratt at Coulommiers. This was especially convenient as the French Chief of Air Staff, General Vuillemin, had his private airport at Coulommiers, and as a result of some special reconnaissances we had done for him, with which he told me he was well satisfied, he had offered us the use of it. We were also near his headquarters at Meaux.

I preferred using French airfields for two reasons; first, we often experienced hostility at R.A.F. airfields because station commanders resented not being told what we were doing, and secondly over security, which was difficult to maintain in the face of searching questions and careless talk. Vuillemin eventually gave me *carte blanche* to use all his airfields, backing this up with a letter, and from then on we always used them, no questions ever being asked once I produced Vuillemin's letter. Often a hangar would be cleared and sentries posted within minutes of our landing. Vuillemin even had a special hangar built for me at Coulommiers in the shape of a haystack, camouflaged with straw, big enough to house my Lockheed and the two Spitfires. To reach the hangar we had to taxi along a cart track into a hayfield about 200 yards from the airfield boundary, and in all the blitzes which followed that hangar escaped.

Demands for photography of the main areas of the Ruhr were frequent at this stage, but neither the R.A.F. nor the French were able to cover this area successfully, although many attempts were made. It was of course an unusually difficult task as the target area was almost continually obscured by cloud and smoke haze and the defences were among the strongest in Germany. Barratt, who told me that whenever he sent the Blenheims out on this sort of reconnaissance he had to face losses of between 30 and 80 per cent, asked if we could help. What we needed, I felt, was an airfield in northeastern France, as near the Ruhr as we could get, and on 30th November I flew to Nancy with Niven, Longbottom and a new pilot named Hugh McPhail, a First World War pilot of great experience, to select a site for a second mobile unit. We settled for the airfield at Essey, some fifty miles west of the border at Strasbourg, and early in December we moved our second Spitfire across from Heston. We were still operating with the two aircraft lent to us by Dowding, and although on 7th December, at a meeting I had with Peck, the plans I put forward for expanding my unit were approved in principle – I was to have a total of eight Spitfires – plans in those days were a long time reaching fruition. Indeed Peck told me that neither the Spitfires nor the pilots to fly them were likely to be available for many months.

I was extremely depressed about this as I knew there was a great deal of vital reconnaissance work waiting to be done. The reason why I could not get the priority necessary for a speedier expansion could only be that our work was not fully appreciated at the Air Ministry, and from this time on I made it my business to bombard them with requests for action and reminders of the work we were doing. I was hopeful that photographs of the Ruhr, when we could get them, would be a strong argument in our favour, but for practically the whole of December the weather closed in. Then at last, on 29th December, in a period of better weather, Bob Niven did a beautiful job of photographing the southern areas of the Ruhr asked for by the French, although he was actually over the target for less than half an hour. I was very excited at the results of this and other sorties flown during this cloudless period; Cologne and Dusseldorf were photographed, and large areas of the Siegfried Line were covered for the first time since the outbreak of war. The R.A.F. and the French had been trying to get these pictures for weeks at dreadful cost, and now Niven had produced them at one go. I was elated as I felt sure we would get the support we needed when these results were known.

Meanwhile the Spitfire at Lille–Seclin was suffering from almost continual 'compass trouble', judging from the excellent progress being made with the 'X' series of sorties, as the flights over Belgium were known. The task was completed early in 1940, and the entire series of photographs handed over to Gort, suitably annotated by Hemming's outfit, but we could not do any boasting about this. However, I felt that our pictures of the Ruhr would be enough, and early in January I pressed Peck again for action on our proposals. Peck said that the pilots simply couldn't be spared, or the Spitfires, but Blount offered to let me have some Battle pilots, who were ideal for reconnaissance work as they were qualified navigators, so back I went to Peck. My proposals now included the merging into my unit of Hemming's Aircraft Operating Company, with all his trained interpreters and such valuable equipment as the *Wild* photogrammetric machine (pronounced Vilt), of Swiss manufacture, an elaborate machine for recording precise measurements from aerial photographs. I also asked for a trained administrative officer to relieve the load on my shoulders at Heston. But Peck was unconvinced, and there were still no more Spitfires.

Vuillemin's headquarters at Meaux also housed the French School of Photographic Interpretation, and early in January I was introduced to the commandant, Colonel Lespair, who showed me over the school. I was shown beautiful dossiers full of photographs, and it was plain from the detailed annotations and analyses that the French were a long way ahead of the R.A.F. in interpretation, and that even Hemming's men could learn a lot from them. When Lespair offered me full facilities for an exchange of ideas I asked if I could send one of Hemming's men over to work with them for a time and take the French interpretation course, and Lespair agreed. Douglas Kendall, who had been in aerial survey for some time and had worked for Hemming before the war in South Africa, besides studying forestry and geology at Oxford, went over shortly afterwards, and he was followed by others. He later became one of the foremost air photographic interpreters of the war.

Encouraged by Lespair, I now began to send many of our photographs straight to the French school at Meaux for interpretation, saving valuable time. Meanwhile I continued to urge the Air Ministry, as I had from the beginning, to take interpretation seriously. They still regarded it as a job that any intelligence officer ought to be able to do without special training. I could not resist telling the French of the low priority still accorded to the requirements and expansion of my unit, and some days later Lespair produced a chart showing enemy areas photographed from the outbreak of war to mid-January, together with the losses incurred in the process. It seemed to me that this chart would be decisive in arguing my case. In summary it amounted to the following:

The R.A.F. had photographed 2,500 square miles of enemy territory in three months for the loss of 40 aircraft, mostly Blenheims.

The French had photographed 6,000 square miles of enemy territory in three months for the loss of 60 aircraft.

The detachment from Heston had photographed 5,000 square miles of enemy territory in *three flights* without loss.

The figures given for my unit did not include the 'X' series over Belgium covering 12,000 square miles, which we could not mention, but they included some of the most heavily defended areas in Germany, and we had not been so much as challenged by a single aircraft. All that anyone had seen of us was an occasional condensation trail very high up.

On 26th January 1940 I produced this chart in Peck's office. Peck glanced at it, prepared to brush it aside, and then studied it. I watched his expression change as the figures sank in.

'Where did you get this?'

'From the French.'

'I knew you'd produce something like this sooner or later.'

Without another word he took me in to see Peirse. No one ever queried the figures, so they must have been about right. Next day I heard that the Air Council had at last accepted my proposals for the expansion of my unit; this was the greatest encouragement I had received up to that time, and I see it now as the real beginning of what later became the famous P.R.U.

Approval was given by Peirse on Monday 29th January for Farnborough to give priority to modifying our new Spitfires, and the first one arrived at Heston on 7th February. Several pilots, mostly volunteers from the Battle squadrons in France, were also posted in. But in the meantime I was again reminded that it was one thing to get proposals agreed and quite another to get them all implemented. The first difficulty was over an administrative officer, and eventually I asked Barratt if he could help. He told me that he had a very fine administrator on his staff in France named Geoffrey Tuttle: he could not really afford to let him go, but it was an indication of his opinion of our work that he agreed to do so. The Air Ministry then intervened, saying quite categorically that we could not have Tuttle, but I persisted, Barratt backed me up, and Tuttle reported to me at Heston on 9th February. The second and more serious difficulty lay in getting the decision not to requisition Hemming's company reversed. In spite of the fact that the Air Staff were supposed to have agreed to all my proposals, which included the absorption of the Aircraft Operating Company, nothing was done. I was forced to go on using Hemming's facilities privately, as I had been doing for many weeks, delivering highly secret negatives to be printed and interpreted by a civilian organization about which the Air Ministry were apathetic because they did not understand its value.

Although the Admiralty had assumed control of the Fleet Air Arm on its formation in 1937, they were still entirely dependent on the R.A.F. for photographic reconnaissance. Early in February the Naval Intelligence Divison received a report that the *Tirpitz*, which up till then had been in graving dock at Wilhelmshaven, was out, but the R.A.F., to whom they appealed, were unable to get photographs or to confirm or deny the report by visual reconnaissance. On 6th February I was rung up by Charles Drake and asked what I could do. The weather was bad for the next three days, but at 11 a.m. on 10th February Shorty Longbottom took off for Wilhelmshaven. At the same time I rang Hemming and asked him to keep some of his men on duty that night for an urgent job.

It was a cold, clear day, and the Spitfire, stripped of all armament, streamlined to our pattern, and polished so that it shone, climbed rapidly away from Heston. At 3.20 that afternoon Shorty was safely back, having photographed Wilhelmshaven and Emden from more than five miles up. I took the film straight to Hemming at Wembley, but the special processing for ship recognition took some hours, and it was two o'clock on Sunday morning before the film was ready for interpretation. Hemming's photogrammetric expert was a brilliant young engineer named Michael Spender, a brother of Stephen Spender; he had studied physics under Professor Lindemann at Oxford, but he had always been deeply interested in aerial photography, and after leaving Oxford he had taken part in several expeditions as a geographer. He had joined Hemming's staff just before the war, and it was obvious to me that because of his flair and intuition he would become an important influence in the development of the art of evaluating photographs. He had always been fascinated by ships, and he was soon able to declare that the *Tirpitz* was in fact still in graving dock after all. However, it was obvious to us all that to do a satisfactory job of interpretation on all these photographs, not only of the ships but also of the port installations, he would require naval assistance. I told Hemming I would get someone from the Admiralty in the morning, but his answer was that he had just received instructions from the Air Ministry that, pending a final Air Council decision, he was to deal with the Air Ministry only and on no account to contact the Admiralty.

I rang the Air Ministry at ten o'clock on Sunday morning to ask their permission to deal direct with the Admiralty but was forbidden to do so. I daren't disobey this order as I feared it might react on Hemming, whose company had still not been taken over. I was told to deliver the pictures as soon as possible to the Air Ministry, where they would be interpreted and sent on to the Admiralty, and I took a set of prints over personally.

I learned later that the Air Ministry interpreters wasted most of that day trying to find a copy of the *North Sea Pilot* (which gives information about ports, etc.) and other essential charts before they could even begin the task of interpretation and the re-drawing of maps and plans. One thing that especially bothered them was the appearance of a cluster of objects at Emden which looked like submarines, and this started a scare, so much so that the Chief of the Air Staff rang the Admiralty and suggested a bombing raid on Emden as there were about 60 U-Boats there. The matter was referred to the Admiralty's Operational Intelligence Centre, and the man who dealt with it was the man who had in fact created this centre just before the war, one of the few men who were fully alive at that time to the possibilities of air reconnaissance and photo interpretation – Lieutenant Commander 'Ned' Denning, who twenty years later was himself to become Director of Naval Intelligence and then Director of Intelligence for the Combined Services in the Ministry of Defence. Denning's reaction was that the report was nonsense. 'It's not a U-Boat base,' he said, 'and it's very unlikely that there would be any U-Boats there.' I didn't know about all this until later, but when I asked that evening for permission to take a set of prints to the Admiralty I got a direct order from Peirse that the photographs were to go through Air Ministry channels only.

I spent most of Monday morning at the Air Ministry trying to get permission to take a set of prints to Drake. He in turn was trying to reach me at Heston. At midday I gave up and went back to Heston, and during the afternoon Drake at last contacted me and I told him of the Air Ministry ruling. He sounded most agitated and said that it was vital that they have the information at once. At this point I decided that inter-Service jealousies had gone far enough and I told Drake I would take him a spare set of prints. I learned later from Peck that the Admiralty had upset the Air Ministry in recent weeks by asking again and again for their reconnaissance work to be done by 'Cotton's unit', as they called it, which the Air Force resented, perhaps not unnaturally. When their hand was forced they were prepared to let me do the job, but they didn't see why the Admiralty need always know who had done it.

I delivered the prints to Drake at 6 p.m. Drake told me that Rear-Admiral J. H. Godfrey, the Director of Naval Intelligence, wanted to see me later, but would I first take Denning down to Wembley to view the photographs on Hemming's equipment. This was the first time anyone from any intelligence branch had been down to Wembley. Spender and Denning had a good laugh over the submarines theory; they could see with the naked eye that the objects were barges. Denning was a frequent visitor to Wembley after that. The

9(a). A group of my pilots in France (wearing Sidcots). Bob Niven is centre left and Shorty Longbottom centre right

9(b). Discussing a sortie with Air Marshal Sir Arthur Barratt

Getting Into Position for the Attack

'C'. Control Aircraft, fitted with searchlight of 70 kilowatts power, against 10 kilowatts of army searchlight, A.1. radio and all equipment necessary to enable interception to be made. 'A'. Fighter Aircraft fitted with a cannon. 'B'. Fighter Aircraft fitted with a cannon. 'X'. Enemy Aircraft.

The Attack

'C'. (Control Aircraft) has signalled 'Attack' and switched on light. 'A'. has dived in and opened fire. 'B'. awaits completion of attack by 'A'.

10. Aerial Target Illumination

(*See page 204*)

correct interpretation in this case could have been made available
to the Navy some thirty-six hours earlier.

When I went back to the Admiralty that evening, Admiral Godfrey took me straight in to see Sir Dudley Pound. Pound explained
that it was vital that the Admiralty had regular up-to-date information on the whereabouts of German naval units, to enable our own
warships to be deployed to the best advantage. Without this precise
knowledge too many warships had to be tied down to ensure adequate cover of the various enemy units and bases. Keeping track of
these ships, he said, had been a requirement of the highest priority
since the outbreak of war, but the R.A.F. had never been able to
meet it. He then took me over to a wall-map of the North Sea and
pointed out the various ports where German ships might be. I said
that my medium-range Spitfire, with a range of 1,250 miles, could
cover all these targets in one flight. We would be able to cover more
distant areas, I told him, with one of our new Spitfires, for which
Supermarine's were fitting special tanks in the wings to give a
range of 2,000 miles. This had been my idea; we were having baffle-
plates fitted in the leading edge with non-return valves, and I had
already cabled America to get the rubber sealing compound which
would prevent the petrol from leaking. I met the bill for this
compound myself. Pound was delighted with my answers, and he
said he wanted me to attend the War Room meeting later that
evening, when he proposed to take the matter up again with the
Air Staff.

I asked Pound if he thought it was wise for me to be there. 'Don't
you think the Air Staff might resent it?' I said. 'I'm told they're
sick of hearing about me and the work of "Cotton's Unit". I'm especially anxious not to upset them at the moment,' I added. 'They've
just approved a new establishment for my unit, and it looks as
though they're going to back me up fully at last. If I upset them they
could take over my unit and we'd be back where we started.' Four
Spitfires had arrived at Heston on the previous day, Sunday 11th
February, which with two others delivered in the previous week made
eight in all, and I had sent one of them down to Supermarine's at
Southampton for the special modifications while the others went to
Farnborough. The outlook at last was bright.

'I'll discuss it with the First Lord,' said Pound; 'it was he who asked
for you to be there.'

I was left to digest the news that Churchill wanted to see me; I

G

had heard before from Drake that he was taking a keen interest in our work. Then I got a message from Pound. 'The First Lord wants you to be there,' he said. 'He's coming himself and he says he'll handle the situation.'

I arrived at the Admiralty at 9.30 p.m. and reported to Commander Drake in the D.N.I.'s office. We went up to the War Room and found a number of senior naval officers already there. Pound greeted me and told me that the First Lord had been summoned to see the King but that he would be there later. I was taken aback at this as I felt that my presence would need statesmanlike handling, and I was about to suggest that I await the arrival of the First Lord when the Air Staff officers walked in. Among them were Air Marshal Peirse, Air Marshal Joubert de la Ferté and Air Commodore Stevenson. When Peirse saw me his reaction was exactly as I had expected – those thick, expressive eyebrows shot up in surprise. He crossed the room towards me.

'What are you doing here, Cotton?'

Pound managed to intercept him before I could answer. 'I'm sorry about this, Peirse, but we sent for Cotton in rather a hurry and there wasn't time to get permission from the Air Staff for him to attend. We're hoping he may be able to help us with a matter we want to discuss tonight.'

At these meetings the C.N.S. sat in a high-backed armchair, flanked on either side by a similar high-backed chair, one for the senior R.A.F. officer present and the other for the senior Army officer present. The remaining officers sat in well-upholstered but low-backed armchairs. As the various officers sorted themselves out I stayed with Pound, waiting for him to indicate where he wanted me to sit. I saw Peirse making for one of the high-backed chairs next to Pound, and he was about to move round in front of it when Pound tapped him on the shoulder. 'Oh, I'd like Cotton to sit there, Peirse,' he said. 'Would you mind moving down one?'

This was embarrassing for me and no doubt infuriating for Peirse, and for a moment I thought he was going to explode; but he said nothing and moved down. Pound himself looked ill-at-ease for a moment, and he told me afterwards that he realized he'd committed an unfortunate *gaffe*. I wondered if Peirse would ever forgive me. It was a bad start to a meeting that promised to be a stormy one anyway.

I had armed myself with a set of the scale drawings and interpretations done by Hemming's men with the *Wild* machine of the photographs Longbottom had taken two days earlier, and when Pound opened the meeting by mentioning them I passed them round. All the naval people present agreed that these were magnificent and gave all the information required. Peirse, too, remarked on their excellence. 'How were these results obtained?' he asked.

Not wanting to embarrass Peirse still further by saying that they were made with Hemming's equipment, which the Air Ministry had been offered five months earlier but had continually refused to requisition, I answered as vaguely as I could. 'With a special photogrammetric instrument, sir.'

'Then why weren't the Air Staff told about it?' demanded Peirse. 'We would have requisitioned it at once.'

In my pocket I had a piece of paper recording the Air Ministry's refusal to do this very thing; this was the decision that I had been fighting to get reversed. But I saw no point in further upsetting Peirse, and I let his question go unanswered, accepting the implied rebuke. Pound then wound up his introductory statement. 'We have consistently pressed for information on the whereabouts of these ships and been put off for one reason or another. We're not prepared to accept that situation any longer.'

'I thought we had made it clear,' said Peirse, 'that this is a most difficult task, and that some of the best brains in the Air Force are working on it.'

'Perhaps,' interrupted Pound, 'you might get better results if you tried some of the lesser brains for a while.'

It was a harsh comment, and Peirse, already upset at being interrupted, was speechless with annoyance. Pound turned to me. 'Cotton, you've heard what we've been discussing. Can you get this information?'

'Yes, sir,' I said, 'quite easily.'

I suppose I should have been diplomatic and hedged a bit and said how difficult it was and that I thought it might be possible and so on, but instead I spoke the truth. Peirse found his voice again and jumped from his chair. 'I'm not accepting that just because Cotton says it. There are scores of difficulties that he probably hasn't even thought of.'

'Surely the proof of the pudding is in the eating, sir,' I said. 'May we not try?'

'That sounds reasonable enough. What about it, Peirse?'

'How do you propose to carry out this operation?' asked Peirse. 'I shall want to know a lot more about it before I'm convinced it's feasible.'

The next twenty minutes or more were taken up by my explanation of how I would do the job and Peirse's repeated cross-questions and doubts. I described what I called my 'H' plan, in which I intended to use a Hudson in conjunction with a Spitfire. I wouldn't want to risk the Spitfire in bad weather because of navigation difficulties in a one-man aircraft, so the Hudson's role would be to take off on the same route as the Spitfire would take, flying in cloud cover, and to send the appropriate signal – whether it was suitable for the Spitfire to operate or not – when it reached a pre-arranged point. If the weather ahead was reported clear by the Hudson, the Spitfire would take off and climb to its operating height. There would then be a fair chance that the weather over the distant target would be clear.

Peirse objected that the Hudson was quite unsuitable for such work, that it would be shot down as soon as it used its radio, and so on. He suggested a Blenheim. I reminded him that it would be the Hudson's mission to go out in bad weather, that this would reduce the chances of interception, and that in any case we would arrange for the Hudson to change course immediately after any radio transmission. The real value of the Hudson, I added, would be that it was well heated inside and that the crew were comfortably situated and could therefore attend properly to their duties. I did not believe this was so with the Blenheim.

Peirse's next objection concerned the Spitfire's range. I had spoken of reaching Kiel with the Spitfire that had already been modified by Farnborough, but Peirse doubted very much if this could be done. I told him about my plan for carrying additional petrol in the wings, and although Peirse was still sceptical I felt I had come through a tough cross-examination fairly well.

'What do you think of this plan?' asked Pound.

'I shall have to consider it.'

'Don't you think it's worth letting Cotton have a go at it right away?'

'Very well, if you wish it.' Peirse turned to me. 'Come and see me tomorrow morning and we'll work out the details. And bring me the information on the equipment you mentioned earlier.'

Pound leaned across to Peirse. 'Are you going to requisition this equipment now, Peirse? Because if not we propose to do so ourselves.'

'Yes. I should have been told about it before.'

Next morning Peirse agreed to let me go ahead with the 'H' plan, promising all the support I needed. When I told him that the photogrammetric equipment in question was Hemming's, he asked why I hadn't told him this the previous night, and I reminded him that the minute rejecting Hemming's equipment was still unrescinded; specific mention of it at last night's meeting, I had felt, might be embarrassing for him. He agreed then and there to requisition it at once and to allow Hemming's organization to be absorbed into the Photographic Development Unit, as my unit was now called. There was a second *Wild* machine stored at Southampton, and I asked him to requisition that as well. It was many months, however, before these promises were made good.[1]

---

[1] The Air Ministry, although ready to engage some of Hemming's staff, still refused to take over the company as a unit. 'It was eventually made to do so,' says the Air Historical Branch narrative *Photographic Reconnaissance* 'by a letter from the First Lord of the Admiralty, then Mr Winston Churchill, to the Secretary of State for Air informing him that the Admiralty would take over the unit if the Air Ministry did not do so.'

18

The Fall of France

O<small>NE</small> of the most difficult targets to photograph was Heligoland. It was heavily defended and often obscured by cloud. A week after Shorty Longbottom's flight to Wilhelmshaven, on Sunday 18th February, I learned from the Air Ministry that the R.A.F. were making regular flights over this target and that at 2 o'clock that morning all the necessary information had been obtained and the P.D.U. were not to go near it unless it was with the Spitfire at height. As this had been the principal target given me by the Admiralty I felt obliged to check with Drake, and he said that the Navy were certainly not satisfied with visual evidence obtained by moonlight, which was all they had got from the Blenheims, however useful in some circumstances this might be. Co-operation between the R.A.F. and the Navy was clearly not what it might be.

I was even more upset when I learned of the R.A.F.'s losses in obtaining their information–in five days they had lost three machines out of five. I regarded this slaughter as entirely unnecessary and little short of criminal. We went ahead in the next few days with our 'H' plan and photographed Heligoland several times, and only once was the Hudson attacked by enemy aircraft, when it sustained only slight damage. The flights were not without their dangers, but we had succeeded in minimizing them. By the end of that month, February 1940, we had photographed all the targets given us by the Admiralty, most of them several times, and the soundness of the 'H' plan was proved. Meanwhile I had recommended two of my pilots, Bob Niven and Shorty Longbottom, for the D.F.C., and they received the awards a month later. The Air Ministry press release announcing the awards stated that these two officers had been decorated for their part in developing a new system of photographic intelligence, a frankness which I found both disturbing and annoying after our conscientious efforts to keep news of these developments secret.

The demand for photography had already outstripped the R.A.F.'s processing resources, and we particularly needed our own plant in France to make our two mobile units self-supporting. I still hadn't managed to get the two photographic trailers I had been asking for, but with Barratt's help I got hold of sufficient equipment to start a static photographic unit in France. I wanted to site this at Meaux, but Barratt queried this at first, saying that it would be cheaper to install the equipment in the Château at Tigeaux. I didn't much like the idea of disfiguring a historic building unless it was essential, but in any case I regarded Meaux as the more practical choice; there was an airfield there, and we would be near the French interpreters, who were giving us their full co-operation.

While I was stating my case to Barratt, a message came in to say that two more Blenheims had just been lost on reconnaissance. Feeling rather put out at the way Barratt had queried the cost of my new photographic facilities, I couldn't help asking him how much a Blenheim cost, and what the lives of the crew were worth to the nation, not to mention the grief that would be caused to the families. I told him of the three Blenheims out of five recently lost on the Heligoland sorties from England, and I'm afraid I exploded at the shocking waste of sending Blenheims on tasks for which they were not fitted, whereas my unit could cover all photographic demands in comparative safety if the conversion of our new aircraft could only be speeded up. We had been promised priority, but we still had only one Spitfire operational, as I was obliged to keep the other at Heston for training new pilots and as a reserve. Barratt, grieved by the loss of the Blenheim crews, did not answer at first. Then, in contrast to my outburst, he spoke quietly. 'Sidney,' he said, 'I'm bringing all the pressure to bear that I can.' I apologized for what I had said, and Barratt agreed that I should site my photographic unit at Meaux.

Early in February a new pilot joined us at Heston named Dennis Slocum, nicknamed 'Slogger', a carefree young man who had formerly been an airline pilot. We needed a Hudson pilot, and Slocum flew for us at first as a free lance, taking a day or two's leave from his squadron, which was based in Scotland, and flying one or two sorties before hurrying back. His commanding officer, who must have been a tolerant man, eventually allowed Slocum to join us permanently. Not all the men who came to us proved to have the right temperament for reconnaissance work – the essential thing was to avoid combat and to get home with the pictures – and I had to be ruthless in posting men who proved unsuitable. Slocum, however, soon showed his

ability, and on the afternoon of 29th February he landed back at
Heston with some wonderful pictures of naval targets, including
Cuxhaven, Brunsbuttel and a number of submarines in that area.
Soon after he landed I had a phone call from the Admiralty to say
that the King would like to see some of our pictures, so we worked
until four o'clock next morning processing Slocum's pictures and
making them up into a dossier. I delivered this dossier to the Air
Ministry at 8.45 next morning, and I asked that I might be allowed
to go over them with Sir Cyril Newall before they were shown to
the King, but my request was refused. I also asked permission to
take a second dossier to the Admiralty, but this too was turned
down.

It was clear from my contacts with members of the Air Staff and
others that jealousy of my unit's reputation was mounting and that
it had become impolitic for men lower down the scale to profess
confidence in me. I was aware that there were men in the Air Ministry
intriguing against me; but apart from repeated requests for speeding
up the expansion of my unit I took no action except to appeal to
senior officers not to listen to gossip but to back us up fully. By this
time I had made many visits to the department of the Director of
Intelligence, Archie Boyle, and he at least professed himself 100 per
cent behind me.

Another important contact I made in February 1940 was with Air
Chief Marshal Sir Edgar Ludlow-Hewitt, C.-in-C. of Bomber Command. Ludlow-Hewitt had personal experience of the value of aerial
photography, both in the First World War and between the wars in
India, and he had appointed an imaginative and knowledgeable
regular officer named Peter Riddell to organize a photographic and
interpretation section for him at High Wycombe. Ludlow-Hewitt's
difficulty was the same as the Admiralty's had been – he could not
get the photographic cover he needed to compile target material.
Although the bombing of Germany had not then been begun, it was
clear that when the shooting started the main targets of strategic
bombing would lie in the Ruhr. When I mentioned to Ludlow-Hewitt
that I needed an experienced wireless operator for my Hudson, he
was kind enough to lend me his own personal operator.

Towards the end of February our first new Spitfire was delivered
to us from Supermarine's, giving a range of up to 2,000 miles, so we
were now equipped to photograph the entire Ruhr and targets further
afield. For several days the cloud over Germany was solid, but at

last, on 2nd March, Bob Niven took off from Heston bound for the Ruhr. From 30,000 feet he started his cameras over Duisburg, then flew eastwards above the Ruhr valley as far as Dortmund. 'He looked back, and down, and all round: not an Me 109 anywhere,' records Constance Babington Smith in *Evidence in Camera*. 'He banked right over, and turned for a run back to the Rhine, flying parallel to his previous run so as to cover the whole of the industrial area. He kept his cameras on right up to the German frontier; then turned south for the trek round the edge of Holland and Belgium and so home. Over the hills and woods of Luxembourg the German fighters put in an appearance at last, three of them. Niven opened right up and felt as if he had been given a blow in the back as the Spitfire leapt forward. When he looked back the Messerschmitts were out of sight.

'Niven's photographs were exactly what Cotton had hoped for, and he had already made his plans how to use them. This was an occasion when not only a detailed plan but a "mosaic" could best serve his purpose, because when the overlapping prints were pieced together by the interpreters and re-photographed, the full extent of the cover could be displayed with dramatic effect. When Sidney unrolled his great mosaic of the Ruhr before Ludlow-Hewitt, and stood back triumphantly, the Commander-in-Chief's long face seemed to grow longer than ever, and by silence he showed his amazed delight.' Ludlow-Hewitt was in fact so impressed by the value of this kind of intelligence that he put forward an immediate proposal that Bomber Command should take over the P.D.U., but I felt obliged to oppose this on the principle that it was unwise for a major customer to run the show, and the idea was turned down.

If 2nd March was a great day for the unit, 3rd March was a black one. My diary is headed 'Black Sunday'. First one of my new pilots crashed our training Spitfire, which seemed tragic enough at the time. Then real tragedy overtook us with the news that Dennis Slocum's Hudson had been shot down over Kent by Spitfires from Biggin Hill. My diary records: 'They say our rear turret opened fire. We have no turret.' Slocum was killed, and so was the wireless operator lent to me by Ludlow-Hewitt. These were the first casualties suffered by the P.D.U. The only man to escape was the second pilot, a man named Reid, who was pushed out of the starboard window by Slocum as the machine dived in flames. Fortunately his parachute opened. This was the second time Reid had been shot down by his own side, the first time being over the Firth of Forth a few months earlier. He suffered serious burns on this occasion, and he told me wryly that he thought he might do better if he changed sides.

On 21st March our photographic trailers were delivered to us and they were operating in France within a few days. Barratt was an almost daily customer, always firm in supporting us, and the 'X' series for Gort was nearly complete. The *Deuxième Bureau*, who ran' the French interpretation school, were also pleased with our work, and they wrote to Barratt to say so. But policy decisions that I had thought were behind us were still apparently being made in London, and the future organization of the P.D.U. remained uncertain. We had only four converted Spitfires, and the order had still not been given to take over Hemming's outfit. I was trying to requisition Kodak plant made redundant by the war in both Paris and London, as this was the only hope of a rapid expansion of our processing facilities, but I was not getting the backing I wanted from the Air Staff. Barratt told me that he had almost as much difficulty with the Air Staff as I did, over a very much wider field. He advised me not to be upset by the creaking of Air Ministry machinery. 'It's rusty and cumbersome,' he said, 'but in your case that works in your favour. Go ahead and make your own decisions and act on them, and they'll take ages to catch up with you.' This in fact was how I was forced to operate – it was the only way to get results.

It was consoling to know that I wasn't the only one who was fighting on two fronts – the Germans and the Air Ministry. Another man who was always sympathetic was Air Commodore Douglas Colyer, then the British air attaché in Paris. He advised me to handle the Air Force machine much as a good mechanic would handle a troublesome motor-car engine; keep tickling the carburettor, and if one spanner didn't fit, try another. Sholto Douglas, whom I met about this time, told me much the same thing. The R.A.F., he said, was full of regulations which had been thought up over the years by people with nothing better to do, and which gave those who studied them the chance to delay and sabotage anything they could get their hands on. 'But take my advice, Sidney,' he added, 'learn how the machine works and you can beat them. You can rise to any heights if you study the machine and use it properly.' It seems he knew what he was talking about, for he subsequently became C.-in-C. Fighter Command, C.-in-C. Coastal Command and C.-in-C. British Forces in Germany before becoming Chairman of British European Airways.

On 30th March I gave Barratt a report on the progress made so far with the expansion of my unit, and I impressed on him that unless we could get an Air Ministry decision immediately we could not continue to meet all the demands being put upon us. He promised to do what he could. At the end of that day I wrote in my diary: 'The attitude of the Air Ministry appals me. God help the Allies unless our leaders wake up or we get new leaders.'

In asking for more aircraft and bigger processing and interpretation facilities and staffs I had continually advanced the theory that photography of important targets should be frequent and regular, backed up by detailed and methodical interpretation, and not just something that was ordered as a panic measure whenever unusual activity was suspected or feared. This had been borne out right from the Schillig Roads photographs before and on the outbreak of war. A single photograph of a port might be useful, but its value would be nothing to the intelligence obtainable from a comparison with recent cover. The truth of this precept was heavily underlined in April 1940. Early on Sunday morning, 7th April, I had a message to say Barratt wanted to see me. He told me that Bomber Command Whitleys over Germany that night had reported intense activity in Hamburg, Lübeck and Kiel. Streams of traffic were said to be moving north from Hamburg and Lübeck and there was a build-up of shipping in Lübeck and Kiel. Could I get some pictures? I left soon afterwards for Heston in the Lockheed to arrange some sorties from there, and that afternoon Shorty Longbottom got some good pictures of the town and harbour of Kiel. From this and other sorties we were able to confirm the reports of the Whitley crews, but in default of recent cover for comparison we could not tell how abnormal this activity might be. We knew two days later when the Germans invaded Norway and Denmark.

On 11th April I got a message from Drake asking me to go to the Admiralty. I was there at ten o'clock and was taken straight in to see Admiral Godfrey, who impressed upon me the importance they attached to finding out what German ships if any were limping back into Wilhelmshaven and Kiel. The Norwegian campaign was in full swing, *Scharnhorst*, *Gneisenau*, *Hipper*, and many other German ships were at sea, and the *Lutzow* had been torpedoed early that morning and was thought to be making for Kiel. Both Drake and Godfrey mentioned another matter – the fact that the Admiralty were worried about air attacks on British naval units in port. They feared an air strike similar to the one with which the Japanese later opened the war against America, completely upsetting the balance of naval power. They were not satisfied about the efficiency of the warning system for the approach of enemy aircraft, particularly in the Portsmouth area. I was then taken in to see Pound.

Pound told me that the Admiralty's fears had been put very forcibly to the Air Staff, who had been reassuring, but he was still not satisfied that the Fleet could depend on proper warning. 'What's your experience?' asked Pound. 'You're always coming and going. Do you ever get intercepted?' I said that I didn't, and that I had often wondered about this. Service aircraft carried a secret device called I.F.F. (identification friend or foe) which enabled friendly aircraft to be distinguished from hostile, but this device had never been fitted in my Lockheed, simply because no one had ever suggested it. The only warning I gave of my movements was the cryptic 'White Flight taking off', so on re-entering the country I was in much the same position as a hostile aircraft. It was true that my Lockheed was easily recognized, but surely I should have been challenged somewhere along the line. I owned to having serious doubts about the system.

'Can you prove anything?' asked Pound.

'I think so, sir – if you'll lend me a naval man to come as observer.'

'What do you propose to do?'

'I think you'd better not know that, sir.'

'Don't go taking any chances, Cotton. I don't want that.'

I assured Pound that I never took chances, which seemed to amuse him, and he promised to have someone to join me at Heston next day.

It turned out to be one of those lovely warm spring days, with cotton-wool clouds lazing by. We took off without submitting a flight plan, climbed to 14,000 feet over the Welsh Harp, started the cameras and headed south. We circled Portsmouth for fifteen or twenty minutes to give the warning system plenty of time to pick us up. One flight across the town proved enough to take in all the naval objectives and I then flew west along the coast, passing over Bournemouth and on to Portland, where after a run across the town I headed back to Heston. There was no evidence that anyone had seen or noticed us. On landing at Heston I took the film across to Hemming at Wembley and asked him to treat it as top secret and mount the mosaic on linen, showing the route of the flight as well as the objectives. Twenty-four hours later the work was finished and I took the evidence up to the Admiralty.

Pound took one look and then groaned. 'Good God,' he said, 'you've got all my secret asdic stations!' He seemed quite upset at the success of his own probing. No one seemed to know quite what to do about it. Eventually a memorandum was sent to the Air Staff. 'Reference Sound Locator Problem,' it began (the warning system was still referred to as the sound locator system although radar was coming into use), 'we have today received information from a reliable source that unidentified aircraft were flying in the vicinity of Portsmouth and Portland yesterday. What can you tell us about it?'

The Air Staff reply was short and to the point. I took some rough notes of it at the time, as follows: 'You have brought up this question on a number of occasions in the past, and you have not accepted our assurance that our warning system is adequate. We are glad you have brought it forward again at this time for not only were no enemy aircraft flying in the areas referred to on the day in question, but no British aircraft were in that vicinity either.' This gave the Admiralty the ammunition they wanted, and I was told afterwards that the argument was vigorously pursued that night at the War Room meeting. The Air Staff insisted that the warning system was reliable and the Admiralty insisted that it was not. When the atmosphere was at its thickest Pound produced his evidence. Peirse took one look at the pictures and exploded into a single word – 'Cotton!' But when tempers had cooled down the Air Staff finally had to admit that the system wasn't working as it should.

From my simple outlook on life I couldn't understand why the battle that was being waged between the Air Ministry and the Admiralty at that time was of such importance that it could induce anyone to take such risks. The Air Ministry must have known the shortcomings of the warning system but must have been simply unwilling to admit them. It seemed to me that more energy was being put into this private war than into the war against Hitler, so fierce had the battle become.

I am told I was severely criticized in some quarters for my part in this episode, on the grounds that my action was disloyal to the R.A.F. This, I believe, is just the sort of muddled thinking and confused idea of loyalties that a handful of very senior officers in all services were suffering from. My only interest had been to prove or disprove the efficiency of the warning system, on which the safety of the country depended.

Although we still had only four Spitfires, the number of sorties we were called upon to fly from our various bases was becoming so great, and my own cross-Channel flights to our two mobile units and to Coulommiers and Meaux were so frequent, that I decided to move from my flat at Arlington House to Heston, taking Kelson with me. There were many matters to attend to at Heston, and I should not have been able to spend so much time in France but for Geoffrey Tuttle. I never regretted the day Barratt released Tuttle to me. He took all the administrative load off my shoulders, and he also had a flair for following up the many schemes and systems which we were developing and applying on both sides of the Channel.

On a visit to France on 21st April I got a message to go and see Commander Bill Dunderdale, the British liaison officer attached to the *Deuxième Bureau* in Paris. Bill told me that the French had put several people forward from my unit for special decorations and he wanted full names and ranks for the citations. My first reaction was that we should decline, but it occurred to me that an award of honours by the French would help to stimulate the support and equipment we were striving to get from the Air Ministry. However, for the next few days I was completely absorbed in the affairs of the unit, first in France and then in England, and it wasn't until four days later that I was reminded of the request by Flt. Lt. Mark Diament, the man I had put in charge at Tigeaux. Diament had had a visit from General Vuillemin's chief of staff, and he told me that Vuillemin wished to award the following honours:

Commander Legion d'Honneur and Croix de Guerre with Palm – F. S. Cotton.
Officer Legion d'Honneur and Croix de Guerre with Palm – Niven, Longbottom and Diament.
Croix de Guerre with Palm – Milne and Taylor.

Although I was most anxious that the pilots of my unit should receive the honours they deserved, I didn't want to offend Barratt, so I asked that the request should go through him, and made a mental note to discuss the matter with him. However, next morning when I visited the French School of Interpretation Colonel Lespair pressed me again for names and I gave him Niven, Longbottom, Diament, Milne and Taylor. Then I got a message that Bill Dunderdale wanted to see me urgently. When I called on him he told me that the *Deuxième Bureau* had been on to him again about the decorations, and I handed him a copy of the list I had given Lespair. 'Why isn't your name on the list?' asked Dunderdale. 'The French have got it on theirs.' I told him I was not a gong-hunter and that frankly I couldn't see what I'd done to earn decorations anyway. Bill said the French would be most upset if I refused them, and we left it at that.

On Tuesday 7th May I heard that we were all to attend a special parade of the Alpine Chasseurs at General Vuillemin's Headquarters to receive our decorations. This was indeed an honour. I had to see Barratt that morning on a number of points and I told him about this, saying that I felt he ought to have been consulted. He said it wasn't really essential because the Unit was not a part of B.A.F.F., but that perhaps he had better have a word with the Air Ministry. Later he told me that the Air Ministry had refused, adding that they would much prefer all decorations to be exchanged between British and French Forces on Bastille Day, 14th July. More than two fateful months thus separated my pilots from the honours the French wanted to award them. They never got them.[1]

It was on this visit, 7th May 1940, that I showed Barratt the wet negative from a sortie of the previous day by one of our Spitfires along the Luxembourg–German border, taking in some of the wooded country on the German side of the border which was really an extension of the Ardennes. Douglas Kendall had identified a number of German tanks hiding up in a wood in this area. Barratt at once saw the significance of this and asked if we could carry out a low-level sortie to confirm our findings; he was afraid that otherwise no one would credit that there were tanks in this area.

Barratt had explained to me in November 1939, when I first went to see him and we arranged the 'X' series of sorties over Belgium, how the French regarded the Ardennes forest as altogether unsuitable for the employment of tanks and armoured forces, a virtually impassable barrier, and how the whole Allied defensive strategy had been

---

[1] These honours were offered again by the French immediately after the war, but were again refused by the Air Council.

built on this assumption. Here, in the wet negative that I had brought in to show Barratt, was evidence suggesting that this assumption might be false. I ordered a low-level sortie to be flown at once, and it fully confirmed the evidence we had, the interpreters estimating that there were some 400 tanks visible in the area.

The original German plan had been to develop their main armoured thrust in the north, across the Belgian plain between Namur and Antwerp, exactly as the Allies expected. But in January 1940 an incident had occurred that was to have far-reaching consequences: a German plane carrying secret papers giving full details of the plan was forced down in Belgium. Thus the Allies were forewarned. It does not seem to have occurred to the Allied military leaders that the Germans, knowing the Allies to be in possession of these plans, might change them. No doubt the argument was that the Germans had no alternative; if they were to attack at all, they would have to come through the north. But there were a few isolated military experts, among them the historian and strategist B. H. Liddell-Hart, who had expressed doubts more than ten years earlier that the Ardennes forest was as formidable a barrier to tanks as the French believed. And on 1st May 1940 – although this was unknown to me personally at the time – the French military attaché in Berne had sent the following report: ' . . . the German attack will occur between May 8 and May 10; the main effort will be made in the Sedan.'[1] The Sedan was in the heart of the French Ardennes. Thus the photographs my pilots had taken were the apex of a soundly-based pyramid of intelligence, pointing unmistakably to an imminent and major armoured thrust from the direction of the German–Luxembourg border.

Barratt was clearly disturbed by what we had found; it was, he said, news of vital importance, because an attack from that quarter was totally unprepared for. He at once informed the Air Staff in London. So far as I could gather from my subsequent visits to Barratt, the Air Staff gave the report little credence; Barratt therefore sent one of his own staff officers to the Air Ministry with copies of the photographs and a personal report. This I believe was on 8th or 9th May. I saw Barratt myself at eleven o'clock on the morning of 9th May, when he gave me the task of going to the C.-in-C. Bomber Command to show him my photographs. 'Unless we can convince them and

---

[1] Alistair Horne, writing in Purnell's *History of the Second World War.*

get them to take appropriate action at once,' he said, 'it might be disastrous.' Barratt's idea was that a strong force from Bomber Command should be briefed to shower incendiaries on the forest areas
beyond the Luxembourg border, starting forest fires which might
develop into major conflagrations. Our photographs showed that
these areas were thick with tanks, ammunition dumps, armoured
vehicles and petrol and oil supplies, which would certainly add to the
blaze.

I left for Heston in the Lockheed soon after two o'clock and then
drove to High Wycombe. Ludlow–Hewitt, who had shown such
interest in the work of my unit and indeed had tried to get control
of it, had been displaced by Air Marshal Sir Charles Portal in the
previous month. I had met Portal only once and he hardly knew
me, which I felt in the circumstances might be a disadvantage.

My position as a kind of emissary of Barratt's was a strange one,
entirely unofficial. Barratt had no authority to call in the heavy
bombers of Bomber Command, though when the shooting started he
could ask for their help. Here he was asking for a bombing attack on
German soil before any German ground or air attack against the
Allies had developed. It could not be done without the authority
of the War Cabinet. However, I knew that Barratt had sent the
photographs and an appreciation to the Air Staff, and I could only
assume that the War Cabinet had been consulted and that the Air
Staff would have been in touch with Portal. It seemed when I got to
High Wycombe that this was not so, but Portal agreed to see me.

My task as I saw it was to convince Portal that the tanks were
there, and this is what I tried to do. But the interview proved an
unfortunate one. Portal clearly regarded me as a nuisance – his
orders for the targets he was to bomb were given him by the Air
Staff after they had been approved by the War Cabinet, and he
pointed out that his plans were laid days, weeks and even months
ahead; Bomber Command didn't just decide to lay on that night's
raid the same afternoon. When the shooting started his targets might
change, but he would hope to be bombing the Ruhr. I pointed out
that I had come specially to England at Barratt's request to convince him, and I showed him the photographs; but I could see that
my task was hopeless.

I stayed that night at Heston, and early next morning came the
news that the Germans had violated the neutrality of Belgium,
Holland and Luxembourg and were attacking on all fronts; the

'phoney' war was over. People in the towns and villages along the Moselle, on the Luxembourg border, afterwards described the invasion as uncanny: the contrast between the silence and peace of the previous night and the spectacle of a modern mechanized army pouring across the Moselle was shocking and unreal. With the help of the forests the Germans had successfully masked their intentions – from all but the prying eyes of the P.D.U.

I have often wondered since what might have been achieved if a determined fire-raising attack had been mounted against the hidden German armour on the Luxembourg frontier on the night of 9th–10th May, by the 200 heavies that then comprised Bomber Command. It may well be argued that not much damage would have been done in such an attack with the weapons and aircraft then available; but not long afterwards a project for a fire-raising attack on the Black Forest was seriously canvassed. However, whether such an attack would have achieved material damage or not, I believe it would almost certainly have postponed the assault that opened on the morning of the 10th, because it would have served notice on the Germans that their plans were known. It could quite possibly have resulted in a drastic revision of the Ardennes plan, a plan in which the German military leaders had little confidence, as we learned after the war. What might their fears and apprehensions have been if their armour on this front had been bombed that night, only two or three hours before it was due to roll forward? The whole course of the war might have been changed.

As it happened, of course, seven of Germany's ten panzer divisions were concentrated in the Ardennes. The forest, as Liddell–Hart had warned, proved no obstacle at all to tracked vehicles, and the German armour moved rapidly towards an area that was regarded by the French as a safe sector and was therefore only lightly defended, by elderly reservists at that. Meanwhile the Allies were hurriedly reacting to a plan which the Germans had abandoned some months previously.

I attended urgent meetings in London on the morning of 10th May, in which I gathered that under the pressure of events I was going to get the support I wanted, and I was naïve enough to write in my diary: 'I think we see eye to eye now.' Early that evening I was airborne again for Coulommiers, where I found that 212 Squadron, as my detachment in France was now known, had already flown several sorties over Belgium to determine the extent of the German

advance. Our airfields at Lille and Nancy had both been bombed and
our detachments had evacuated to Coulommiers and Meaux according to plan. Kendall had moved to Tigeaux from the French school
at Meaux so as to be on the spot at our forward headquarters for the
interpretation of sorties from either airfield. Rapid interpretation
was now essential, as information more than a few hours old was
often useless. There was a message for me to go and see Barratt, and
I thought I knew what he wanted.

'I've lost a lot of my precious aeroplanes today,' said Barratt, 'and
I shall lose a lot more if I can't get up-to-date information on Belgian
aerodromes. The Air Staff can't produce anything, and I'm afraid
I'm going to have to ask you to do something that may be disastrous
for your crews. Will you send one of your Spitfires to "dice" the
Belgian aerodromes?' To 'dice' meant to fly very low. 'We simply
must have this information if we are to operate from Belgium.'

The Allied plan to swing northwards through Belgium to meet
what was thought to be the main German advance was still being
put into operation; the danger in the Ardennes was not yet realized.
In any case, plans of the Belgian airfields were essential. While
Barratt was talking I pulled from my brief-case an album of fifty-two
photographs of Belgian airfields taken during the 'X' series of sorties
over Belgium, sorties which had been flown against the express orders
of the Air Staff. I had had these photographs extracted, and each one
was accompanied by *Wild* readings giving all possible information –
compiled by Hemming's company, against an account guaranteed
by me, since the Air Staff had been so tardy in recognizing the company's value. The shock of finding exactly what he wanted right there
within his grasp almost brought tears to 'Ugly' Barratt's eyes. He
spoke in a whisper.

'Sidney, where did you get these from?'

I reminded him of the pictures we had taken for Gort and he asked
how soon we could get more copies. I had had thirty-six copies made
in all, Barratt gave me a list of the units who needed them, and with
some help from Barratt's headquarters in aircraft and transport we
made all the necessary deliveries before dawn next day, 11th May.

Even at this late stage it should not have been beyond the wit of
the Allied air reconnaissance forces to determine the true strategy
of the German assault, and to divine, from the giant phalanx of
armour breaking through the Ardennes, where the main danger lay.
But the Ardennes front was a French responsibility, and the French,

with a total of only fifty reconnaissance crews to cover the entire front, many of which were quickly shot down, appear to have mounted no intensive reconnaissance of this sector. The British, whose forces in any case were small compared with the French, had more than enough to cope with in their own sector. All we could do was to carry out the tasks given to us: it was too late for personal interventions of the kind Barratt and I had attempted on 8th and 9th May.

Another urgent concern of the French was that Mussolini, emboldened by the news of the German advance, might attack them simultaneously in the south, and the *Deuxième Bureau* asked me if my unit could help. Barratt agreed to my going south, leaving Mark Diament and our pilots at Meaux and Coulommiers to fly what sorties he wanted, and I went into Paris to discuss the French requirements. I signalled Heston for two Hudsons and a Spitfire, sent an advance party including a mobile radio van to Le Luc, near Toulon, to make ready for our arrival, joined up at Meaux with the Hudsons and the Spitfire, and then took off in the Lockheed for Le Luc, carrying a spare pilot for the Spitfire. All this was done on 11th May. As some consolation we spent the evening in Cannes.

I took off for Corsica next day in search of a suitable airfield – I wanted to shorten the distance to Italian objectives still further – and I eventually decided on Ajaccio, roughly 200 miles south of Genoa and 300 miles west-north-west of Naples. I then flew back to Le Luc. On this and the following day the two Spitfire pilots, Longbottom and Le Messurier, flew sorties over Italian naval bases and the Brenner Pass. Next day, 14th May, I sent one of the Hudsons back to Heston with the bulk of the photographs we'd taken so far, and we all flew down to Ajaccio, where Shorty took off in the Spitfire and photographed Bari in southern Italy. Next morning the Spitfire radiator was leaking, however, so I sent Shorty back to Heston in it, preceding it in the Lockheed, and the Hudson followed, thus closing down the Southern detachment for the moment. We had got, I hoped, some useful results.

On the way back to Heston I called in at Coulommiers and Tigeaux to make sure Barratt was getting what he wanted. I learned that Kendall, 'Wally' Walton, the sergeant in charge of my photographic team, Flight Lieutenant Pippitt, who acted as my liaison officer with Barratt's headquarters, and the Spitfire pilots, had been working at full stretch. It is difficult now for anyone to appreciate how little information was available at Headquarters on the state of the battle, and the chaos that prevailed. Barratt's intelligence staff were in dire need of information and Kendall was interpreting direct from the wet negatives as Walton turned the drum, while Pippitt scribbled down Kendall's interpretations and phoned them to Headquarters. To begin with the bridges across the Meuse were supposed to have been blown, but it was known that the Germans had captured some of them intact and it was vital to know which. Fairey Battle bombers were being launched against those thought to be still in use. My pilots got some excellent pictures, albeit small in scale, of the whole length of the river, from which Kendall produced a report showing the precise condition of each bridge; some of the bridges that were actually destroyed looked intact to the untrained eye, but by viewing the photos in stereo Kendall was able to pronounce with certainty that in several cases they were unusable. He then had the greatest difficulty in persuading B.A.F.F. Headquarters that his interpretations were correct as the intelligence officers there could not see the damage, and he feared that some of the Battles were being sent to bomb bridges that were already down instead of concentrating on those that were still standing. Bridges, however, made poor targets for 100-lb. bombs, and the real tragedy was that with our small resources we could never get more than a fraction of the whole picture, without which it was impossible to weigh the intelligence properly and relate it to the overall battle.

On the morning of 16th May there was a really big flap on in London. The Dutch had capitulated and General Gamelin had ordered the general withdrawal of French forces from Belgium. In response to a desperate message from the French Prime Minister, Churchill had flown to Paris. It seemed that the battle was lost and the first orders for evacuation were being given. Instructions had been passed to my unit to evacuate, but they were awaiting orders from me.

I signalled Diament to sit tight and said I'd be over that afternoon. When I got to Meaux I drove straight over to see Barratt. Like everyone else he was looking very tired. I stressed that the sort of information we could get would be even more vital to him now, and that since we could evacuate our personnel quickly and easily in the Hudsons whenever we wanted to, we ought to remain and help him for as long as we could. He agreed that we should stay. Next day, however, we again had orders to evacuate, this time from B.A.F.F., so I sent all the men I could spare back to Heston by Hudson, which I hoped would pacify B.A.F.F. for the moment. We could move our mobile units by road and keep them occupied so long as there were airfields to operate from, and I had good radio contact with Heston and could send for a Hudson at any time. In addition I kept in continual personal touch with all sections through my daily flights in the Lockheed. I checked back with Barratt and he gave me a free hand to do whatever I thought necessary to cope with his requirements while being ready to evacuate at short notice.

In all these moves I always took Kelson with me, civilian though he still was, and on 18th May as I arrived at Meaux from Coulommiers with Kelson driving an air-raid started. There were several heavy crumps and much scattered machine-gun fire on the aerodrome, so I told Kelson to drive in under the trees on the edge of the field, near a ditch. We stood beside the ditch for a while, and I told Kelson that if any aircraft headed our way he was to jump into the ditch immediately. 'Will you be jumping in too, sir?' he asked. One has no secrets from a gentleman's gentleman, and I admitted that I would be. Kelson began to rummage in the car, and I asked him what he was doing. 'I'm going to place the rug in the ditch, sir,' he said. I hadn't the heart to stop him.

We continued to operate in the next three weeks from Meaux and Coulommiers in the north and from Le Luc, Hyeres and Ajaccio in the south, flying several sorties a day in the north to keep pace with Barratt's demands. This period included the ten days from 26th May onwards in which the main evacuation of ground forces took place at Dunkirk. Within fifteen minutes of a request from Barratt's headquarters for a sortie I would get a message back from our mobile radio van to say that a Spitfire was airborne. 'I don't know what I'd do without your help, Sidney,' Barratt said to me at this time, and I couldn't help asking him what he would have done if I had obeyed the order to evacuate. 'I was only passing on an order from London,' he reminded me. I told him he should have seen the look on the faces of all ranks when that first order to evacuate was given; abandoning the job was the last thing they wanted to do.

On 6th June I received a report from Bill Dunderdale, the British liaison officer with the *Deuxième Bureau,* that the French had blown up Borgo airfield at Ajaccio because they were afraid the Italians were about to come in the war and might use this airfield in an airborne invasion of Corsica. I decided to go and see for myself, and to select another site if necessary. I arrived over Le Luc after dark, and there were no landing lights, but our mobile wireless vans had been in contact and Longbottom and Le Messurier were expecting me; they had sited two vans facing each other 400 yards apart and I landed in their headlights. The *Deuxième Bureau* in Cannes denied the story about Borgo, but I took off at five o'clock next morning for Ajaccio, staging on my way at Hyeres, where I wanted to meet Lt.-Commander Drummond, the commander of the Fleet Air Arm Squadron based there. Drummond's job was to bomb naval targets in northern Italy if the Italians attacked; his aircraft were Fairey Swordfish 'Stringbags', capable of a top speed of about 120 m.p.h. They were to complement a squadron of Wellingtons which would fly out from England and refuel at Marseilles before attacking Italian industrial targets. I promised Drummond any help he needed in reconnaissance, then went on to Borgo, which was undamaged. Next day I got the Spitfire off on flights over Naples and Gaeta, rushed the film back to Le Luc for processing, and then flew back to Paris, landing at Coulommiers at 6.30 that evening, Saturday 8th June. There I learnt that Barratt was using the lull between the German offensive which had culminated in Dunkirk and the forthcoming battle for France to withdraw his forces to the Orleans–Le Mans region, preparatory to final evacuation from Nantes and St Nazaire.

It was nearly midnight when I reached Tigeaux and I at once held a conference with the officers of the unit. The Old Mill was still untouched, but we had virtually been bombed out of Coulommiers and Meaux. Several sorties had been flown during the day south of Paris for the express purpose of reconnoitring the escape routes and determining which were clear and which were clogged with refugees; Barratt's headquarters were making for Châteauneuf, near Orleans, some 100 miles south-west of Coulommiers, and we of course did the same. Our total remaining complement in France was ninety men. The convoy moved off at five o'clock next morning, and I followed soon after in the Lockheed.

We spent the rest of that day and most of the next getting organized and flying our first sorties from Orleans, keeping only a

small nucleus of essential personnel and evacuating the rest by
Hudson to Heston. Barratt's principal concern now was to give
what support he could to the retreating ground forces while ensur-
ing his own escape route, and among our targets were the Seine
bridges, which the French were supposed to destroy but over which
German tanks were still pouring. 'Wally' Walton had organized his
photographic team in a little mill on the Duke of Orleans' estate, and
the film from these sorties was actually washed in a trout-stream on
the estate.

Late that night we got the news that Norway had capitulated and
that Italy had declared war, so the following day, 11th June, I flew
down to Marseilles. There I found the R.A.F. detachment in great
confusion: the Wellingtons had arrived from England, but the French,
fearing that reprisals would be more likely to fall on French than on
British cities, had forbidden bombing operations against Italy. I
then visited Drummond at Hyeres, found that his orders to bomb
naval installations at Genoa and La Spezia had not been rescinded,
and organized a reconnaissance of these two targets right away.
While we were waiting for the Spitfire to return the aerodrome was
machine-gunned by fifteen Italian aircraft, and to my dismay the
Lockheed disappeared in clouds of earth and smoke; but when the
dust cleared I found she had escaped damage. Only then, when she
was threatened, did I realize what an asset she was and how impossible my task would have been without her.

Drummond and his crews duly bombed Genoa, and Le Messurier
took off to photograph the damage. Meanwhile the R.A.F. Wellingtons, after many hours of argument and consultation, finally had their
orders confirmed by Churchill only to be prevented from taking off
by obstructions in the shape of lorries driven on to the airfield by the
French. My own detachment, however, was working well and without
obstruction, so after making arrangements for evacuation of the
party by Hudson if that should become necessary I flew back to
Orleans on 14th June. The Germans had entered Paris, and Orleans
was crammed with aircraft. Barratt's headquarters were preparing
for the final evacuation, and I asked his permission to send my Spitfires back to Heston, from where they could continue to operate in
greater safety, and to find a quieter aerodrome to get the residue of
my unit away from. He agreed, and we moved 120 miles south-west
to Poitiers.

That evening I flew back to Heston, where Geoffrey Tuttle met me with the news that the Air Ministry at last seemed to realize the value of our system of photographic intelligence, so much so in fact that they were planning to take over the P.D.U. and put it on a service footing, replacing me when they did so. The latter suggestion I found hard to credit, and I went to see Archie Boyle, Director of Intelligence, who ridiculed the idea, which was reassuring. I was given broad details of the evacuation plan for the R.A.F. elements in France, I passed on what I knew of the current situation, and I returned to Poitiers in the late afternoon. Under my instructions the boys had been looking for a more suitable airfield to get away from, Poitiers being a long way from the coast and too small for the Hudsons, and they had selected Fontenoy-le-Conte, an inconspicuous grass field near La Rochelle. We got our convoy fuelled at four o'clock next morning, 16th June, and moved off towards the coast. I followed in the Lockheed, circling the convoy several times to make sure they were not held up by road-blocks or refugees. This at least proved to be good for morale.

By ten o'clock that morning we were all at Fontenoy, where I laid final plans for getting the troops home, involving a Fairey Battle which we had acquired at Poitiers (where it had been abandoned), the Hudson, my Lockheed, and a ship from La Rochelle, requisitioned with the aid of General Vuillemin's letter. I chose La Rochelle because a quick reconnaissance of Nantes and St Nazaire in the Lockheed the previous day had shown that they were already crowded and at full stretch.

On the way back from La Rochelle to Fontenoy that afternoon I had another look at St Nazaire and chanced to witness one of the great tragedies of the war. The *Lancastria*, bombed a few minutes earlier by the Luftwaffe, lay on her side, surrounded by a black mass of bobbing heads, the survivors of the 5,000 troops who had been on board. Other ships were going to their aid and there was nothing I could do. I was glad I had chosen La Rochelle.

That afternoon I made a final visit to Le Luc. The Hudson had been shot up on the ground by the Italians and was a total wreck, so I told Le Messurier to get his whole party over to Hyeres by road and to attach himself to the Fleet Air Arm, who would get them home. Drummond had earlier promised to do this for me if it should become necessary. I then flew back to Poitiers, where I had left Kelson holding the fort in case the Hudsons tried to land there as originally arranged: I picked Kelson up and finally got back to Fontenoy at

8 p.m. In the circumstances the morale of the unit remained incredibly high. We slept that night at Fontenoy under the trees.

Throughout the final stages in France I had kept in close touch with Marcel Boussac, the French textile magnate and race-horse owner, who was a friend of mine, with the idea of doing what I could to keep abreast of French opinion and to stimulate efforts to continue the war as far as possible. So next morning, 17th June, which happened to be my forty-sixth birthday, I flew east to Châteauroux to confirm that the Boussacs had got away. The French Government had moved to Bordeaux, and I guessed the Boussacs would be there, so I flew to Bordeaux and soon found Marcel. He told me it was all over; it was impossible for France to continue the war and the Cabinet had asked for peace terms. The town was crammed with staff officers and with refugees, many of them British, Bordeaux and the Gironde estuary having become the best remaining escape route from Western France. The British Embassy staff had also reached Bordeaux, and I saw Douglas Colyer and Bill Dunderdale, who were most concerned because no arrangements had been made to get their staffs out of France. I promised to send my two Hudsons down to pick them up immediately.

I got back to Fontenoy late in the afternoon, allowed several of my officers to return in a Bombay that was refuelling at Nantes, sent the remainder of my party to La Rochelle, where a boat was waiting for them, and prepared to take off with Bob Niven in the Lockheed. We finally got away at 16.50 that afternoon. I had four passengers with me, including a girl secretary who had been left behind by her employer and who had refused to leave without her Collie dog – a defiance of which I thoroughly approved. The dog seemed to enjoy the flight.

As it happened, however, we did not get back to England that day. We ran into thick fog over the English coast, and with the safety of my passengers in mind I returned to Jersey, where we managed to get rooms in an hotel. At daybreak we were awakened by a loud clatter, as though someone was playing in the garden outside with a machine-gun, and a dotted line of holes was rapidly punched along the wooden wall of my room. Then I heard the whine of an aeroplane as it climbed away. This was far more efficient than any alarm clock, and we got up, had a hurried breakfast and took off for Heston. There were reports of German planes all over the Channel, so I filled up with ten hours' fuel, flew due west at low level into the Atlantic and then turned

north, finally coming in via Bristol and thence to Heston. I sent my
two Hudsons to pick up Bill Dunderdale and his party, then rang the
Admiralty and told them of the crowds of people still stranded at
Bordeaux, adding that I had seen a large number of ships at the
mouth of the Gironde and suggesting that these could be used to
assist the evacuation. Ian Fleming, who had gone over to France on
13th June to put pressure on Admiral Darlan to bring the French Fleet
to England, and who had also reached Bordeaux, then persuaded the
captains of the neutral vessels in the Gironde to co-operate, personally
supervising the evacuation of refugees from Point Verdon at the
mouth of the estuary.[1] I also rang the Air Ministry and gave them the
same information. I then went into London for the wedding of Bob
Niven and my young cousin, an attachment which I had pretended
not to notice for some time. I had completely forgotten in the previous
forty-eight hours that I was coming home to a wedding.

The biggest thing about my arrival back at Heston, however, was
the letter that was handed to me as I stepped out of the Lockheed.
It had been written two days earlier, on 16th June, and delivered on
the previous day – my birthday. It made a strange birthday present.
I reproduce the text in full:

> Air Ministry, Dept.OA,
> London, S.W.1.
> 16th June 1940.

SECRET

S.58864/S.6.

Sir,

   I am commanded by the Air Council to inform you that they
have recently had under review the question of the future status
and organization of the Photographic Development Unit and that,
after careful consideration, they have reached the conclusion that
this Unit which you have done so much to foster, should now be
regarded as having passed beyond the stage of experiment and
should take its place as part of the ordinary organization of the
Royal Air Force.

   2. It has accordingly been decided that it should be constituted
as a unit of the Royal Air Force under the orders of the Commander-
in-Chief, Coastal Command, and should be commanded by a

---

[1] See *The Life of Ian Fleming*, by John Pearson (Jonathan Cape, London,
1966).

regular serving officer. Wing Commander G. W. Tuttle, D.F.C., has been appointed.

3. I am to add that the Council wish to record how much they are indebted to you for the work you have done and for the great gifts of imagination and inventive thought which you have brought to bear on the development of the technique of photography in the Royal Air Force.

> I am, Sir,
>
> Your obedient Servant,
>
> Arthur Street

Wing Commander H. L. Cotton, A.F.C.,[1]
Royal Air Force Station,
Heston, Middlesex.

However the pill was coated, nothing could hide the fact that this was a letter of dismissal, and coming as it did at the end of a long period of great tension in which I had worked and flown myself to a standstill, it was a blow that for the moment I could hardly absorb. Whatever the merits of the case, the timing of that letter, and the manner of its delivery, seemed to me then, and still seem to me now, to be cowardly in the extreme. For many weeks I had been much too preoccupied to defend myself, nor had I been properly aware that such defence was needed, and the decision to dismiss me had been taken at the precise moment when Barratt, for whom most of my work had been done in that hectic if unhappy period, was neither in full control in France nor yet safely back in England. Many times since agreeing to form what had become the Photographic Development Unit I had suffered experiences which had filled me with resentment, but I had never felt quite so sickened as now.

I had of course always known that the time would come when the P.D.U. would pass beyond the development stage and be incorporated as a regular unit of the R.A.F. Now, with the fall of France, the clamour for intelligence was increasing while most sources other than the P.D.U. were either drying up or declining to a trickle, so that many agencies coveted possession of my unit. They were also envious of our reputation. 'There was a great deal of prestige attached to it,' wrote Air Chief Marshal Sir Philip Joubert after the war, 'as the principal supplier of hot news. . . .'[2] Yet with the lessons that had to

---

[1] The Air Ministry got my initials wrong, and added a decoration to which I was not entitled.

[2] In *Rocket* (Hutchinson, London, 1947).

be digested from our experience in France and the reorganization that must result, it was an astonishing time to dispense with my services. I had carried the unit on my shoulders and no one, not even Tuttle, had my grasp of the many problems still to be solved. In any case I had hardly expected to be summarily struck off the roll in this way.

There were a number of things, I'm afraid, for which the Air Staff never forgave me, and for which they had resolved to get rid of me when they could. There was the disastrous meeting in the Admiralty War Room, on which Pound had insisted, which I felt had seriously antagonized the Air Staff. They had always hated the references to 'Cotton's Unit'. These references were not of my seeking, but it was inevitable that the successes of the unorthodox P.D.U. should be contrasted by the Admiralty with the failures of orthodox reconnaissance by the R.A.F. There was the way I had got my first Spitfires, the use of Hemming's company before it was requisitioned, the continual war I had waged on apathy and delay, and so on – all these things marked me down, from the Air Staff's point of view, as a nuisance. The fact that this had been my brief from the Chief of the Air Staff, that it had been the only way to get things done, and that it had succeeded, probably angered them still more.

I had many consolations. The principles of high-speed, high-altitude reconnaissance which I had preached, in the face of widespread opposition and even ridicule, had now become part of official policy. I was immensely proud of the work of my unit in France. The members of that unit had supported me absolutely, and I felt that I in turn had not let them down. I didn't lose a single man in France. When they heard of my dismissal the men of my unit got together, or so I'm told, and put forward a recommendation for me for a D.S.O. That, coming from my team, was higher than any other reward I could ever receive. It wasn't awarded, and I didn't deserve it anyway, but the thought was worth more than any medal. I was eventually awarded the O.B.E.[1]

Geoffrey Tuttle, who was nominated to take over from me, probably felt worse about the affair than anyone. He had warned me of what was in the wind, but I had hardly credited it. He is now Air Marshal Sir Geoffrey Tuttle, R.A.F. retired, while I am a retired

[1] Author's note: Except for awards for gallantry, among which the Distinguished Service Order might indeed seem not inappropriate in this instance, this was the highest award for which a wing commander could qualify. – R.B.

R.A.F. volunteer reserve officer with the substantive rank of squadron leader; but he still calls me 'sir' when we meet.

It was no good continuing to be depressed about being sacked, and I was thankful in the knowledge that the good work would go on in the capable hands of Geoffrey Tuttle. There would be many jobs in the war effort which I could turn my hand to – or so I imagined. I did not then know how vindictively I was going to be pursued.

19

Bureaucracy Hits Back

M<small>Y</small> efforts to get myself reinstated with the P.D.U. proved abortive, and I was posted to the pool depot at Uxbridge, though Peck told me there was no need for me to live there. When I asked if the intention was to give me some other appointment on the photographic reconnaissance side, perhaps overseas, Peck said that the R.A.F. had 'other plans for my considerable abilities' – but he didn't specify what these plans were. I reminded him that I had joined the Service at the invitation of the Chief of the Air Staff for one specific purpose – to introduce and develop the theory and practice of new air reconnaissance methods. I would naturally expect to continue to be employed in a similar role. The war was only just beginning, the need for air reconnaissance was world-wide, and I fully expected that I would be offered another worthwhile job.

I went back to my flat at Arlington House, and there I stayed. I never heard a word from Uxbridge. I was still being paid as a wing commander. July came and went, then August, the Battle of Britain was fought and won, and in all these great events I was allowed to play not even a modest part. Then the nightly bombing raids by the *Luftwaffe* began, and it soon became clear that Britain faced a new threat to her ability to continue the war. The great successes that our fighters had achieved in daylight were not repeated at night. Our defence against night attack was in fact entirely inadequate, and German bombers ranged all over Britain under cover of darkness, while successful interceptions were rare. I turned my mind to thinking how the challenge of these night raids might be overcome. A new system of air radar interception called A.I. had been developed, but the early equipment was not very sensitive, besides being unreliable, and the aircraft in which it was installed, the Blenheim, was too slow. Improved equipment and faster aircraft were planned for the future, but the problem was an immediate one. I asked myself what advantages we already had, and decided that they were:

(*a*) our ground radar stations were able to give warning of the approach of enemy aircraft;

(b) with this information, fighter controllers were able to direct our fighters to the vicinity of enemy raiders.

Getting the fighter within range for the final visual contact, however, was not possible except under conditions of bright moonlight, unless by chance.

It seemed to me that the best immediate solution would be for the attacking aircraft to be fitted with a powerful searchlight with which to illuminate the target. This, however, would so overload the attacker that its speed would be reduced and the raider would easily escape. Two or more aircraft would therefore be needed – a master or control aircraft big enough to be equipped with A.I. and a powerful searchlight, and a slave aircraft in attendance. The master aircraft, which would have to be unusually fast for its size, would make its approach under A.I. to within about 600 yards, when the pilot would switch on the light. The attendant fighter or fighters would then close in for the kill. The light need only be on for twenty or thirty seconds, minimizing the risk of counter-attack by enemy machines.

I began by trying to interest the Air Staff, but I could not get anyone to take a constructive interest in the idea. I was told that similar projects had already been considered but that after thorough investigation they had been discarded as impracticable. The main objections were that any aircraft flying round at night with a searchlight would be immediately shot down; that a sufficiently powerful light could not in any case be carried; and that fighters could not keep station at night. None of these arguments convinced me, the German night raids on London intensified, and I became more and more determined to test my idea under operational conditions and try to get it through.

My long experience in aviation gave me confidence in what I was putting forward. As for the searchlight, I believed that the normal candle-power in use at that time could be greatly increased and that air cooling would eliminate the dangers of over-heating. However, this was a task that I could hardly undertake as a paid wing commander in the Royal Air Force, so on 3rd October 1940 I obtained my release in order to be free to go to other interested parties without running the risk of being considered unethical. Authority was given for me to retain the acting unpaid rank of wing commander and to wear R.A.F. uniform when my duties made it necessary. On the same day I went to see Lord Beaverbrook at the Ministry of Aircraft Production, and he passed me on to his chief production director, Trevor

11(a). My post-war Lockheed

11(b). Myself in the Lockheed cockpit, showing the tear-drop window; more than 100,000 were manufactured for the RAF during the war

12. Unloading medical supplies after the 'mercy' flight to Hyderabad, July 1948. Sidney Cotton with back to the camera on the left

(*See page 244*)

Westbrook. Westbrook thought the idea should at least be tried, but Air Chief Marshal Sir Wilfred Freeman, who represented the Ministry of Aircraft Production on the Air Staff, turned it down. The opposition that I had already encountered at the Air Ministry was thus confirmed at the highest level.

Crackpot ideas for winning the war, or for solving special war problems such as night interception, were numerous at this time, and some resistance to new inventions was natural, but I felt that my record in the P.D.U. ought to raise me above the crank level and ensure me the support I needed. The main trouble, I found, was one that I was already familiar with. The basic idea of searchlights on aircraft had been finally rejected by the Night Interception Committee in July 1940, and getting Service chiefs and civil servants to admit that they have been wrong is one of the hardest tasks in bureaucratic life. An attempt had been made to introduce a paper on the subject at this July meeting, although the idea had already been discarded once, and the committee had merely reiterated the views expressed at an earlier meeting. Sir Henry Tizard, indeed, had voiced his deprecation of a demand to reopen a question which had already been carefully considered and turned down: such a procedure, he felt, implied that the considered opinion of the technical and operational staffs must be wrong! He argued most strongly that there was no foundation for such an implication and that if the Committee were to work on such a basis nothing would ever be done; the Chairman and the rest of the committee, in self-righteous indignation, backed him up. It was decided to record the committee's opinion that the paper re-stating the idea for searchlights on fighters held no basis on which to justify a reversal of their previous conclusion, and that no further experiments in connection with searchlights on aircraft were necessary.

I was at a loss to know what to do next until I remembered an old friend named Wing Commander W. Helmore, a first-class honours man in mechanical sciences and Ph.D. of Cambridge University, who was now back in the Service as an assistant to Sir Henry Tizard. I felt that if I could get the approval of Helmore the project might become respectable in the eyes of the Air Staff. Helmore was pessimistic at first, because the idea had already been rejected, but after he had taken a couple of days to consider my proposals he pronounced them feasible and promised his full support. The only stipulation he made was that we should develop the plan together as 50/50 partners, to

H

which I agreed. I did not in any case intend to make a claim myself for this or any other wartime invention. Patents were at once applied for in our joint names; one never knew when it might be important to establish one's rights in a particular process. As it turned out, it was just as well for me that this was done.

We called our plan 'Aerial Target Illumination', and Helmore, who was well known to the air marshals, took it to Sir John Salmond, a retired Marshal of the Royal Air Force who was now working under Beaverbrook at M.A.P. and who was also chairman of the Night Defence Committee, who promised his support. On 18th October both Salmond and Helmore took the plan to Beaverbrook, who said that provided Dowding thought well of it he would provide facilities for a series of trials. We were asking for a Douglas DB 7 Boston light-bomber, fully equipped with the appropriate instruments and A.I. radar. Helmore went to see Dowding at Stanmore next day, and although Dowding expressed doubts that the scheme would work, he promised that 'if you and Cotton produce a searchlight machine and tell me that it works, I will give you the fighters to try it operationally'. He gave Helmore a letter to this effect to take back to Lord Beaverbrook which I copy below:

Dear Lord Beaverbrook,　　　　　　　　　　　　　19.10.40

Helmore has been to see me about a scheme for searchlight interception which Cotton has devised.

The proposal has frequently been made before and always turned down. At the same time I am a believer in trying anything which *may* be useful, and I cannot think of two people better than Cotton and Helmore to put such a project through. If you agree to let them go ahead with their plan, I will provide a fighter or fighters to give it a practical test when it is ready for trial.

Yours sincerely,
H. C. T. Dowding

PS. Helmore is a friend of mine and I have a great admiration for him which I would like you to share. He wants nothing for himself – neither pay nor position.

As a result of this letter, Lord Beaverbrook promised to let us have a Boston DB 7 as soon as one could be obtained, and a Boston was delivered to us at Heston before the end of that month, October 1940. The Douglas Boston had been ordered in quantity by the French in 1939, and Britain had become heir to them on the fall of France. I then asked Salmond for the formation of a special unit with its own establishment, as had been done with the Photographic Development Unit, so that we could carry out the development work, train our personnel, and perfect the interception technique before handing the unit over to Fighter Command, assuming that the plan proved practical, but I could get no action on this request. I was also asking for various items of A.I. and other equipment, night-flying instruments and so on, but these also proved impossible to get quickly.

The development of the searchlight was undertaken by the General Electric Company under Bill Helmore's direction, and contracts were let to Airwork of Heston for the mounting of the searchlight in the Boston. We decided that Helmore should design a new searchlight as we did not believe that any existing beam was powerful enough for our purpose. This development work, of course, took some time, so as soon as the Boston was delivered to us I ordered an existing searchlight for trial purposes, so that we could investigate the problems and clear as many snags as we could while we were waiting for the one we intended to use operationally. This order, too, was subject to counter-orders and delays, but a Stelmar light was installed at the end of December. Helmore's searchlight was also nearing completion, but the Boston still lacked nearly all the items of equipment we had been pressing for, although we had had the plane for two months.

Anyone who remembers the bombardment we were subjected to in the winter of 1940-1, and the ineffectiveness of our night defences, will understand my anxiety to get a higher priority accorded to this project. It seemed to me that only one man could inject the kind of urgency we needed to get the job done, and that man was Churchill. I decided to approach him through Ernest Bevin, and I had an interview with Bevin in the second week of January 1941. Bevin suggested that I should see the Air Minister, Sir Archibald Sinclair, but I pointed out that all Sinclair could reasonably do would be to refer the matter to the Air Staff, who had already decided that the idea wouldn't work and who seemed determined not to go back on that decision. Bevin then agreed that if I would put up a short description of the system in writing he would explain it to the Prime Minister and try to get me an appointment.

At about the time of my meeting with Bevin, on 10th January 1941, Salmond wrote to say that Air Chief Marshal Sir Philip Joubert, then an Assistant Chief of the Air Staff and the man in charge of night interception, wanted me on his staff. The scope of my work, wrote Salmond, would be far wider in this appointment. I went to see Joubert and told him that Helmore's new searchlight had just been delivered by G.E.C. and that my engineers had just started on the necessary modifications to the nose of the Boston; I wanted to see the job through. After a discussion it was agreed that I should join Joubert's staff when my current work was done, and I reported this to Salmond on 14th January.

Meanwhile I had been preparing documents and drawings on my A.T.I. scheme for Ernest Bevin, and I delivered these to him on 15th January. I also contacted Professor Lindemann and gave him details of the scheme. So far as our own work on the Boston was concerned, everything was going well, but what we wanted was the delivery and fitment of the A.I. and other equipment as a matter of urgency. I was hopeful that the Prime Minister would intervene, as he had done to my knowledge on more than one occasion back in the P.D.U. days, to see we got the right priority. But this time things worked out rather differently. Ernest Bevin, instead of passing my documents to Churchill, gave them after all to Sinclair, who passed them on to the Air Staff. (I did not learn this until some months later.) The Air Staff, incensed no doubt by my action in going over their heads on this project from the beginning, and in finally trying to enlist the help of the Prime Minister, told Salmond that they had found me difficult and unsatisfactory to deal with and advised him to have no further dealings with me. My relations with Salmond up to this point had been good; now they deteriorated rapidly. Finally, on 24th January 1940, I was told that I had been discharged from the A.T.I. project. I was asked to leave the station, and when I went down a day or so later to collect my kit I was arrested. I asked to see whoever was in charge and was escorted to a new Wing Commander who had been appointed as No. 2 to Geoffrey Tuttle. He told me how upset they all were at the order, but that it had come from the Air Ministry and there was nothing they could do about it.

I had an appointment at the end of that week, at 10.30 a.m. on Sunday 27th January, with Air Marshal Sir Sholto Douglas, who had replaced Dowding at Fighter Command two months earlier. I had always been on very good terms with him. On Saturday 26th January, his P.A. telephoned me as follows: 'The C.-in-C. says he hopes you will understand if he asks you not to come down to see him for the present.' The same thing happened with Joubert, whose staff I had been about to join. 'Sir Philip regrets that owing to the action taken by the Ministry of Aircraft Production it will be no use your seeing him again.'

In the face of such persecution I decided it would be best if Helmore and I went our separate ways, he remaining to progress the job while I did what I could to push it through from behind the scenes. I knew well enough that this would probably make me even more unpopular, but I had come to the point where I was not much concerned with that aspect while the country was still being bombed with impunity and the A.T.I. project was still held up. It was in this period that I contacted Bevin's secretary for news of progress only to learn that my papers had gone not to Churchill but to Sinclair. That explained everything.

On 3rd March the Air Ministry wrote to me as follows:

Sir,

I am commanded by the Air Council to inform you that as it is no longer necessary for you to retain the acting unpaid rank of Wing Commander, or to wear Royal Air Force uniform, the authority granted in this Department's letter of the 3rd October 1940, numbered as above, is hereby withdrawn with effect from the date of this letter.

You will, therefore, remain on the Unemployed List of Officers of the Royal Air Force Volunteer Reserve in your substantive rank of Squadron Leader, but as it seems unlikely that your services will again be required on the active list of the Royal Air Force, the Council would be prepared to give favourable consideration to an application by you to resign your commission, in order that you may feel entirely free to follow civilian employment.

I am, Sir,
Your obedient Servant,
Arthur Street

I interpreted this letter as a request to me to resign my commission; it seemed that I had no alternative, and I did so. My subsequent

letters to Lord Beaverbrook, Sholto Douglas and the Chief of the Air
Staff urging rapid progress with the A.T.I. project and offering to do
all I could to help brought only assurances that the project was highly
regarded and was going ahead at all possible speed; Portal thanked
me for the offer of my services but regretted that he had no appointment to offer me. I also tried again to lobby the Prime Minister, this
time making an approach through Clement Attlee, and eventually
Churchill put his seal of approval on the plan and insisted on a high
priority. It was my lobbying of Churchill, I am convinced, which resulted in the Air Ministry letter of 3rd March 1941 inviting me to resign my commission.

Meanwhile Helmore continued to make progress on the technical side
and his searchlight was eventually installed in the Boston. A special
unit, which had been consistently refused when I had asked for it,
was at last authorized, with a famous test pilot named A. E. Clouston
to lead it, and tests were begun at Hunsdon, near Ware. Ten special
units were to be formed to put the plan into operation, but before
these plans could bear fruit the main German night offensive had
petered out. In my view the Helmore Turbinlite, as it came to be
known, could have been ready to go into operation months earlier,
certainly by February 1941, and would have resulted in a timely
stiffening of our air defences. When it was finally introduced, however, opportunities were limited by the scarcity of targets, which
also had an adverse effect on training, and A.I. equipment had become more sensitive, lessening the need for target illumination.

The concept of searchlights on aircraft was meanwhile being developed on a parallel course by Wing Commander H. de V. Leigh at
Coastal Command. I had pointed out the possible application of this
method for anti-submarine work to Sir Philip Joubert at the outset,
and he had shown considerable interest, so the idea was not originally
Leigh's; but Leigh was the man whose persistence got the idea
through for coastal aircraft. He had to face all the opposition that I
had faced, developing the idea in his spare time against orders and
getting a civilian firm to work without contract, while the Air Staff,
with unconscious irony, pressed the claims of the Helmore Turbinlite,
which would have needed modifying for this kind of work. The whole
story of the Leigh Light is a repetition of the frustrations and delays
which attended the introduction of the P.D.U. and the Turbinlite,
and Leigh certainly deserved the credit for finally getting it to the
operational stage, over a year after successful trials had been com-

pleted and nearly two years after I first put the idea to Joubert. It is acknowledged by historians as being one of the greatest single contributions towards the defeat of the U-boat.

Now that I was out of the R.A.F. I decided that the proper thing for me to do was to join the naval air arm. Pound, Godfrey and others at the Admiralty had always said that if ever I were to leave the R.A.F. they would welcome me, and when I told Pound what had happened he arranged for me to be reinstated as a naval officer, offering me the rank of commander, which I accepted; on his instructions I ordered my naval uniform. I would be back in the same uniform in which I had served in the First World War, and I was excited at the prospect.

My first task, I was told, would be to work on the development of air equipment under Rear-Admiral A. L. St G. Lyster, Fifth Sea Lord and Chief of Naval Air Services, particularly in the field of photographic reconnaissance. Before my commission was confirmed, however, the Air Staff got to hear of my impending appointment, and the result was a call from Admiral Lyster asking me to go and see him. 'Cotton,' he said, 'I'm afraid I've got bad news. The Chief of Naval Staff has had a letter from the Air Staff, and he's asked me to show it to you.' I took the letter. It said that the R.A.F. had had a great deal of trouble with me and that if the Navy used my services the Air Council would consider it an unfriendly act.

'Sir,' I said, 'could you let me have a copy of this letter?'

'I wish I could, but I'm afraid that's not possible.' It was, I realized, a great privilege to have been shown the letter at all. 'You see,' went on Admiral Lyster, 'we have to kow-tow very much to the Air Staff. We foolishly gave up the right to operate land-based aircraft before the war and now we're paying for our folly. The knees of my trousers are worn out crawling to the Air Staff to beg for equipment, and if we don't take notice of this letter the task of getting equipment will be harder still.'

I could see that the Admiralty were not prepared to stand up to the Air Staff on this point, and I offered to serve in any capacity without a uniform if that would help. From that moment on I worked as a civilian, without remuneration, helping the Admiralty as far as I could with their problems, and they were grateful to me. But I must admit to being disappointed at their passivity when dealing with the Air Staff. I did not want them to make difficulties for themselves on my account, yet I could not help remembering that much of the Air

Staff antipathy towards me had resulted from the work I had done for the Admiralty.

It was clear to me now that the Air Staff were determined to obstruct me in anything I might attempt, and about this time I learned that they were actually contemplating positive action against me. I could not imagine what they could possibly do, until someone reminded me that under Emergency Regulation 18B, which provided for the internment for the duration of persons whose liberty was likely to be prejudicial to the national interest, I could be put away without specific charges and without trial. I went to see my good friend Duggie Colyer, who had been air attaché to the British Embassy in Paris up to the fall of France and who was now Director of Personal Services at the Air Ministry; this department had the general supervision of the R.A.F. Provost Services. I told Colyer what I suspected and he confirmed that a special dossier was in existence. 'If that's the case,' I said, 'I don't see what I can do about it. Under 18B the Government can lock me up when they please.'

'I don't think it's as bad as that,' said Colyer. 'As long as I'm D.P.S. I'm bound to be consulted, and as often as the file is minuted to me I shall minute it back with my comments on what I know of your record. In any case your enemies would have to convince the highest authorities of their case against you.' But although he said he would do all he could to protect me, Colyer warned me to go carefully. It was clear that I was under surveillance and that the smallest indiscretion might be seized upon.

The Admiralty's dissatisfaction with their dependence on the Air Force for photographic reconnaissance remained; a few months earlier they had tried to form a new unit of their own only to have the project vetoed by the Air Staff. Now Lyster told me that they were especially concerned about the lack of long-range reconnaissance aircraft in the Mediterranean and the Far East. These fears had been intensified by the German attack on Russia, which had left the Japanese free to develop their expansionist aims southwards to Saigon in French Indo-China, threatening Malaya and Singapore. Lyster asked me if I could suggest any means of bridging the reconnaissance gap, and I thought at once of the Boston DB 7; although in my opinion a good aircraft, the Boston was not over-popular with the Air Staff, and this no doubt was why I had been able to get one for the Turbinlite project. I suggested to Lyster that there might be a good chance of getting some to form a naval unit for the Far East.

After we had drawn a blank at the Air Ministry I tried the Ministry of Aircraft Production, where Beaverbrook was sympathetic; he offered me a Boston that had been damaged but which he believed could be made serviceable without much difficulty. His forecast proved correct, and I was soon able to put in hand the necessary modifications to fit the plane for a reconnaissance role, including 'Cottonizing' to increase speed and all-round vision and the design and fitment of additional fuel tanks to give an operating range of some 3,500 miles. This was an enormous advance on anything in existence in the Mediterranean or the Far East in 1941. I arranged for the 'Cottonizing' to be done by the General Aircraft Company at Hanworth; the long-range tanks were to be fitted at Burtonwood.

What happened to the Boston after that is best described without comment. Someone in Air Force uniform–that was what I was told–came down to inspect it and accidentally pulled the undercarriage handle. All efforts to trace the culprit failed. I got it repaired and flew it to another airfield, but the same thing happened again. Either there was a jinx on that Boston or someone was deliberately putting it out of action. At last the modifications were completed and I flew the Boston to Burtonwood; while it was there someone without any authority to do so flew it to Kinloss, of all places, where it was crashed and completely written off. We had lost our prototype, and weeks of work had been negatived. Whether we could get another Boston at this stage was doubtful, as Beaverbrook had left M.A.P. The Director of Naval Intelligence called in Charles Morgan, the writer, to make a report on this and other matters, and Morgan's conclusions pointed to the fact that the Boston had been sabotaged. It seemed to me at that time that the Air Staff were showing a fanatical determination to stop the Admiralty operating their own photographic intelligence service.

Had we had the right kind of support for this project we could have had a flight of Bostons ready when the Japanese war started in December of that year, and the *Prince of Wales* and the *Repulse* could have had far better intelligence of Japanese intentions. The whole balance of naval power in the Far East in the early part of the struggle might have been changed.

In mid-August I ran in to Bill Helmore at the R.A.F. Club. He, too, had been pushed out of the A.T.I. project, the Service having taken it over completely, and he was very fed up about it. He suggested that I ought to get my American friends interested in the idea–would I consider taking it over to America myself? I said I would see if I could get official approval to do so. A day or so later I lunched with Sholto Douglas, and I asked if I could spend a night at one of his stations to see how A.T.I. was working. I was particularly interested to compare current operational experience with our estimates of the previous year. Sholto Douglas spoke frankly of his interest in A.T.I. and of his annoyance at the many delays, and he promised to arrange for me to go to Hunsdon whenever I wanted to do so. I went there two days later, on Thursday 21st August, and apart from one or two problems such as searchlight after-glow and a shortage of spares I was very satisfied with what I saw. The actual attack was requiring about thirty seconds of light compared with our estimate of twenty seconds, but this was partly due to the slow acceleration of the Hurricanes which were being used as satellites at that time.

Next morning, Friday, I tried to get in touch with Helmore to talk to him about my visit, but I couldn't reach him. Then in the afternoon I had a phone call from the Air Ministry to say that Air Commodore D. L. Blackford, Director of Intelligence (Security), wanted me to call on him as a matter of urgency on Monday 25th August at eleven o'clock. The man who telephoned me was a Group Captain Greenlaw. He went on to say that at Blackford's request he was to advise me to be very discreet about any Air Ministry equipment of which I might have knowledge in the meantime. I asked if he meant A.T.I. and he said yes.

During the afternoon a dispatch rider drove up to my flat in Seamore Place[1] with a letter for me from Sholto Douglas saying the Air Ministry had instructed him to withdraw the permission he had given me to visit Hunsdon or any other of his fighter stations. I tried again to get Bill Helmore on the phone to see if he knew what it was all about, without success. Charles Drake and Ian Fleming came to dinner with me that evening, and I told them about the mysterious summons from Blackford and showed them the Sholto Douglas letter. They were as puzzled as I was.

On the Saturday morning I rang Sholto Douglas to acknowledge his letter. He said I had got him a rap over the knuckles from the

[1] Now renamed Curzon Place.

Air Ministry: he hadn't known that a ban had been placed on my
visiting R.A.F. establishments. I assured him that I hadn't known it
either; this was the first I had heard of it. I began to feel very un-
easy about my appointment with Blackford; it looked very much as
though something was being cooked up against me. I recalled the
warning I had had from Duggie Colyer, and I rang 'Pluto', my most
recent contact with M.I.5 (I don't think I ever knew his real name),
and asked him to lunch, in the course of which I told him what was
happening. I thought his department ought to be put in the picture.

At eleven o'clock on Monday morning, 25th August, I reported to
Blackford's office. There were two other officers present, and a steno-
grapher who took notes of everything that was said. I knew Blackford quite well and thought of him as a friend. 'I hope you're not
going to take this as anything personal,' said Blackford, 'but the fact
is that I've got orders to investigate certain matters concerning you
on the highest authority.' I nodded, wondering what was coming. The
atmosphere was most unpleasant, with the other two men staring at
me suspiciously and the girl scribbling away.

Blackford said that he wanted to know where I fitted into the
A.T.I. project. He understood that I had been called in at some
stage to give certain advice but that there my work had ended, and
that I had been officially told that my part in the project was finished.
Further, I had been ordered not to visit the station where the development work was being done. Now it was alleged that I had visited
an R.A.F. fighter station working on the A.T.I. device in spite of the
fact I well knew that a ban had been placed on me, and it was further
alleged that I had given information on this highly secret device to a
foreign power.

'What was the information?' I asked. 'Who was the power?'

'The power was America,' said Blackford. 'You are known to have
made frequent visits to the company which was doing the development work on the searchlight, and we have information that you
passed details of this development work to the American authorities
in London, and that you took some of them out to Heston to see it.'

'Are you referring to my searchlight-on-aircraft idea, which I
patented?' I asked. 'The scheme I put forward to the Air Staff,
which they turned down as impracticable, and which I then got
through with the help of Attlee and Bevin, by getting Churchill to
put top priority on it? For which I was subsequently asked to resign
my commission?'

Blackford pushed his chair back from his desk and looked at me in surprise. 'This is not the information we have.'

I told Blackford that his information was mistaken. In the first place, I had not been called in to advise on the project; I had originated it. I offered to let him see all my files and papers connected with it. I said that I had certainly visited G.E.C., the company who did the development work on the A.T.I. project, many times, with the full knowledge of the Ministry of Aircraft Production. My visit to Hunsdon had been made at the personal invitation of the Commander-in-Chief. I had never passed any details to the Americans. I knew at an early stage that they had expressed an interest in the idea, and I had referred them to M.A.P. More recently the question of American interest had been raised again and I had written to M.A.P. on 21st August to ask their approval for sending an engineer to brief the Americans. All this, I repeated, could be substantiated by my own files.

For the rest of that morning I was put through a grilling which disgusted me. Where was I on certain dates, where did I go between this date and that, who visited me on such and such a date and why. I had suspected for some time that I was being watched, and I derived a moment's satisfaction from the thought of the number of high-ranking officers of all three Services who had visited me at my flat in Seamore Place. My shadowers must indeed have wondered what I was up to. There were times during the interview when two or three people were questioning me simultaneously, and eventually I gave up trying to follow them and refused to answer. At length, with the warning that I must come back at eleven o'clock next morning, I was allowed to go.

I returned to my flat and pondered deeply on my situation. It seemed to me that the charges against me were astutely framed. They were easy to deny, but in some cases difficult to disprove. I had certainly never taken anyone out to Heston, but I must have discussed the A.T.I. project with a score of people, especially when I was trying to get support for it, and it was quite possible that some Americans had visited Heston or the G.E.C. without my knowledge. Under 18B there was no such thing as a trial, and if the Air Ministry felt they had made their case no doubt the Government would have to act. If the personal vendetta that was being pursued against me could get this far it could certainly go the whole hog and have me locked up.

My dominant emotion at first was one of anger, which gave way to cynicism and finally to resentment and deep-seated unease. I sat alone in my flat for the rest of that day; for once in my life, just when I most needed them, it seemed I didn't have the right answers. By eleven o'clock next morning I would have to find them, and I collected all my files and documents together. I feared, however, that more than this would be needed to expose the Air Ministry case.

My flat at that time was open house to many people, and I suppose it was not really so fortuitous that just when I was wondering where salvation was coming from, two of my friends should come in for dinner and cheer me up no end. The first was an American who was acting as one of Roosevelt's special envoys in the U.K., and he began with a story that seemed to amuse him no end. 'I feel I ought to tell you,' he said, 'that we've had a letter today from the Air Ministry informing us that we should have nothing whatever to do with you.' He laughed uproariously, but for once I didn't see the joke. First the Admiralty, then Fighter Command, now the Americans. It was becoming a circular. I told him what had happened that morning, and at once his manner changed. 'I think I can help you on that,' he said. 'We've got some trainee cadets in London, and a short while ago the Air Ministry invited these boys out to Heston to see some new equipment – I think it was called the Helmore Turbine Light. Could it be the same thing?'

'It not only could be,' I said, 'it is.' I forgot all about my depression and began to look forward to eleven o'clock next morning with relish. This had been the one charge I had feared, and now I had the complete answer to it. I asked for more details, and my American friend promised to bring a list of names early next morning and a copy of the invitation. 'Don't produce them unless you have to, though,' he asked.

I had felt that afternoon that my friends had let me down, but I didn't feel that any more. I had simply made one or two mistakes about who were my friends. And within a few minutes Duggie Colyer joined us, and I told him the story. He didn't show any surprise. 'They've been trying to pin something on you for ages,' he said. 'Don't worry about it. Just answer their questions. There's nothing they can do.'

Next morning, completely out of the blue, I got a letter from the Ministry of Aircraft Production. 'Referring to your application for patents for a searchlight on aircraft,' it said, 'this is to be put on the

Top Secret list and the patent applications are to be impounded for the duration of the war.' Here was further confirmation of my story. And soon after breakfast the list of cadets arrived, together with a copy of the invitation. I felt I now had all the ammunition I needed to deal with Blackford. Curiously enough it had all fallen into my lap in the space of a few hours without any stimulation from me.

I had all the papers in my brief-case when I arrived in Blackford's office next morning. The questioning began as before, but I soon broke in. 'Blackford,' I said, 'this whole thing, as you know well enough, is a frame-up.' He hotly denied it but I waved his protestations aside. 'Here is a letter from the Ministry of Aircraft Production which proves beyond doubt my *bona fide* association with the searchlight project. That's number one. And as for the Americans, you invited them out to Heston yourselves, or anyway the Air Ministry did. If you check up on that you'll find I'm right. In any case if pressed I happen to be in a position to produce documents to prove it.'

'Oh,' said Blackford, looking at the M.A.P. letter, 'then that confirms your story.' The case against me had collapsed, I was allowed to go, and I heard no more about these accusations. Nevertheless, in view of the letter that had been written to the Admiralty, the warning letter from the Air Ministry to the Americans, and my knowledge that the Air Ministry were trying to get me put away under 18B, I decided to place copies of all the relevant documents and papers in the hands of the Australian High Commissioner in London, Mr S. M. Bruce,[1] with the request that, should I be arrested, he demand an inquiry. He took the papers from me with a searching look and put them in his safe, promising that he would not forget what I had asked him.

I continued to help the Admiralty as best I could in an unofficial capacity, but it was not a very satisfactory state of affairs for me and I never got over my disappointment at not being allowed to take a more active part. I tried hard to get on better terms with the Air Ministry, so that they might at least be persuaded to withdraw their ban on the use of my services, but throughout this period I was treated as a suspect and the possibility that some other charge might be framed against me was always in my mind. Then towards the end of 1943 Desmond Morton of the Ministry of Economic Warfare, one of Churchill's personal assistants, who had heard something of my

[1] Later Viscount Bruce of Melbourne.

story through a mutual friend, expressed a desire to meet me. I invited him to dinner and he asked me if the fantastic story he had been told about the treatment I had received was true. I said I didn't know what he'd been told but that very probably it was true enough. He said he remembered very well the value of my sorties to Churchill when he was First Lord early in the war, and he asked to hear more. After dinner I got out my papers one by one and showed him the facts, and within a very short time documents and letters were spread all over the floor of my flat. Morton wanted to see everything, and it was three o'clock in the morning before he left. 'I intend taking this up with the Prime Minister tomorrow,' he told me. 'It's the most fantastic tale I've ever heard. The only story I can think of that compares with it is that of Captain Dreyfus.'

Next day Morton telephoned. 'I mentioned your case to the P.M.,' he said, 'and he remembers you well. He told me to make an immediate investigation from the Prime Minister's Office, which I'm now doing.' His first call, I learned, had been to Sir Arthur Street, the Permanent Under-Secretary to the Air Ministry. 'What would you say,' asked Morton, 'if I said Sidney Cotton to you?'

'Personally, grand, but officially, hell, what now?'

'I'm afraid it's "hell, what now". The Prime minister wants his papers in fifteen minutes!'

My papers were sent over to Morton and they confirmed that there was a plan to shut me up and to oppose everything I did. Morton reported this to the Prime Minister, who ordered a further investigation. A week or so later Morton came to dinner again. 'I reported to the P.M. on the investigation today,' he told me. 'He cleared you entirely and insisted on a paper going on your files to the effect that the Prime Minister's Office has cleared you. He said this should do away with all the trouble you've had.'

A few days later Mr Bruce, the Australian High Commissioner, asked me to lunch with him at Australia House. 'My boy,' he said, 'I owe you an apology. I had lunch with Desmond Morton yesterday and he told me an astonishing story. When you brought those papers to me I promised to look after them because of my friendship with your father, but one doesn't listen to that sort of tale as a rule. All I can say is that you underestimated your story, and I apologize for being sceptical.'

My next move was to write to Sir Dudley Pound again to offer my services. 'Since a new Fifth Sea Lord has been appointed,' I wrote, 'I would very much like to offer my services again to the Admiralty, but before doing so, I would like to ask you if the ban put on the Navy's use of my services by the Air Staff still stands.' Sir Dudley Pound replied that the Admiralty would be highly honoured to use my services, but regretted to have to tell me that the ban still existed. This was disappointing; but here at last was confirmation in writing of the existence of the ban. Sir Dudley's frankness did him credit, but I always wondered how that letter got past the Civil Service machinery at the Admiralty. They must have known what sort of lever it put into my hands.

With this letter I approached an M.P. who was aware of the Air Ministry's attitude towards me—Mr W. J. Brown—and weeks of wrangling followed in which Sir Archibald Sinclair, the Air Minister, did his best to get his Ministry off the hook. Churchill, so Morton told me, said that if I continued to press my case he would be on the touchline barracking for me, but that it would be as well for me to consider another factor. If I were to beat the machine, or the Establishment, as he called it, they would eventually get even with me somehow, I could depend on that. But if I decided to let the matter go and not press the case to the House of Commons, he would do anything I asked of him. After long consideration, and much wise counselling from Desmond Morton, I decided to accept Churchill's advice. No one, I felt, knew more about the Establishment than he did.

I had no call to test the Prime Minister's promise until the following year, immediately after the entry of French and British troops into Paris. But in September 1944 Morton was dining with me and I told him that Marcel Boussac had flown in from France and asked me to go over for a few days. It was a time of great rejoicing, yet under my excitement at the news of the re-taking of Paris was a depression which I could not shake off, a hangover, I suppose, from my personal struggles of the war years. I felt that a change would do me good.

'What do you want to do?'

'I'd like to go over to Paris.'

'How can you possibly do that? Civilians aren't allowed there.'

'Churchill said that if I didn't press my case against the Air Ministry I could ask for anything I wanted. Let's ask him anyway. He can only say no.'

Next day Morton telephoned to ask if I could be ready to leave the following morning. A passage on a destroyer had been arranged for me and rooms booked at the Bristol Hotel. I motored down to New-haven next morning and a naval officer met me and took me aboard. I was the only passenger, it was very rough, and I was not at all sorry to reach Dieppe. I was met at Dieppe and given a very comfortable room in a little hotel for the night and then driven into Paris. It was wonderful to be treated like a V.I.P.

As soon as I got settled in at the Bristol I called on Marcel Bous-sac, who was living in Paris. One of the first things he spoke of was his disappointment at finding that the French-owned race-horses left behind in England had not in his opinion been particularly well looked after, whereas the British race-horses left behind in France had been given fake pedigrees by the French and protected in every pos-sible way. Boussac's most famous stallion, Pharis, had been taken by the Germans, as had another leading French stallion, Brantome, owned by Baron Edouard de Rothschild. It occurred to me that we could redeem ourselves by making some effort to get these stallions back.

When I returned to London three weeks later I thanked Morton for organizing such a wonderful break for me and mentioned the matter of the two French stallions; I suggested that I might try to get these stallions back. He agreed that it would be a nice gesture and said he would put it to Churchill, as a result of which Churchill told Morton to give me full authority to attempt the rescue. I was given letters of authority and told that I should not be specific about where the orders came from but simply say that 'the gentleman smoked a cigar'. This sounded specific enough to me.

It was agreed that I should fly over by the Air Force service that was running daily from Northolt. Morton rang me up next day to tell me about the booking. 'I phoned the R.A.F. Booking Centre in St James's to book your passage,' he said, 'and they rang me back shortly afterwards to say that the Air Ministry had put a ban on your leaving the country.'

'Good heavens,' I said, 'what do we do now?'

'It's all right,' he said, 'the Prime Minister told me to call them up and give them fifteen minutes to take it off. You're on tomorrow's plane.' I felt now that I could just about close my accounts with the Air Ministry.

My credentials, and the aside about the gentleman who smoked a cigar, did the trick and I was able to enlist a formidable array of officers of various nationalities and services to carry out the rescue.

The two stallions were known to be at the German stud farm at Erfurt. The American advance had not quite reached Erfurt, and our plan was to follow up the advance and slip in to Erfurt as soon as the Americans passed through. Our mixed party would give us the necessary liaison with whatever forces we encountered on the way. We got Pharis all right, the bribe being a horsebox full of champagne, and Brantome was returned to Paris shortly afterwards.

When I visited Paris again some time later, Boussac told me that General Gaffy, the American general in command of the armies that took Erfurt, had asked him if he could visit the Boussac stud farm at Falaise. When he saw Pharis there he said: 'That horse belongs to us. We liberated it from the Germans but Cotton's party came in and stole it from us.' In those days, of course, possession was nine-tenths of the law. Other horses liberated by the Americans were sent back to the States, where they have considerably improved the stock, but Pharis subsequently sired many big race winners in France and England in the immediate post-war years, adding greatly to the prestige of French racing and to the fortune of his owner.

20

Blockade

WITH the war over, I began to turn my attention to the problem of earning my living again. I was convinced that there were big profits to be made from the disposal of surplus and unwanted Army equipment in various parts of Europe and the Middle East, but the first essential was mobility: I needed an aeroplane. For choice I fell back on the Lockheed 12A, which I regarded as still the best twin-engined plane built for private use; but it was impossible to buy a Lockheed without dollars, and dollars in those days were impossible to come by. The R.A.F., however, were still using several Lockheeds, and I was told that they had plenty of spares for them. Was it right that the R.A.F. should use these planes when they could be sold for precious dollars? I put this point to Air Chief Marshal Sir Leslie Hollinghurst, then Air Member for Supply and Organization, whom I had met during the war; an American friend agreed to put up the dollars, and Hollinghurst agreed to sell the planes. Under the terms of my agreement with the American we were each to take one Lockheed as a part share in the profits, so Britain got the much-needed dollars and I got a Lockheed and all the spares I wanted without infringing the currency regulations.

The first overseas trip I wanted to make was to Italy, where the bulk of the American army equipment stored at the end of the war was for sale. When I applied for a visa, however, bureaucracy stepped in and I was told that I must first get permission from the Board of Trade: unless my visit was in the national interest I would not be allowed to go. I was required to answer innumerable questions, such as who were my parents and grandparents, why I was going to Italy, did I intend buying anything there, what did I intend paying for it, did I intend selling it to another country, what did I expect to get for it, and what was I going to do with the profits? There were three foolscap pages of this. I told the Board of Trade that they had no authority to refuse me a visa, that I didn't propose to answer any of their ridiculous questions, and that I intended going to Italy anyway.

When they asked how I proposed to do that I told them I had a visa for France and that I would go to Paris and apply to the Italian Embassy there for a visa for Italy, which I would get without answering any questions on payment of the usual fee. A few days later I left London and carried out my programme as planned.

The Italian deal eventually fell through, but other deals followed in the next few months. Then early in 1948 I heard that a large quantity of road-making equipment which had been held in reserve in Calcutta for the laying of roads in wartime might come up for sale. I wrote to the Disposals Officer of the Indian Government, got an intermediary to start negotiations, and meanwhile reached agreement with an American oil company to sell the equipment to them at a very handsome profit; they wanted it for road-making in the Middle East. I eventually left London for India in my Lockheed to complete the deal on 8th February 1948, taking with me my flight engineer and radio operator, a Pole named Mroszczak who had been with Lot Airways, the Polish National airline, before the war and who had since served in the R.A.F. He was a first-class engineer and radio operator as well as being a most likeable character, and I had no hesitation in flying to any part of the world with Mroszczak to look after the engines, work the radio and service the plane.

A word more about Mroszczak; he had been promised British nationality after the war, and from 1946 up to the time he left me in 1952 he was trying to get his papers. He would come to me very proudly from time to time to say that very soon he was going to be a British subject. But eventually, after giving him all sorts of promises, the Home Office refused his application, and he was so upset that he left England and went to Canada, where he got Canadian nationality immediately. He was virtually married to my Lockheed and he looked after it with loving care, so I was very sorry to lose him, and I know he was sorry to go. He had thought the world of the British. For me it was another heavy black mark against British bureaucracy.

Soon after reaching Bombay I received a cable from Miranda asking if I could buy groundnuts for him in India, and on inquiry I found that the only possible source of groundnuts was Hyderabad but that owing to a blockade imposed by the Indian Union they could not export them. I knew little of Indian geography and less about Indian politics, but I soon discovered that Hyderabad was one of the old independent States of British India and that it was completely surrounded by the Indian Union, with no outlet to the sea.

The Socialist Government's plan to divide India and create Moslem and Hindu States had resulted in the passing of the Partition of India Bill in the House of Commons in August 1947, the parties to the agreement being the British Government, India and the new State of Pakistan. The agreement provided that each individual Indian State could decide for itself whether to join India or Pakistan or remain independent. Hyderabad had opted for independence. Although a Moslem State, for geographical reasons it could never accede to Pakistan; and although both Nizam and government were intent on resisting any attempt to transfer sovereignty from Britain to India, they recognized the country's geographical dependence on Indian goodwill and were prepared to compromise and to come to some workable arrangement with the Indian Union outside the realm of accession.

Hyderabad had been a Moslem State for centuries under Moslem rulers and was an admirable example of a peaceful partnership between Moslem and Hindu. Although the rulers were Moslem, the State legislative assembly was roughly half Moslem and half Hindu, with only a small Moslem majority, presided over by a prime minister appointed by the Nizam. With a population of over 18 millions, Hyderabad State was predominantly Hindu, being only 15 per cent Moslem, but Hyderabad city, the historic main centre of Moslem rule in southern India, had a much higher proportion of Moslems. To judge the issue on the proportion of Hindus to Moslems, however, would have been unfair, since millions of low-caste Hindus had crossed into Hyderabad over the years because they got better treatment under Moslem rule.

The friendship of the Nizams of Hyderabad had always been specially valued by Britain, and during the Indian Mutiny of 1860 the Nizam had adhered to the British. At the time of partition, the British Government had promised that they could not and would not in any circumstances transfer paramountcy over Hyderabad to an Indian Government. In November 1947 a Standstill Agreement had been negotiated between India and Hyderabad to allow time to negotiate a fuller agreement, and this expressly provided that 'nothing herein contained shall include Paramountcy functions or create any Paramountcy relationship'; but since then the situation had deteriorated because of the threats and demands made by India. Even before partition the Interim Indian Government, frustrated in its diplomatic manœuvres to gain control of Hyderabad, had taken the matter into its own hands and imposed a blockade to coerce Hyderabad into joining the Union. The question now was whether the British Government would act in support of the rights of Hyderabad under the partition agreement, to which they were a party.

This was the situation into which I would have to thrust myself if I were to follow up the possible export of groundnuts, and I approached it with caution. Eventually I found an Indian businessman who was prepared, for a consideration, to get me a permit for the groundnuts to cross India if I could get them out of Hyderabad. On the strength of this I decided to fly to Hyderabad and investigate the situation at first hand.

We took off from Bombay in the Lockheed on 18th February 1948, flying in brilliant sunshine, although on either side of us huge black thunder-clouds poured forth torrential rain accompanied by vivid flashes of lightning, warning us to stick to our course. After half an hour's flying we passed the British hill station of Poona, and we continued in a south-easterly direction towards the city of Hyderabad, the state capital, 400 miles inland. As we approached Hyderabad the thunder-clouds closed together in an encircling movement almost as sinister as the blockade; yet the city itself was bathed in sunshine, a brilliant white shaft of sunlight raising it into bold relief from the surrounding gloom. Three brightly-tinted rainbows, arched across Hyderabad, flooded the city with colour. I had heard many stories of the fabulous wealth of the Nizam, and I could not help recalling the fairy-tale about gold at the end of the rainbow. We seemed to land right at the foot of one of these rainbows on to Haktimpet Airfield, on the outskirts of the city. I was treated with great courtesy and friendliness and was soon installed in an hotel.

Within a day or so I met Sir Walter Monckton, who had been counsel to the Nizam for many years and who was now trying to negotiate some sort of compromise with the Indian Union, based on giving the Hindus an equitable share in state administration, making certain concessions to India's reasonable requests, and the ending of autocratic rule. He confided in me that he was not very hopeful of the outcome, and he gave it as his opinion that Lord Mountbatten, then Governor General of India, seemed more interested in helping Nehru to achieve his aims than in seeing that the terms of the Partition of India Bill were honoured. Monckton arranged for me to meet the Prime Minister of Hyderabad, the forty-five-year-old Mir Laik Ali, a graduate of Manchester University who was an engineer and businessman, but who had eventually been drawn into politics. Shortly after the signing of the Standstill Agreement the Nizam had asked him to form a government, and he had agreed to do so. I also met the Prince of Berar, Crown Prince and titular head of the Nizam's army, and General Peter el Edroos, the man actually in command. Peter el Edroos had joined the Army as a sepoy at the age of sixteen, and had risen to the rank of major-general; he had served in Burma during the war. All these men confirmed that there were large supplies of groundnuts in Hyderabad State, and the Prime Minister said he would be pleased to negotiate a contract with me if I could find a way of getting the goods through the blockade.

The matter of the blockade inevitably dominated our talks. I found bewilderment was the chief reaction. The citizens of Hyderabad, it seemed to me, very much wanted to keep their independence, the Moslems because they did not want to be absorbed by India and the Hindus because many of them were 'untouchables' who expected to suffer from absorption into the Indian Union. But the material plight of the people as a result of the imposition of sanctions was desperate. Thousands of tons of much-needed supplies were held up by the blockade, and there was a serious shortage of medicines; even chlorine, essential for the purification of water supplies, was under embargo. Cholera had broken out and an epidemic was threatened.

The situation from the military aspect, I was told, was just as desperate. Both Mir Laik Ali and Peter el Edroos expressed the view that sanctions were no more than a prelude to actual aggression, in which event they would be overcome before they could put their case to the United Nations. The Nizam, it seemed, had re-equipped his army during the war at Britain's behest to help fight the Japanese, under the promise that all new equipment thus provided would be replaced; but nothing out of the £80,000,000-worth of equipment that the Nizam had provided had so far been returned. Since the war, the factory making war materials had been closed down by the British and all armaments removed. The only hope for Hyderabad was that the British Government would stand by the terms of the Partition of India Bill and honour its pledges.

I asked Mir Laik Ali and Peter el Edroos why they did not fly modern weapons into the country, sufficient at least to strengthen their hand in negotiations and to defend themselves in the event of attack for long enough to allow the United Nations to intervene. They both said this was quite impossible, as the Indian Air Force would shoot down any aircraft attempting to cross Indian territory without clearing Customs.

'With respect,' I said, 'I disagree. It would be quite a simple operation to fly arms into Hyderabad.'

When I explained how this might be done, both men showed great interest; and they then asked me if I would go to Karachi and discuss the possibility of an airlift with Colonel Iskander Mirza, the Secretary of Defence to the Pakistan Government; it would be essential, we all agreed, to get Pakistan's help.

Before going to Karachi I made what progress I could with my business proposals. Due to a new decree by Nehru that disposals stores were not to be sold outside the Indian sub-continent, the road-making equipment deal fell through; but the groundnuts contract was duly signed, and on 10th March I flew to Bombay in the Lockheed to clear Customs before flying on to Karachi. I presented my letters of introduction to Iskander Mirza, and he began the conversation by assuring me that the Pakistan Government wanted Hyderabad to remain an independent Moslem State but could not see how this was to be achieved unless Hyderabad could be made strong enough to defend herself. 'Would you be prepared,' he asked, 'to help provide the arms and equipment that would be required?' He added that there was a shortage of such items in Pakistan. I said at once that I did not want to get into the arms business, nor to trade in arms in any way. 'In that case,' said Mirza, 'Pakistan would supply them somehow, though they would probably have to be bought abroad. The biggest difficulty would be getting them into Hyderabad.'

I said I would be quite prepared to go into the question of organizing and carrying out an airlift into Hyderabad, and transporting anything that the Pakistan Government delivered to me, provided I was satisfied that it could be done legitimately and provided proper agreements were drawn up. I felt very deeply about the manœuvres to coerce Hyderabad and was quite ready to defer or even abandon the groundnuts contract for the time being if I could help.

Mirza asked me to prepare an outline plan for lifting 500 tons of freight into Hyderabad in three days. I had not envisaged anything so rapid, and I pointed out the difficulties. The average load of the aircraft I had in mind was 9 or 10 tons, and they would have to carry fuel for the return journey; thus a large number of aircraft–twenty

or more—would be required, and such numbers would almost certainly be unobtainable, not to mention the crews to go with them. It
emerged from our talk that both the Pakistan and Hyderabad governments were obsessed with the fear that the operation would be stopped
by the Indian Air Force; this was why they wanted to get it through
quickly, before the Indian Union could react. In vain did I insist that
the Indians would be powerless to interfere with a well-run operation,
even over a long period. I was therefore obliged to work out a plan
for a quick operation.

I flew back to Bombay and then on to Hyderabad, taking with me
letters from Iskander Mirza to Mir Laik Ali assuring him of Pakistan's readiness to give practical help. The Hyderabad Prime Minister
seemed resolved to take all possible steps to defend his country, and
when in testing this resolve I asked him if his Government were prepared to spend £20,000,000 to remain free, he replied: 'You need not
ask that question. The cost will not be counted.' When I asked what
scale of operation they had in mind I was given the same figures as
those mentioned by Mirza – 500 tons in three days.

It was suddenly borne in upon me that I was possibly the only
person at that vital moment who could help the people of Hyderabad; without arms they were doomed to being overrun. Yet to bring
them arms was to encourage them to fight. That night I paced the
floor of my room for many hours, trying to decide what I ought to do.
A decision to help would involve grave risks; that much seemed
clear. I had no responsibilities in the matter and could easily pull
out. Five hundred tons in three days would be impossible–I was
quite sure of that. On the other hand, the Indian Union in applying
sanctions against a friendly and defenceless state had committed a
brutal act of aggression. All around me I could see the evidence of a
contented and well-run country, operating under difficulties because
of India's illegal blockade, and looking to its old ally Britain apparently in vain. The more I thought about it the more indignant I
became, and I knew very well what I had to do.

Peter el Edroos came to see me next morning and I told him I had
decided to go to London to see what could be done. He telephoned the
Prime Minister at once, and we went over to see him. Both men expressed their gratitude, and indeed it seemed that in taking action a
great load had been lifted from their minds. They sent a representative to see Mr Jinnah, founder and Governor General of the State of
Pakistan, to seek his approval of the action they were taking, and

they wished me success in London, adding that they had been greatly cheered by recent messages indicating that whatever the attitude of the British Government, Winston Churchill, Leader of the Opposition, was on their side.

My visit to London had two purposes; first, to sound opinion on support for Hyderabad, and secondly to inquire into the possibility of chartering suitable aircraft. I found that the British Government seemed determined to let Nehru have his own way over Hyderabad, but that the Opposition were very much against it and were just as determined that the Government should be made to honour its pledges. I also made a study of the relevant Air Navigation Regulations, from which it was apparent that British-registered aircraft were not permitted to carry arms and ammunition except when under charter to the Crown. However, since Pakistan was a Dominion and had elected to remain in the Commonwealth, it was evident that if a contract were signed with Pakistan the aircraft would technically be under charter to the Crown. From what I heard in London I believed that the Government would do all they could to stop anyone from operating an airlift, so I kept this point up my sleeve for the time being. It was reassuring, though, to know that with such a contract in existence the British Government would have no case against me.

On 31st March 1948 I came to a provisional agreement with Skyways Ltd. for the charter of twelve aircraft—four Lancastrians, four Yorks and four Skymasters. With these I could certainly uplift 500 tons, though not in three days. The chief points of the agreement were set out in a letter to me of the same day from Captain Ashley of Skyways. The aircraft would arrive at Karachi twenty-four hours after we requested them, ground crews and operations staff would accompany them, and the charter rate would be £1 per statute mile. With these proposals I returned to Karachi on 3rd April, where Mirza expressed his satisfaction with the arrangements, and I then flew on to Hyderabad via Bombay. I was held up for some time at Bombay by the Indian security people, and my Lockheed was searched; so I concluded that I was already under suspicion. When I flourished my groundnuts contract, however, they let me continue.

After I had discussed the situation with Mir Laik Ali and General el Edroos they compiled a list of their requirements and I flew back to Karachi and gave it to Mirza. The original list prepared by General el Edroos had included anti-tank weapons and artillery, but these items were struck out by the Prime Minister, who preferred to concentrate on rifles and ammunition, which he presumably thought would be making the best use of the limited space available.

Mirza asked me to call on the Pakistan Finance Minister, Ghulam Mohammad, who had apparently raised some objections. 'Ghulam Mohammad is a difficult man to deal with,' said Mirza. 'He has a personal interest in a Pakistan air company called Pakair, and he wants them to run the airlift; but they're quite incapable of doing it.' All they had, I learned, was a few Dakotas, which could not carry a worthwhile load over such a distance. I called on Ghulam and was ushered into a small conference room, where presently he joined me. He wore the Mohammedan white trousers, the black coat buttoned up to the neck, and an Astrakhan cap. My interview with him proved completely abortive, but it did serve to show me that I already had at least one enemy. 'Don't worry about it,' said Mirza, 'the operation has been approved by the Cabinet, but it would have made things easier if we could have won him over.' Many of our difficulties in the ensuing weeks stemmed, we all knew, from Ghulam's animosity towards us.

I returned to London to progress the charter agreement, where I was joined on 15th April by Mirza and the financial representative of the Defence Department, a man named Shoaib, and several of their colleagues. Two million pounds had been credited to a London banking house for the purchase of arms, for which the Pakistanis now began to negotiate. At this point, however, Skyways dropped a bombshell by asking to be released from their contract. They said that as a public company they were nervous of becoming involved in this sort of operation: they might get into difficulties with the British Government and lose their licence to operate. There was something in this, and in spite of counsel's opinion that the contract could be enforced I agreed to its cancellation. When I told Mirza and Shoaib what was happening they asked me if I would run the airlift myself, so I got Skyways to agree, as a consolation, to sell me some aircraft.

I had few illusions about what I was taking on. Yet I had studied the regulations carefully and in spite of Skyways' withdrawal I felt I was on reasonably firm ground. The only illegal act I might be committing, it seemed to me, was in over-flying India, but even here I believed I was covered by the Air Navigation Regulations, for the Chicago Convention permitted the over-flying of countries 'except for safety purposes'. The Indians might claim that they wanted me to land in Indian territory for considerations of safety, but I did not think the signatories to the Chicago Convention would wish to see their instrument used to enforce a policy of illegal sanctions, and in any case I hoped I could stall objections until the airlift was completed.

What still weighed with me most was that India, in imposing sanctions on Hyderabad, had committed an act of war, and I thought that this in itself would be a powerful justification for any reasonable action I might take if it came to a legal battle. I therefore concluded an agreement with Mirza and Shoaib under which I was paid a substantial advance on the signing of the contract; I should have to buy a number of aircraft, and big figures were involved. The cost of the aircraft would have to be recovered out of the charter rates, but I did not intend to take undue advantage of the situation in which Hyderabad found herself. We eventually agreed on a charge based on Skyways' rates for European charters plus 10s. a mile. This meant that the charter rate from Karachi to Hyderabad and back, 900 miles each way, would be 30s. per mile. Mirza agreed that the crews should have a special bonus of £500 per trip, there were other heavy incidental expenses, and eventually an aggregate of £4,000 per round trip was agreed as a fair charge. Accommodation was to be arranged for my crews and ground personnel and fuel would be provided by the Pakistan Government. Any idea of completing the airlift in three days, of course, had to be abandoned.

Skyways kept their word and sold me two Lancastrians, and they also helped me to get crews for them. They released Captain Frewin, an Australian and one of their most experienced pilots, and they arranged for another aircraft company, Silver City Airways, to let me have Captain Norton, another first-class pilot. Both these men were offered on loan for the duration of the operation. I then learned that Silver City Airways had a Lancastrian which had become redundant and was for sale, but unfortunately it was on the way to Australia. It was due in Sydney that day. I telephoned Mascot airfield and asked to speak to the chief engineer; he came on the line but he couldn't hear me very well – there was a plane landing as we spoke. It turned out to be the Lancastrian. I asked if she had made a good landing. 'Perfect,' said the chief engineer. 'Then tell the pilot I'll buy her,' I said. I paid the money to Silver City Airways in London, and that was how I got my third Lancastrian.

Within a few hours two more Lancastrians were offered to me, this time by Trans-Canada Airways, and I bought them subject to delivery being made at London Airport, as I had no spare crews to send to Canada. Under Canadian regulations the registration of these aircraft became invalid as soon as they were sold and delivered, so I applied at once for British registration.

I now had five aircraft, on paper at least, which was all I could cope with for the moment; the problem was to find more crews. I read a report that Aer Lingus, the Irish airline, had abandoned a decision to run an Atlantic service, for which they had earlier engaged several crews, so this looked like an opportunity and I flew to Dublin. As I went through Customs I ran into Mike Cusack, one of the senior Aer Lingus captains, and he told me that a dozen crews were threatened with redundancy and there was to be a meeting of the Guild that evening to discuss the situation. I had brought a draft contract, of which I handed him a copy, and he promised to put my proposition to the crews.

Late that night Cusack turned up at my hotel to tell me that eight captains, eight first officers and eight wireless operators would like to join me. Among them were some of the most experienced Aer Lingus crews, including Cusack himself; he said they would all give in their notices next day. This presented a pretty problem to Aer Lingus, who had given notice to a number of their less experienced crews while I had been engaging the more experienced ones. Most of these dismissal notices had to be rescinded, and I believe there was chaos in Aer Lingus for several days; so much so that Captain Kelly Rogers, the old Imperial Airways pilot who had flown Winston Churchill on many of his wartime missions and who was now the Aer Lingus flight manager, was heard to cast doubts on my legitimacy.

Within forty-eight hours of being engaged the crews were in London, getting their kit together and undergoing various vaccinations and inoculations. I had also engaged two executive officers and twenty-eight engineers, which with the ten crews made a total of sixty people in all. The monsoon season was about to begin, so I bought wireless communications and direction-finding equipment for installation at both terminals–Karachi and Hyderabad–to enable us to operate in any weather. The monsoon, I believed, would work in our favour, offering good cloud cover for the avoidance of Indian fighters. The Indian Air Force was equipped with Tempests, which were not much faster than Lancastrians at low altitude, and I doubted if the general standard of flying and of ground equipment was such as to make flying in monsoon conditions possible for them except at great hazard. Another factor that I relied on was that Indian Air Force pilots at that time were unwilling or unable to fly at night. Provided we landed at Hyderabad shortly before dark and shortly after dawn, and unloaded our cargo quickly, the Indian pilots could not observe or attack us on the ground without facing a night landing or take-off at their bases. I did not believe they would take that risk.

As a security precaution I installed a powerful amateur radio set at my home in England, and arranged for an operator to stand by at given times daily so that direct contact could be maintained between Karachi, Hyderabad and London. I did this as I feared that cables sent by ordinary commercial methods might be stopped, or at least intercepted and perused.

Although I had resolved not to traffic in arms, I was prepared to give Mirza and his assistants what help I could to get what they wanted, and on 25th April I flew to Zürich with Mirza to witness a test of an anti-tank gun at the Oerlikon factory. Mirza agreed to buy two for test purposes and I agreed to fly them to Karachi. Through this contact with Oerlikon's, Mirza was able to buy some 30,000 rifles from a third party. To get round the Swiss export regulations, which did not permit the export of arms to Pakistan—presumably out of deference to Britain's wishes—the Oerlikons were consigned to Chile via the free international airport at Bâle-Mulhouse, on the Swiss–French border, where we loaded them on to our first Lancastrian, 'Peter Peter'—G-AJPP.

I got Mirza to issue a certificate for each aircraft showing that it was under charter to the Pakistan Government. These certificates were written on the letter paper of the High Commissioner for Pakistan in London, as follows:

The High Commissioner for Pakistan,
16 Fitzhardinge Street,
London, W.1.
10th May 1948.

This is to certify that Lancastrian Aircraft No. G-AJPP has been chartered by the Government of Pakistan to carry equipment and stores. It is requested that all facilities be given to the aircraft and crew.

This aeroplane will carry some arms and ammunition and I have
already approached the Egyptian and Iraqian Ambassadors in
London who have kindly promised to cable their respective
Governments.

> (Signed) Iskander Mirza
> Secretary, Ministry of Defence,
> Pakistan.

I collected these certificates from Colonel Mirza on 10th May 1948.
With a copy for each aircraft I did not feel that there was much risk
of difficulty or delay at any of the airfields at which I intended to
land *en route* to Karachi. These letters eventually proved to be among
the most important documents in my possession.

Next morning I went to London Airport to take off with Captain
Jerome Frewin in 'Peter Peter' *en route* for Bâle-Mulhouse and Karachi. The news of what we were trying to do had inevitably leaked out
and already I had evidence that people were taking sides. Mirza
and his colleagues, for instance, were finding it impossible to buy
arms in England. Then, passing through the Customs at London
Airport, I was asked by one of the Customs staff to go into the
Chief Customs Officer's room, and I wondered what I was in for. We
had no arms aboard at that stage. Inside the room I found myself
confronted by about a dozen people, and I stepped forward uncertainly. Then the Chief Customs Officer, whom I had known for many
years, handed me a glass of whisky. 'We know what you're doing,
Mr Cotton,' he said, 'and we want to wish you luck.'

I tried to hide my astonishment at this splendid gesture. It showed
that there were some people at least who, like myself, disagreed with
the Government's passive attitude over Hyderabad, and I felt that
in a small way my decision to help was beginning to be confirmed by
public opinion. I touched the glass to my lips, for I drink very little
and I don't touch spirits at all, and for a few moments I forgot the
many difficulties which I knew must lie ahead.

At Bâle-Mulhouse we found that the Oerlikons and other armaments had been packed into cases which were far too big to load into
the Lancastrian; we had to break them open and stack the contents
in the fuselage, without proper packing. Everyone on the airfield
could see what we were doing, and I wondered what reports would be
made and what repercussions would follow. The runway at Bâle-Mulhouse was a short one and we had to take off with a light load of

fuel, but I planned to make my first refuelling stop at El Adem, keeping clear of British civil airfields in case they had been warned of what we were carrying and tried to delay us. Before we reached the heel of Italy, however, we got the news that El Adem was in the middle of a sandstorm and would not accept us, so Frewin and I had a conference and decided to make for Rome. Then Rome refused us because of fog, and the last safe alternative was Malta, which I had been anxious to avoid. They accepted us, and we landed at Luqa.

'What are you carrying, Mr Cotton?' asked the Customs men.

I had landed at Malta many times in the Lockheed, and I knew the Customs officials there fairly well. Frewin too had flown in and out on various services. The best thing to do, I thought, was to tell the truth and hope for the best.

'We're loaded to the roof with arms and ammunition.'

The Customs men laughed politely at my joke and stamped our papers without comment. We took on a full load of petrol and were airborne again within the hour. Soon we were on our last leg into Karachi.

13. On board the *Amazone* with the Duke of Windsor

14. Bunty and the children, Sally Anne and Charles

21

The Fight for Hyderabad

WE duly arrived in Karachi at noon on 13th May. The second
Skyways Lancaster, Jig Oboe, arrived two days later. At
first I was subjected to strong pressures to start operating into Hyderabad immediately, not from the Hyderabad end but from Pakistan,
but I was determined to organize the flights properly. The impatience
of Pakistan, I believed, was dictated by nervousness–they wanted to
get the airlift over before the Indian Union guessed how deeply they
were implicated. Then, within a few days, all kinds of difficulties were
put in my way, I suspected by Ghulam Mohammad. I wanted to use
the civil airport at Karachi so that I could operate under cover of
genuine freight schedules, but we were eventually forced to use the
military aerodrome at Drigh Road. The agreement to provide accommodation and transport was not honoured and I was forced to
buy the lease of an hotel and two villas to house my crews and staff,
hotel accommodation being impossible to find. I also bought a building for use as offices. These four buildings, together with furniture,
transport and petrol, cost me over £70,000, and I insisted on (and
received) a written undertaking that this sum would be refunded. In
all these frustrations I could trace the hand of Ghulam Mohammad,
but there was no doubt that there were elements in the Pakistan
Government who feared repercussions and who were not inclined
to act openly to defy the Indian Union.

Early in June I received word from Hyderabad that negotiations
with India looked like breaking down and that they wanted the airlift to start immediately. All our plans had been laid, Jig Oboe was
serviced and loaded with the Oerlikon equipment and ammunition,
and we took off at eight o'clock next morning, 4th June. Frewin
was the pilot, and in view of the importance of this first flight I went
with him. Many people in both Karachi and Hyderabad remained
sceptical of our ability to operate without being intercepted, and we
went to great pains to ensure success. Failure would inevitably be

I

followed by loss of confidence, and Hyderabad's last hope of resisting aggression might be gone.

I decided to follow the direct route into Hyderabad rather than try to disguise our intentions by taking an indirect course. I felt that the Lancastrian was fast enough to take care of itself, and in any case Frewin was a wartime bomber pilot and knew his evasive action. But I guarded against the possibility of a planned interception by announcing a test flight and keeping our destination and departure time secret. In practice it proved to be an uneventful flight. Soon after take-off we went into cloud, which I had of course relied on, and even in the occasional clear patches there was little to be seen, and certainly no other aircraft.

We landed at Warangal, about fifty miles north-east of Hyderabad, and Peter el Edroos and his personal staff were there to meet us. They gave us a great welcome. I sent Frewin straight back to Karachi in the Lancastrian as soon as it had been unloaded, as I didn't want it to be spotted on the ground, and then General el Edroos took me into Hyderabad in his jeep. It was an extremely hot day, and after twenty minutes or so the petrol in the carburettor vaporized and the engine stopped. I was impressed by the ingenuity of the driver, who damped a rag from a water-bag in the jeep and wrapped it round the carburettor, which kept us going for another few minutes. When the water-bag gave out I was equally impressed by the alternative method employed to damp the rag, at which we were expected to take our turn. It seemed to work just as well.

When I met Mir Laik Ali I found him pessimistic about the negotiations with Nehru, and he said that Sir Walter Monckton took the same view. In spite of the fact that a complex agreement had been worked out and substantially agreed by both sides, Nehru was still making inflammatory speeches demanding accession. Mir Laik Ali now felt that the original figure of 500 tons would be nothing like enough, and he suggested a fresh target of 3,000 tons. He then left for Delhi at the head of a three-man delegation, with Monckton as constitutional adviser. A day or so later I returned to Karachi with a new agreement, in a Lancastrian that flew in specially for me. The agreement was quickly ratified by the Pakistan Government, and a special envoy was sent to London to inform Mirza and Shoaib and to open further credits.

On 7th June Mir Laik Ali had a long session with Mountbatten, who urged the Hyderabad Prime Minister to agree to a solution on democratic lines by means of a referendum, based on the simple question of whether Hyderabad should accede to India or remain independent. It was clear that Mountbatten believed that the small Muslim minority was standing in the way of the natural wishes of the Hindu majority; the result of a referendum under neutral control must surely be inevitable. The demand for such a plebiscite had often been made from Delhi, though they did not believe for one moment that Hyderabad would ever agree to it. But Mir Laik Ali, confident that the Hindu population valued their freedom no less than the Muslims, and resigned to the inevitable if they did not, surprised Mountbatten by giving his agreement. Detailed minutes were then drafted by Mountbatten's own Secretariat and agreed.

The effect of Mir Laik Ali's acceptance of a plebiscite showed clearly which side was acting in good faith and which was not: Nehru's first reaction of astonishment quickly gave place to fear. Suppose he didn't win? His attitude changed at once. If Hyderabad could be absorbed by democratic means, well and good; if not, she must bow to India's will. That was Nehru's considered reaction, and negotiations were thus at an end.

In the fortnight following our first arms flight into Hyderabad sixteen further flights took place. I now had three Lancastrians operating—the two from Skyways and the one I had bought from Silver City—and they were well able to cope for the moment with the diminishing stockpile of freight at Karachi. The major difficulties now seemed to be in London, where Mirza was facing what he termed a crisis in the supply of arms, and where British registration of the two Canadian Lancastrians, which had meanwhile been delivered to London Airport, was still held up. Leaving Frewin to run the airlift with two Lancastrians, I flew back to London in the third on 12th June to see what I could do to help.

Mirza and Shoaib were still having difficulty in getting what they wanted, but they were confident of buying enough material to make the employment of up to ten aircraft worth while. I then took up the question of the Canadian aircraft. My intention had been to re-register them in England, putting them into the ownership of my British Company, Aeronautical and Industrial Research Corp. Ltd., but when I found that the Canadian certificates of airworthiness would first have to be validated by the Air Registration Board in London I hesitated. Rumours of an airlift into Hyderabad were already circulating and there were indications that the British

Government would do all they could to put obstacles in our way. I therefore decided to fly the machines to Karachi under their Canadian markings. This would be contrary to Canadian regulations, but I hoped that the British authorities would be unaware of this.

Both aircraft were ready to take off on Saturday 19th June. The captains were Mike Cusack and W. H. (Bluey) Gardner, both of whom I had engaged in Dublin. Cusack got away at 9 a.m., but Gardner, who had followed Cusack out to the end of the runway, was recalled by the Controller and told to report to Air Vice-Marshal John d'Albiac, Commandant of London Airport. D'Albiac apologized but said he had been instructed to check the papers of the aircraft and crew; and when Gardner produced them, d'Albiac pointed out that Gardner's licence was not validated to fly Canadian-registered aircraft. This was a mere technicality, as many airline pilots did not have their licences so validated. Gardner was a fully qualified Lancastrian pilot, but this was enough for d'Albiac to delay him. Cusack's licence had been exactly the same but he had got off before the Ministry could stop him.

As it was a Saturday the Ministry of Civil Aviation may have calculated that we should be held up at least until the Monday, when some other pretext might have been found to delay us. However, it did not take us long to dig out someone at Canada House and get Gardner's licence suitably endorsed, together with a letter to cover Cusack in case he was held up *en route*. Early on Sunday morning we were back at London Airport, and d'Albiac himself was there to greet us. I showed him the endorsement, and he grinned. 'All right Cotton,' he said, 'Gardner is free to go.' Had it been appreciated in London that registrations of Canadian aircraft were automatically voided when they were sold, both planes could have been held legitimately.

When I got back to Karachi I found that newspapermen from all over the world were congregating in Hyderabad to report on the blockade. For security reasons we were now landing and unloading at Bidar, some eighty miles north-west of Hyderabad city: I had always believed that the success of the operation depended very much on good security, inasmuch as it was difficult for anyone to act against us if they were not sure what we were doing. Then an American newspaperman applied for permission to visit Bidar; his idea, we learned, was to measure the width of any wheel-tracks he could find and from them identify the type of aircraft landing there. I arranged for the field to be swept and for a Beechcraft to make a series of landings, and a pattern of tracks was left which duly deceived the reporter.

My security problems in Karachi were looked after by some forty or fifty Pathan troops who had been on leave in Pakistan and who had been refused permits to cross Indian Union territory into Hyderabad when the blockade was imposed; they were living in a refugee camp outside Karachi. They guarded our planes, our stores, our offices and our villas, and they even guarded our persons, as I had been warned that my life was in danger. They were splendidly loyal fellows and they proved their value daily. When they told me that the office of the Indian High Commissioner in Karachi was trying to bribe them to hand over the contents of my waste-paper baskets, I decided that here was a chance for them to make a little extra money, so I had special baskets prepared for them to gather up and sell. Out of this little deception arose many fantastic stories of how arms were being delivered to Hyderabad, one of which involved the use of an aircraft carrier, with a schedule of aircraft taking off at hourly intervals and refuelling in Portuguese Goa. These and other distractions, we hoped, would occupy the Indians while we got on with the job.

The only thing I really feared was the possibility of effective intervention by the Ministry of Civil Aviation. I did not expect that they would leave matters where they stood, and under date of 1st July 1948 I received a formal complaint from them, which was followed up on 7th July by a letter to my London office complaining of infringements of Indian air regulations by specified Lancastrian aircraft belonging to me. The letter further alleged that these aircraft had carried arms and munitions contrary to the Chicago Convention, and asked for my observations. At the same time I heard from my London office that two of my staff had been summoned to appear before Lord Pakenham, the Minister for Air, and Mr Noel-Baker, the Minister for Commonwealth Relations, and had done so on 9th July. Although threatened with arrest if they failed to answer various questions whose object was to incriminate me, they had rightly insisted that they knew nothing apart from the fact that the aircraft were being used for freight services.

After receipt of the second letter I cabled back admitting that my

aircraft had carried urgently needed medical supplies into Hyderabad but denying any association with smuggling activities. The basis
of my denial was this: I was certain that no one had definite evidence
of specific flights into Hyderabad, and until such evidence could be
brought I was quite prepared to hide behind two 'medicine' flights
that I had already made. We were certainly over-flying India, but
legal opinion was that it was very doubtful if we could be prevented
from doing so. When we had carried arms it had been under contract between the Pakistan and Hyderabad Governments, and this
was not smuggling.

In order to remove my aircraft completely from the jurisdiction of
the M.C.A. I decided to form a company in Pakistan which would buy
the aircraft from my London company, who were the registered
owners. I registered my new company in Karachi on 14th July and
called it 'Onzeair', onze being French for eleven, and the eleventh
commandment being generally understood to be 'Thou shalt not be
found out'. Immediately the registration was completed, an agreement was drawn up with my London company under which 'Onzeair' would give notice of purchasing the five Lancastrians. At the
same time I urged the Pakistan Government to give our aircraft
Pakistan registration without delay, as the transfer could not be
completed until this was done. Ghulam Mohammad's fingers were
still turning obstructive screws, however, and the transfer was
delayed.

Having by these manœuvres put a stop–as I hoped–to any M.C.A.
action to prevent the flights continuing, I began to complete plans
for a well-publicized 'mercy' flight of medicines into Hyderabad. The
object would be to serve humanitarian ends and to draw attention to
Hyderabad's plight. In this way I felt I could do almost as much for
Hyderabad's cause as by flying in arms. I offered Sri Praksha, the
Indian High Commissioner in Pakistan, full facilities for inspecting
the plane, and I took newsreel and newspapermen into my confidence
and promised that we would warn them when the flight was about to
take place and even take some of them with us.

The reaction of the Indian High Commissioner was sympathetic,
and on 12th July I received a cable from the Indian Government
agreeing to the flight on condition that the aircraft landed at Bombay
for inspection *en route*. This seemed reasonable and I agreed; the

aircraft was loaded on 15th July with all the appropriate medical
supplies we could lay our hands on. I regarded this as my personal
contribution and I footed the bill, which for the record came to about
£3,500. Meanwhile we were flying urgently-needed serums in daily as
part of the routine airlift.

We were all ready to go when I received a telephone call from a
Hindu friend in Bombay. *'Don't land here,'* he said. *'We have orders to
arrest you and your crew if you do.'* The line then went dead.

Why hadn't I thought of this before? It squared up with everything else in the treatment of Hyderabad so far. I didn't want to risk
implicating my Hindu friend, so next morning I called on the Indian
High Commissioner and told him that my wireless operator had
intercepted a signal from Delhi to Bombay instructing the airport
authorities to arrest me and my crew on landing. I proposed cabling
Nehru himself to say that unless I received his personal assurance
of safe conduct, subject to no contraband being found on the aircraft at Bombay, I would have no alternative but to fly the supplies
direct to Hyderabad. Sri Praksha agreed and we sent the cable. For
the next four days, with crew, aircraft and pressmen standing by
ready to go, we waited for a reply. I didn't intend to wait much
longer.

Each night after dinner it was my custom to join the party of a
rich young Sindi in the garden of the Palace Hotel before retiring.
Coffee and drinks would be served and we would talk until a late
hour. For three nights running, while I waited in vain for an answer
from Nehru, an Indian attached to Sri Praksha's office would join
the party soon after I did. Next day the young Sindi would tell me
that shortly after I left the party the man from Sri Praksha's office
had left as well. It was obvious that I was being watched. The reason
must surely be that the Indian Union planned to intervene if I
attempted the flight direct.

On the fourth night, 18th July, I decided that I had waited for
Nehru's answer long enough and that we would take off soon after
midnight to reach Hyderabad just after daybreak. After dinner I
joined my friends in the garden as usual, and my host arranged
that when my 'shadow' came in there was a vacant seat next to me.
Soon I started to yawn, and my shadow remarked that I seemed
tired. 'I'm afraid I am,' I said. 'I was up early this morning hunting
gazelle.'

For the next hour or so we talked in a general way while I yawned with increasing frequency. When I judged that my display would be spoilt if it went on much longer I said that I really must get to bed. 'I have to be up again at four in the morning to go hunting,' I said, 'and I don't want to miss it.' He wished me good luck, and I left the party and walked slowly across the garden towards the hotel annexe.

Once out of sight I walked quickly down the back stairs of the annexe to the street, got into my car, and drove to the offices of the *Dawn* newspaper, where I told the editor that we would be taking off in an hour's time for Hyderabad. I asked that no news release be made before the morning editions. I picked up the *Dawn* reporter and carried on to the airport, where Norton and Cusack were waiting for me. We cleared openly for Hakimpet airport, which caused considerable excitement at Karachi, where everyone wished us luck. A newsreel cameraman had been alerted, and as soon as he arrived we took off. We were under cloud cover all the way and we landed safely at Hakimpet at first light.

We hadn't sent any signals about our coming for security reasons, but on arrival we telephoned General el Edroos and he came out to the airport. Soon afterwards the head of the Hyderabad hospital service also arrived; exemplifying the good relations that existed in Hyderabad between Hindu and Moslem, he was a Hindu. When all the officials had collected, a ladder was brought and placed under the forward freight compartment so that the medicines could be unloaded. The newsreel cameraman then insisted that I climb the ladder and bring out the first case and hand it to the Hindu doctor. This was done and pictures were duly taken. (See Plate 12.)

That evening I sat in the Peters Hotel in Hyderabad with General el Edroos listening to the news broadcast from Delhi. Nehru, it appeared, had been given a rough time in Congress that day because of my medicine flight, and in answer to a question he had said that plans had been laid to intercept the aircraft but that these had foundered because the flight had been made at night. Nehru went on to say that fresh plans had been made to prevent any repetition but it would not be in the public interest to disclose them. This was no more than an excuse to cover the fact that the Indian Air Force was powerless to interfere, and it caused a good deal of amusement in Hyderabad. In this spirit I asked el Edroos if he could get a telegram off for me to Delhi, with a copy to the Indian newspaper *Statesman*, and when he agreed I drafted the following cable:

Prime Minister Nehru, Delhi.

I am sorry to hear over the radio of the rough time you had in Congress today. In order to make it easier for you this will inform you that I am taking off for my return flight to Karachi at 3 o'clock tomorrow afternoon, local time.

Sidney Cotton

I was of course counting on cloud cover from the monsoon, so I was horrified next day to find that there wasn't a cloud in the sky. The direct route from Hyderabad to Karachi would take us right over an Indian Union fighter airfield from which Tempests were operating. I didn't know what weather we might encounter *en route*, but it was obvious that we should have to take some alternative precaution as having made the challenge I was determined not to change my plans.

When, on partition, Hakimpet Airport had been handed over to Hyderabad, the wireless room had been left in the hands of the Indian Union. This was a curious anomaly, and it was one of the reasons why, on our routine arms flights, we used the airfields at Bidar or Warangal. When I had landed the previous day the Controller had reminded me of the existence of this wireless room and warned me that my arrival would be reported at once to Delhi by the Indian Union operators. 'Good,' I said, 'that suits me fine.' The subsequent heckling of Nehru in Congress was the result of the efficient reporting of our arrival by radio. It now occurred to me that these operators could again make themselves useful.

I took up a position near the wireless room from which I was sure I could be overheard, and I called the Controller over. 'By the way,' I said, 'I've decided to fly the long way round on my way back, so can you let me have another 600 gallons of petrol?' 'Ssh!' hissed the Controller, putting his finger on his lips and pointing to the wireless room. I led him away to another part of the building and dropped my voice. 'Yes,' I said, 'I know. I don't really want any more petrol, but I know these operators will report what I've said to Delhi, and they in turn will send instructions to the Indian Air Force. You'd better at least pretend to put some more petrol in to substantiate my story.' I then sent my own wireless operator across to the aircraft to listen for any signals that might be sent.

We took off half an hour later, and no signals had been sent up to that time, but after we'd been in the air for about fifteen minutes the wireless operator leaned over and beckoned to me. I went forward and read what he was writing:

> 'Civilair, Madras. Sidney Cotton has just taken off in Lancastrian G-AHBV for Karachi. Before taking off he asked for 600 gallons extra petrol because he intended flying the long way round. Signed Operator Hyderabad.'

I turned to Norton, who was piloting. 'Steer 300.'

'For goodness sake!' he said. 'That'll take us right over their fighter airfield!'

'Yes,' I said, 'I know. They won't be there!'

He grinned, set the new heading on the compass, and altered course. We climbed to 8,000 feet, and there below us an hour or so later we saw the empty airfield. The Tempests had scattered far and wide, looking for us 'the long way round'.

I handed my wireless operator a signal routed via Delhi Airport to Nehru. *'We are flying above your Tempest airfield in a cloudless sky,'* I said, *'and there are no Tempests in sight. Where are they? Regards. Sidney Cotton.'* We heard later that three Tempests made forced landings while looking for us that day.

We got back safely to Karachi, and as I walked to my usual table at the Palace Hotel for dinner there was an increase in the volume of talk, and I heard shouts of 'Bravo' and 'Well done'. It was obvious that the diners approved of my defiance of Nehru. After dinner I joined the young Sindi's party in the garden, and later my 'shadow' from the High Commissioner's Office came over and paid me a most generous tribute. 'By the sound of the cables we're getting from Delhi, though,' he added, 'Nehru is very angry with both of us.' He then told me that after each of the first three of our after-dinner talks he had rushed off to his office as soon as I turned in and cabled Delhi that I was about to take off. 'The only night I didn't inform them that you were taking off,' he said, 'was the night you did.' He said I had looked so tired that he had been quite certain I wasn't going any-where. 'I'm in hot water over it,' he said, 'but I'm glad you did it all the same. I'm only carrying out orders.' I took quite a fancy to him after that–although I knew he was still paying my guards for the contents of my waste-paper baskets.

The next thing was to get the newsreel film to London, and I left Karachi with it in Lancastrian BV next day, arriving in London the following afternoon, 22nd July. The film was delivered at once to the Movietone Laboratories, and next evening Movietone News was ready to show the 'Hyderabad Mercy Flight' on all its newsreels. The Indian High Commissioner in London tried to stop the showing but failed.

From the point of view of public opinion the timing was ideal. On 27th July Nehru was quoted in *The Times* as saying: '*If and when we consider it necessary, we will start military operations against Hyderabad State.*' Meanwhile His Majesty's Opposition were considering what action they ought to take to call upon the Government to honour its pledges, and letters were passing between Mr Churchill and Mr Attlee which led to a debate in the House of Commons on 30th July.

Opening for the Opposition, Mr Selwyn Lloyd referred to the Indian Independence Act of twelve months earlier and reminded the House that this act gave the Indian States the right to join either India or Pakistan as willing partners or to remain independent.[1] 'To that position,' said Lloyd, 'which I submit was sound in law, this House and the Government are in honour bound.'

After describing the sufferings of the people of Hyderabad, and Nehru's threats of military action, Selwyn Lloyd demanded to know what the Government intended to do to honour its pledges. He was followed by Churchill, who stressed that Hyderabad had a perfect right, legally and materially, to maintain its independence. Of the 54 existing member states of the United Nations, 39 had smaller populations, 20 smaller territory and 15 smaller revenues. The fact that Hyderabad was surrounded by Indian territory and was completely land-locked and had no access to the sea did not affect its right to independence. Switzerland was in a similar situation but had maintained its independence for hundreds of years.

Churchill then referred to the report of Nehru's threat to start military operations. 'It seems to me,' he said, 'that this is the sort of language which really might have been used by Hitler . . .' He concluded by calling on the Government to support Hyderabad's readiness to have their future decided by a free plebiscite with adult suffrage, under the auspices of the United Nations, the result to be accepted by all parties.

Mr Attlee's reply to the Opposition's case was mainly confined to a personal attack on Mr Churchill. It was a bitter disappointment to

[1] See *Hansard*, 30th July 1948.

those who, like myself, regarded the British Government as honour-bound to stand by Hyderabad's right to independence. It was obvious that the Government were as determined as ever to let Nehru have his way over Hyderabad.

Unfortunately the debate in the House of Commons did not arouse public opinion to any great extent. Nor did the newsreel pictures of my medicine flight, although they were shown on all Movietone newsreels in Great Britain during that week. The Russian blockade of Berlin, which involved only $2\frac{1}{2}$ millions against the 18 millions of Hyderabad, attracted more interest because it was nearer home, though there was little enough interest even in that in August 1948. It seemed that the British people, exhausted by the war, had too many problems of their own to worry much about the troubles of others, even when Britain's honour was at stake.

There was only one thing left to do, and that was to carry on with the job of rearming Hyderabad. 'Get on with it as quickly as you can,' I was told in London. 'Indian troops and tanks are being concentrated on the borders of Hyderabad and there isn't much time.' On 31st July I returned to Karachi.

22

Hyderabad Falls – and I Stand
in the Dock

W HILE I was in England I learned that the Ministry of Civil Aviation were building up a case against me under the Customs Act of 1876, under which no article can be exported without a permit. This resulted from the agreement under which my London company was in the course of selling the five Lancastrians to Onzeair so that we could get them registered in Pakistan; I was thus exporting five aircraft without a permit. The penalty for this, I found, was severe – a fine of three times the value of the goods, plus a gaol sentence of two years for each item. As the Lancastrians were valued at £15,000 each and there were five of them, I was liable for a fine of £225,000 and a sentence of ten years. My solicitors were extremely perturbed about this because in their opinion I could offer no defence against such a charge.

When I got back to Karachi the first thing I did was to cancel the draft agreement, which fortunately had not been finalized, though the Crown solicitors were not aware of this. I substituted another agreement which provided for my London company to retain ownership but to charter the aircraft to Onzeair, giving them only an option to buy. This covered me under the Customs Act, but it put us back where we started on the question of getting the aircraft into Pakistan registration, which had been the main object of forming the new company.

I now discovered, however, that some years previously Orient Airways, a Karachi-based company which had operated throughout India, had chartered some Dakotas from B.O.A.C. To simplify matters they had put the Dakotas into Pakistan registration, although they were still owned by B.O.A.C. Ours was a similar situation and we decided to follow suit. If objections were made we could cite the British Government instrument, B.O.A.C., as having set the precedent. I was very relieved at this turn of events, but after making these changes we lay low and did not disclose that the aircraft were now only under charter. It was better to let the M.C.A. go on wasting their time building up a case against me under the Customs Act, diverting their energies, perhaps, from some more promising course. If the case came up we had the answer.

There was very bad news awaiting me when I got to Karachi. As I walked down the steps from the aircraft I saw that the tarmac was littered with newspapermen, and I learned soon enough that one of my Canadian Lancastrians, which had been flying rifles and equipment from Rawalpindi to Karachi as part of the build-up for the airlift, had crashed that morning as it came in to land, killing the crew of four. The pilot, Jerome Frewin, had been the first man I had engaged. The Pakistan Defence Ministry had immediately thrown a screen round the airport, but one reporter had apparently got through, and he reported seeing rifles 'scattered all over the desert'. The Indian papers seized on this and reported that the aircraft had been taking off for Hyderabad, citing this as proof that the Lancastrians were in fact carrying arms. The Pakistan Government issued a denial, saying that the aircraft had been on an internal flight, which was true, but it was doubtful whether anyone would believe them.

We had all considered Frewin to be an outstanding pilot and one of our best. He was a mixture of natural flier and slide-rule specialist, and it was hard to understand how such an accident could have happened to him. One theory put forward by the other pilots was that the handling of the Canadian-built Lancastrians was different from the British, which Frewin may not have realized. The incident cast a gloom over the camp, but the necessity of getting on with the job eventually brought spirits back to normal.

We were faced with continual rumour and counter-rumour of plots and coups behind the scenes in India, Hyderabad and Pakistan. Nehru, following up his threat of 25th July and the troop movements which had accompanied it, stepped up the political pressure on the Nizam. There were stories that the Nizam was by-passing his Cabinet and negotiating direct, and threats of resignation by several Hyderabad ministers were rumoured. There were people who sat on the fence, trying to maintain some sort of reputation with both camps, lest Hyderabad should give in after all. Many times our operations were stopped for days on end on the orders of Ghulam Mohammad and others. Right through August and the early part of September the game of power politics went on. Meanwhile the British Government continued to support Nehru and to do their best to stop help reaching Hyderabad; I had bought two more Lancastrians, but both were languishing at Blackbushe awaiting export permits.

'Soon after the middle of August' [writes Mir Laik Ali in his book *Tragedy of Hyderabad*][1], 'I wrote a letter to the Prime Minister of India and formally communicated to him that in view of the continued tension between India and Hyderabad, the complete blockade enforced by India which was disrupting the civil life of the population and growing raids on the Hyderabad territory by Indian armed forces, failure of all attempts to come to an amicable settlement and refusal of the Government of India to place the matter before any arbitration as provided in the terms of the Standstill Agreement subsisting between India and Hyderabad, the Government of Hyderabad had decided to solicit the good offices of the United Nations Organization in order that the dispute between India and Hyderabad might be resolved and a peaceful and enduring settlement arrived at. The Government of India was also requested to provide the necessary facilities to the Hyderabad delegation to proceed through India to Lake Success. Within a week of sending this request, a reply was received saying that the Government of India regarded the Indo–Hyderabad dispute as a purely domestic matter and that Hyderabad neither historically nor in its present position had a right to make any approach to the United Nations and accordingly they were unable to provide any facility to the Hyderabad delegation to proceed to the headquarters of the United Nations.'

This point-blank refusal was not entirely unexpected, but Monckton continued to prepare the Hyderabad case for presentation. Meanwhile the Nizam wrote a personal letter to King George VI, which after much delay in transit was briefly acknowledged, on the advice of Mr Attlee, with a note expressing the hope of a peaceful solution of the Hyderabad problem.

The only friend that Hyderabad seemed to have was Pakistan. But if the Indian armies invaded Hyderabad, what would Pakistan do? Jinnah had said on more than one occasion that in the event of armed aggression by India against Hyderabad, Pakistan could not remain a silent spectator. But what precisely did this mean? The bulk of the Indian armies and armoured forces that were not in the Kashmir area were now concentrated around Hyderabad, and the Hyderabad Government felt the need for a concrete plan, so early in September we flew Mir Laik Ali to Karachi, where he conferred with Ghulam

[1] Pakistan Co-operative Book Society, Karachi, 1962.

Mohammad. Did Pakistan mean business, asked Mir Laik Ali? The only man who could answer that question, said the Finance Minister, was Jinnah; but Jinnah had been ill and was convalescing at Quetta.

I cannot do better than describe Mir Laik Ali's visit to Quetta in his own words. 'I could see anxiety on everyone's face when I reached the Quaid's residence,' he wrote. 'There were two or three doctors in consultation. I was told that an hour ago some injection had been administered which had caused very severe reaction, and at the moment he was in great agony and in a state of semi-consciousness. A little later I met Miss Jinnah. She was having a very anxious time, naturally, and said that it was not the first time that the reaction of the particular injection had been so severe. It was hoped that in a couple of hours he would feel more restful and I should be able to meet him.

'It was a little before eleven o'clock in the morning that I had reached Quetta. Every minute was hanging heavy on me. At one o'clock I was served with some luncheon. Most of the time I had spent with Miss Jinnah, hoping all along that the Quaid would soon recover enough to spare me a few minutes. Miss Jinnah kept frequently going into his room and returned disappointed each time that he was no better. Finally, she was able to convey to him that I was in Quetta and had been waiting for a long time in the other room. The Quaid, she told me, only with great difficulty, waved his fingers indicating that his agony was too great.

'Around three o'clock in the afternoon I gave up all hopes of meeting Jinnah. . . .'

Mir Laik Ali records that back in Karachi the Pakistan Government seemed surprised to hear that Jinnah was so ill. Had Jinnah deliberately avoided seeing him? Mir Laik Ali was quite sure that his illness was genuine. 'A straight answer to my question as to what Pakistan would do in the event of the invasion of Hyderabad was not forthcoming from anyone of those present,' writes Mir Laik Ali. He was again told that the final word rested with Jinnah. However, Pakair had now put two Halifaxes on to the airlift, and although their operations were an embarrassment to us because of the haphazard and insecure nature of their organization, it seemed that Pakistan would do everything it could for Hyderabad short of war. Buoyed up by messages of encouragement from other Moslem states, Mir Laik Ali returned to Hyderabad in hopeful mood, and he requested me to organize a further stepping up of the airlift. The Agent General for Hyderabad in London, I was told, would be authorized to provide substantial funds for this purpose.

Early in September I took off for London to try to find some way of getting the two Lancastrians released from Blackbushe. I had already tried several ruses to no avail. Landing in Paris *en route*, and telephoning my solicitor, F. W. Ratcliff, of Gordon, Dadds and Co., to say that I would be over later in the day, I was astonished to hear his strongly-worded advice to me not to set foot in England. Word had reached him, he said, that the authorities intended to find some way of preventing me from returning to Karachi if I did so. What could they possibly do? Ratcliff feared that they might find some excuse for demanding my passport and then delay giving it back to me. That way I could be held up for weeks. I thought I knew a way round this, however, and I flew to Dublin, left my passport there, and travelled to Belfast by train, carrying nothing more than an identity card, which was all I needed between Northern Ireland and England. On arrival in England I said I had mislaid my passport, and I applied for a new one. I knew I wouldn't get one, but my application would lay a red herring, and when I wanted to return to Karachi I could travel via Belfast and Dublin, retrieving my passport on the way.

In London I called at once on the Agent General, but his attitude to stepping up the airlift was lukewarm. He professed not to have heard from Mir Laik Ali, which I could not understand in view of the Prime Minister's urgent request to me. This blowing hot and cold between various officials was one of the most exasperating features of the whole operation, the temperature of enthusiasm varying according to the individual's personal assessment of Hyderabad's chances and the latest piece of pressure from Nehru.

Nehru's attitude to Hyderabad was now openly hostile, and in the first week of September he demanded that the Nizam permit Indian troops to be stationed in the old British Army garrison town of Secunderabad, five miles north of Hyderabad city. On 10th September he issued an ultimatum which said that 'with great regret we intend to occupy Secunderabad'. As this was deep in Hyderabad territory it meant armed incursion. He excused this by claiming that Hyderabad was in the grip of Communist risings, which had a familiar ring. It was true that a few border disturbances had occurred, but the responsibility for these lay more with the Indian Union than with Hyderabad.

The Nizam rejected the ultimatum, describing the threatened entry of Indian troops to Secunderabad as a violation of Hyderabad's independence and a repudiation of the Standstill Agreement. Meanwhile on the night of 9th September a delegation left Hyderabad to put its case before the United Nations. Nehru still refused to allow them to cross Indian territory, so we flew them out.

Zero hour for the invasion of Hyderabad was believed to be some time between 20th and 23rd September, and the main concern of the Nizam was how long the invading armies could be prevented from reaching the capital. Peter el Edroos, the Army commander, estimated about two months. Mir Laik Ali was less optimistic but thought they could be delayed for at least a month. The Nizam decided that even if they could only hold out for a fortnight it was worth doing, as that would give the Security Council time to take effective action. This, of course, had been the whole purpose of our work in the previous three months.

The British Government now started to evacuate British subjects from Hyderabad, and at the same time they ordered all British officers to resign from the Hyderabad Army, on the basis that they could not be asked to take up arms against one of His Majesty's Dominions. No such order was given to British officers in the Indian Army. Thus Hyderabad was denied the experience and calm of British officers just when these qualities were likely to be most needed. However, I had engaged as my liaison officer with Peter el Edroos a soldier named Colonel Graham who had until his retirement a short time earlier been el Edroos's chief of staff, and on Mir Laik Ali's request Graham agreed to make himself available for consultation and advice up to the time of the actual outbreak of armed conflict. I had also helped to recruit several other former British Army men of the commando type whose advice would be available.

Then on 11th September came an event which lay outside everyone's calculations, which had no connection whatever with the dispute, but which had the most profound impact upon it. On that day the world heard with sorrow of the death of Mohammed Jinnah, Founder and Governor General of Pakistan. Nehru, counting on the inevitable shock and confusion that would ensue in Pakistan, lost no time in giving orders for the invasion of Hyderabad, and at four o'clock on the morning of 13th September several hundred Sherman and Stuart tanks and thousands of troops and vehicles crossed the borders of Hyderabad State, while Bidar, Warangal and other airfields were

heavily bombed. The politicians in Karachi fulfilled Nehru's expecta-
tions and played no further part in the dispute, but the Hyderabad
forces, consisting of about 30,000 regulars and an army of 'Razakars'
or volunteers some 200,000 strong, stood ready to fight. The main
units of the Army were deployed at strategic points to take full
advantage of natural obstacles on a perimeter of about 300 miles round
the city, and the role of the volunteers was to harry and delay the
advance as much as possible, a task for which they were well suited
although poorly equipped. There were two main Indian thrusts, one
from the west and the other from the south-east, supported by three
minor incursions in the north.

Meanwhile the airlift went on. Because of the bombing of Bidar and
Warangal we now used Hakimpet, and the only hold-up was just before
the invasion started when my wireless operator at General el Edroos's
headquarters decided he had had enough and left by train for Bombay.
My pilots rightly insisted on radio contact with Hyderabad if the airlift was to continue, and Hamblin, one of my managers in Karachi and
also an expert radio operator and engineer, flew into Hyderabad immediately to fill the gap. This set a fine example and ensured the con-
tinuance of operations.

The important thing in Hyderabad now was that the Government
and the Army commanders should not lose their nerve. The Indian
Army units were advancing steadily but slowly, sticking to the
obvious routes and thus making the task of the defenders that
much easier. Everywhere the indications were that determined resistance would hold them up. The delegation to the United Nations
had arrived in London that day after several delays *en route*; they
were due to leave for Paris next morning, 14th September, by the first
available plane. If the Hyderabad Army could hold on for a few days,
perhaps a week, there would be time for the Security Council to
intervene.

The sequence of events that had extended over many months now
moved with sudden rapidity towards its climax, while a dangerous
loss of confidence developed in Hyderabad between Government and
Army, and particularly between Mir Laik Ali and Peter el Edroos. Mir
Laik Ali in his book blames el Edroos: according to him it would
appear that the Army Commander was incapable of taking decisions
and that logical plans for the defence of Hyderabad were non-existent.
From my own knowledge of el Edroos, however, and from the subsequent reports I received from the men I had flown in to help him, I

cannot accept this. He was I believe a most able officer, though no doubt he was severely handicapped by the withdrawal of his chief of staff and other British officers. My experience in previous weeks was that it was Peter el Edroos who had shown his awareness of Hyderabad's weakness by continually demanding an increased airlift, together with heavier arms and ammunition, and Mir Laik Ali who had applied the brake.

Certainly the situation of Hyderabad by the morning of 17th September was desperate. Pakistan seemed to have failed them. News had reached them that the Security Council had met in Paris the previous afternoon and had postponed consideration of the Hyderabad issue until the 20th, which might be too late. (The Hyderabad delegation were working for the convening of a special meeting on the 18th, for which the response had been heartening, and a cease-fire resolution by the Security Council within forty-eight hours was a distinct possibility, but this was not known in Hyderabad.) Meanwhile the Indian armies were still advancing.

Early that morning there came what seemed to Mir Laik Ali the final blow – a report that Indian troops had reached a point less than thirty miles from the capital and were advancing along an entirely undefended road. If the report was true, it meant that all defending forces to the north of Hyderabad had been by-passed or wiped out and that Hyderabad would be overwhelmed within hours. The Prime Minister checked with Army headquarters, who had had the same report a minute or so earlier but could not believe it was true; they had sent dispatch riders to check up.

From this point on, Mir Laik Ali and the Hyderabad Government seem to have panicked. Their minds were dominated by fears of the horror and bloodshed that might follow when the advancing Indian units reached the capital. The mass massacre of the civilian population, with special vengeance against Moslims, was regarded as certain. What good would a Security Council resolution for a cease-fire do, asked the Nizam, if they were all shot dead in the meantime? The only thing that would save the country, it seemed, was surrender.

This was the course that Mir Laik Ali now urged on his Cabinet. A resolution was drafted stating that the Government had done their best to save the country but that surrender to brute and overwhelming might of arms now appeared inevitable; the Government was therefore tendering its resignation to the Nizam. The resolution was passed unanimously and dispatched at once to the Nizam.

Meanwhile the Army dispatch riders had returned to say that no trace of Indian forces could be found where they had been reported, nor was there any sign of Indian penetration many miles beyond that point. The Hyderabad defences remained unbroken. Two staff officers were sent at once to the Prime Minister with this news, and when he emerged from the fateful Cabinet meeting they were there to intercept him. They then learned of the surrender.

'Why, sir,' said the staff officers, aghast at what was happening, 'we could still fight and hold the Indian armies' advance for some time.'[1] 'Bravo!' answered Mir Laik Ali – yet the decision to surrender was not revoked.

There is little doubt that the false report was inspired by members of the Indian High Commissioner's Office in Hyderabad; it certainly had the result that was intended. It is easy to criticize the Government for their panic, and to ask why they didn't wait for the dispatch riders' report, but this would be to ignore the almost intolerable pressures they were being subjected to. To blame the Army Commander, though, as Mir Laik Ali appears to do, is unfair. All the evidence that came to me from eye-witnesses confirmed that the bearing and outlook of Peter el Edroos were firm and confident right up to the moment his government surrendered. Indeed his behaviour was interpreted by Mir Laik Ali as over-confidence. The collapse that occurred inside Hyderabad was political rather than military in origin, and Mir Laik Ali's own account confirms this. The fact is that long before the Indian forces were anywhere near Hyderabad city, even before they had clashed with the main army defences, the Government gave in. Hyderabad had fallen from within.

Early on the morning of 18th September, two British officers found General el Edroos lying exhausted across his desk. 'All is over,' he told them brokenly, 'I am ordered to surrender. I have no choice.' In his great distress he did not forget the pilots who had helped him and his country, and he had already sent word to Hakimpet airport, where one of my Lancastrians had been standing by for two days in case it was decided to evacuate the Nizam, telling the pilot to leave at once as Hyderabad had surrendered. The Lancastrian took off at 07.45 that morning, and as it took off on one runway a Tempest dropped a bomb on the other. The Tempest pilot can't have seen the Lancastrian or he

[1] As reported in *Tragedy of Hyderabad.*

would surely have shot it down as it took off. For this flight the crew received a special bonus of £1,000.

Hamblin stayed at his post until the end. He then passed himself off as a technician and after several months managed to get back to Karachi. During all this time his wife was unable to make any move to contact him in case suspicion was aroused and his whereabouts discovered. Another of my men who was left behind, an engineer named Rowan, was not so lucky. He was shot in the back after the surrender, no doubt because he knew too much.

On entering Hyderabad itself General Choudhry, who commanded the Indian troops and who had also fought in Burma, ordered that there were to be no reprisals, and his action certainly saved much bloodshed. But plans had been made to eliminate all possibility of further resistance, and no quarter was given to the Razakars, or volunteers. For days on end large numbers of Moslems who were trying to get out of the country were hauled off trains, accused of being Razakars, and killed on the spot. Many thousands of Moslems were done to death in this way.

When the invasion began I had been in England, and I hurried back to Karachi to find that the Hyderabad Government had given formal notice that the airlift was to end. We had fulfilled our task of rearming the Hyderabad Army, and we watched the situation closely, hoping that the Security Council would intervene in time. Then to our consternation and chagrin came news of the surrender; all our work over the past few months had been in vain. But we had to accept it, and my object inevitably became to get my aircraft and crews employed on some other work as quickly as possible. While we had been flying in and out of Hyderabad the Berlin Airlift had started, civil aircraft were now being incorporated into it, and my Lancastrians, I knew, could make a useful contribution. A great deal of money was owing to me for the Hyderabad operation, but my charter agreement had been with the Pakistan Government and I anticipated no difficulty in a quick settlement.

I soon found, however, that all kinds of restrictions were being placed on me, my crews and my property. My aircraft were impounded, Ghulam Mohammad was trying to confiscate them for Pakair, and Iskander Mirza advised me to take the matter up with the Prime Minister, Liaquat Aly Khan. From what Mirza told me I gathered that the Pakistan Government were suffering acute embarrassment from the questions that the British, Indian and Canadian Governments were asking about the organization of the Hyderabad airlift, and in self-defence they were formally denying all knowledge of my operations and suppressing all details of their part in them.

My feeling was that this ought to make a quick and reasonable settlement all the easier to arrive at, and after I had written to Liaquat Aly Khan, as Mirza had suggested, reminding him that I had organized the airlift at the personal request of the two governments and that I had documents to confirm this, an agreement was reached and signed on 23rd November 1948 which provided for the payment of £57,500 as the balance due to me; I was to retain the properties and the aircraft, although the Pakistan Government indicated their wish to purchase the latter when the settlement was completed. This was a good deal better than having them confiscated.

Payment was to be made in Dublin on an agreed date in December, but the solicitors for the Pakistan Government failed to keep the appointment, so back we had to go to Karachi, where the settlement was confirmed. I was then offered a further £50,000 for the four Lancastrians, which was not unreasonable. The Government estimated that the properties would bring in another £75,000, which made a total of £182,000 in all. The settlement was something of a compromise, but I had already received about £300,000 towards my very considerable expenses over the past four months and in the circumstances I had no choice but to accept it.

In the next few weeks it became clear that obstacles were still being put in the way of final payments being made, so Ratcliff–my London solicitor–and I made a further visit to Karachi. After three weeks of negotiations Ratcliff told me that final agreement was near and that he expected it to be confirmed at a Cabinet meeting which he had been asked to attend that day. He duly went to the meeting at six o'clock that evening, while I awaited his return. The long fight to get what was owing to me, I hoped, was nearing its end.

At six-thirty a Moslem whom I had once befriended appeared at the door of my villa and demanded to come inside. He said he didn't want to be seen. 'Master, master,' he said excitedly, 'you are to meet with an accident tonight. I have seen the orders, and I have come to warn you.' He then told me he had rounded up twenty of my former Pathan guards and they were surrounding the villa to protect me. He begged me not to go out without an escort.

It occurred to me that from the point of view of a number of people this might be a convenient moment for my demise. I recalled how Rowan had been disposed of, and I was thankful for my Moslem friend and the loyalty of my Pathan guards. The question was, what ought I to do? I would have to wait for Ratcliff, and because of the uncertainty over the agreement we had made no plans for an early departure. I needed time to make some sort of plan.

I remembered that in a thriller I had once read the intended victim gave a party on the principle that nothing would be likely to happen to him while the party was in progress. I decided to give a party to celebrate the 'settlement'. The other thing the intended victim needed, I felt sure, was a plan for a quick get-away. As it happened I had lunched with an Australian pilot that day who was making an air survey of the route to England for one of the big Australian airlines, and he had said that anything he could do for me would be a pleasure. I remembered that he was leaving for Cairo at eleven o'clock that night, and I resolved to be on that plane.

While I was organizing the party, Ratcliff came in looking very depressed. 'I'm afraid I didn't get very far after all,' he said. 'They finally reduced their offer of a settlement to a total of £55,000 only, and then they gave me a list of fines and charges which brought the net amount down to about £6,000. They say they must have your agreement to this by eight o'clock tomorrow morning.'

'I'm not interested any more in what they have to offer,' I said. 'We're going to have a party.' I invited everyone I could think of, and at ten o'clock that night, with the party in full swing, I drew Ratcliff and another man named Wade aside. 'I'd like you to come outside a minute,' I said. We slipped quietly out of a side entrance and into my car and drove to the airport. I explained the situation to Ratcliff and Wade on the way.

As we arrived at the airport the first person I saw, by great good fortune, was the pilot I had lunched with. 'Can you get me on the plane?' I asked. 'I'll explain later.'

'Meet me here in twenty minutes.'

I went inside to see who was on duty at Security—I would have to get my passport stamped. Again I was lucky—it was a man I knew. I reminded him that he had asked me some time back if I could get his son into Vickers. I told him that I was leaving immediately for Cairo to meet the managing director of Vickers and that if he would give me particulars of his son I would take the matter up when I got there. He

wrote the details down and then stamped my passport. Had he known
the truth I am sure he would have forgiven me. I expect he guessed the
reason soon enough.

A few minutes later, to my great relief, we took off, Ratcliff staying
behind to press my case. We did not think there could be any danger
to him. Next morning we landed in Cairo and I wired Ratcliff of my
safe arrival. I then flew on to London.

Meanwhile I was in serious trouble with the Ministry of Civil Aviation.
Ratcliff had already told me that the Crown were pressing charges
under the Customs Act of 1876, and he believed my position was hopeless. 'Why didn't you keep me informed of what you were doing?' he
asked. 'I might have been able to help.' But when I showed him a copy
of the final agreement between my London company and Onzeair,
under which the aircraft had been chartered, not sold, he cheered up
a lot. 'This puts a different complexion on things,' he said. 'It's a
complete answer to any charge under the Customs Act.' He sent a
certified copy of the agreement to the Treasury solicitor, and when the
case came up it was adjourned *sine die* at the request of the Treasury,
who now had no case.

I was quite sure, though, that the Government would try another
tack, and on 5th May 1949 the next move against me by the M.C.A.
came to light. I was issued with a summons to appear at Bow Street
Police Court on 17th May for a flight made on 10th July 1948 carrying
arms from Karachi to Hyderabad in contravention of the Air Navigation Regulations. Once again, however, the Treasury solicitors were
a step behind. The certificates I held from the Pakistan High Commissioner's office, saying that my aircraft were under charter to the Pakistan Government, covered me under these regulations, which permitted
the carrying of arms and ammunition in British aircraft when under
charter to the Crown. The Treasury solicitors, of course, did not know
that I held these certificates, but I had always been fully aware of their
value. My case was clear and unanswerable, and the Treasury's case
was bound to collapse.

At this juncture, however, I had a visit from a Detective-Inspector
Howard of Scotland Yard. He showed me a list of names and asked me
if I knew or recognized any of them. I knew them all-they were influential members of the former State of Hyderabad. One of them had
been Mir Laik Ali's secretary. Nehru, said Howard, had flown all these

people to London to give evidence against me. 'Have you any idea why he should go to so much trouble?' he asked.

'He must have some good reason. No doubt he'd like to see me convicted.'

'There's more to it than that,' said Howard. 'If these men appear as witnesses, they will give evidence which could quite possibly be used against them on their return to India.'

I knew something of the expropriation of property that had been going on in Hyderabad. If these men gave evidence that implicated them in the airlift, which they might well do under cross-examination, they would be lucky if they lost no more than their estates.

My solicitors had briefed two able counsel, a junior named Patrick Browne, who was an expert on the Air Navigation Act and is now a High Court Judge, and Russell Vick, a famous advocate who had been a member in the previous year of the Lynsky Tribunal. In addition I had the advice of Sir Walter Monckton. I asked Russell Vick how we could stop the witnesses from Hyderabad from being called to give evidence. 'We can't,' he said. 'At least, there's only one way that we can, but that would be a course that I wouldn't allow you to take.'

'What is that?'

'You would have to plead guilty.'

I was not prepared to see my friends from Hyderabad, who had had enough to put up with already, implicate themselves and jeopardize their futures in this way, so I told Russell Vick that I believed I had the best counsel in England and that if I pleaded guilty I was confident he would be able to get across to the magistrate the Machiavellian game that was being played. Thus it was that, with all the necessary documents to prove my innocence of the charge, and in spite of much persuasion not to do so, I decided after all to plead guilty.

At the hearing at Bow Street, on 17th May, Mr B. M. Stephenson, prosecuting for the M.C.A., spoke of 'a fantastic story in which truth is sometimes stranger than fiction', and described me as 'a man of adventurous nature'. Later he was kind enough to add that I was 'a gentleman of the highest character', but it was left to my own counsel to speak of my excellent record and to point out that I had believed I was acting legally. In spite of Russell Vick's protests I was referred to as a gun-runner, and the sum of £400,000 was mentioned as having been paid to my company in London. Russell Vick pointed out that most of this had been expended on aircraft and in operating costs. My defence was well managed, and in spite of my plea of guilty I was fined only £200, with £300 costs, my company being treated similarly. The prosecution asked for further costs of £2,500 to cover the expense of flying the witnesses from Hyderabad, but the magistrate refused them. It was clear that he considered I had committed no more than a technical offence. I felt well rewarded by his leniency, and by the knowledge that in pleading guilty I had frustrated a plot to implicate many old friends in Hyderabad. The gratitude of these old friends – the party of Hyderabad witnesses called on me after the trial and said they realized why I had pleaded guilty – made the whole thing worth while.

The final task was to get payment of the outstanding sums owed to me by the Pakistan Government. We started legal proceedings, whereupon the Government reopened negotiations, and the money for the confiscated Lancastrians was paid. But shortly afterwards my properties in Karachi were requisitioned, despite the Government's agreement not to do so, and rents and monies due to me were seized to cover spurious tax claims.

In 1958 came the military *coup d'état* effected by General Ayub Khan. I decided once again to take legal action against the Government to recover what was owed to me. Many attempts were made to beat me down, and although my solicitors often urged me to settle I always refused, believing that on this particular issue the Pakistan Government could never let the matter go to court, however much they might wrangle. When President Ayub Khan visited England in 1962, and just before the court case was due, a compromise settlement was finally signed. It had taken me fourteen years to get the money.

23

Saudi Arabia – and the Wreck of the 'Bessie'

For a year after the Hyderabad venture I did not feel at all well,
and my doctor, Tom Creighton, insisted that I have my gall-
bladder removed. Eight days after the operation, while I was still in
hospital, my sister was dining with Creighton and the surgeon who
had done the operation when she suddenly had a strong premonition
about me. 'Tom,' she said, 'please go to Sidney at once. There's something wrong.'

'Nonsense,' said Creighton. 'I've been in to see him this evening and
it's only an hour since I left. He's perfectly all right.'

'No. I'm sure there's something wrong.'

Perturbed by my sister's vehemence and aware of her reputation
for occasional flashes of clairvoyance, Creighton left the table and
hurried to the hospital. When he got there he found that I had had a
thrombosis. The clot had settled in a lung, the one place, Creighton
told me, where it could be easily dealt with. This kept me in hospital for
several months. Tom Creighton is still marvelling at my sister's intuition.

One morning during my convalescence I was sitting in the sun
aboard my motor-yacht *Amazone* in the yacht harbour at Cannes
reading the London papers. The *Amazone* was a 250-ton yacht which
I had bought just before my illness and which I had since had refitted
in Malta before bringing it to Cannes. I also had my Lockheed at
Cannes, and I had made several flights to London to study and buy
charts for a projected cruise. Now I read in the papers that Mr Attlee,
then Prime Minister, had said in the House the previous day that
Australia had no right to go off petrol rationing without first consulting
Britain. It seemed to me that it was time Australia got her own oil
supply, independently of Britain, and I flew to London next day in
the Lockheed to discuss the possibilities with Lord Bruce.

'I believe there's oil available in Saudi Arabia,' I told him. 'British
specialists said there was no oil there and an American Company got
the concession. They soon found oil and formed the Arabian–American

Oil Company–Aramco. They have rights on four hundred thousand square miles of Saudi Arabia but there's still quite a large area not taken up.'

'Do you think you can get a concession?'

'I can try.'

Bruce said he would write to Menzies and Casey at once and let me know their reaction. Shortly afterwards he informed me that the reply was favourable and advised me to go ahead.

I started negotiations with the Saudi Arabian Embassy in London, and the Ambassador, Hafez Wahaba, confirmed that several areas were available and that the Government would be pleased for me to visit Jedda, where most of the government offices were located. I flew the Lockheed to Cairo so as to have it within striking distance, then returned by civil airline to Cannes. Some time earlier I had engaged an Italian captain named Monti to look after crew and navigation worries, and at my sister's suggestion I had offered the post of secretary to a girl named Bunty Brooke-Smith whom we had met while refitting in Malta, and she had accepted it. Her father was the Lloyd's Register representative in Malta, and Bunty had been out there on holiday. She had lived in South Africa during the war, had finished her schooling there, and had then worked as a secretary in the offices of the British High Commission. She quickly proved to be an asset, and with secretarial worries thus also taken care of I sailed for Jedda, taking Jill, my daughter, with me. After a leisurely cruise through the Suez Canal and the Red Sea we anchored off Jedda on 14th December 1950.

Next day the Deputy Finance Minister, Najib Salha, a charming Lebanese with a most agile mind, came aboard and welcomed us and said that the Finance Minister would like to see me in a few days. I went ashore and called on the British Ambassador, telling him confidentially that I had come to negotiate oil concessions in which Australia might be interested. I found him rather off-hand.

I had been warned before leaving London that negotiations in the Middle East could be interminable and that I should need all the patience I could muster, so I was pleasantly surprised when Najib Salha called for me next day and took me to see the Finance Minister, Abdulla Suleiman. Suleiman, a Saudi, was much more guarded and less voluble than Najib Salha, but he was not unfriendly. I outlined the proposals I had in mind, specifying the general areas in which I would be interested plus any areas relinquished by Aramco. Suleiman gave his general approval and offered to send me copies of the latest

Aramco and other oil agreements so that I could see the sort of terms that might be negotiated. I promised to study these agreements and then put forward my proposals in detail.

The Saudis had promised that transport would be made available for me during my visit, but none was forthcoming, so I decided to make another call at the Embassy to ask their help. I had to walk for over a mile through the extreme heat, well over a hundred in the shade, and when I got there the Ambassador was again very off-hand. No transport was available in Jedda, I was told, nor could he help me, so back I had to walk to the jetty. Altogether I was most dissatisfied with the Embassy's attitude, and I later heard a story that the Ambassador, when asked by his French counterpart what I was doing in Jedda, had said he didn't know but that it 'could possibly have something to do with a breach of the Finance Regulations'. I wrote at once to Ernest Bevin, then Foreign Secretary, and I soon had a reply to say that he had sent instructions to the Embassy. From that time the Ambassador's attitude changed, but I was already meeting procrastination from the Saudis, and I feared that damage had already been done.

During this period the head of the Alireza family, a powerful commercial Saudi family with headquarters in Jedda, invited me to meet Prince Faisal, the second son of King Ibn Saud. Prince Faisal was Viceroy of the Hedjaz and Saudi Foreign Minister.[1] When we met he said he would like very much to visit the *Amazone*, so I invited him to come aboard for dinner and he accepted. I said that with his permission I would like to invite several of his friends, and I asked if one of his staff could advise me on precedence, as I had little experience of Arab custom. Prince Faisal then treated me to a delightful example of Arab wisdom. 'Precedence and protocol are always difficult,' he said, 'but if you give a buffet dinner instead of a set dinner, people soon sort themselves out. Those who think they are important will sit where they think they ought to be. Those who are important will sit where they like and enjoy the dinner.' I took the Prince's advice and the dinner was a success. On similar occasions since then I have adopted the same procedure and it always works well.

More than a week passed and I still heard nothing from Najib Salha. The *Amazone* was still anchored about a mile off-shore and the seas were big enough to present a considerable risk when stepping from the yacht into a small boat and back again. I had still not been provided

---

[1] In 1964 he succeeded his brother as King.

with a car, and walking any distance in the heat was intolerable. I would not allow my daughter or my secretary to go ashore and walk about Jedda as it was against Saudi custom for women to be seen in the streets, and we soon began to feel like prisoners. It was impossible to find out what was going on, and I decided that I had little hope of making any real progress without local partners. The Alireza family suggested the formation of a founders' syndicate, which would give them a small stockholding in the operating company when it was formed and a share in the management side, and I agreed. During this period I flew to Cairo by civil airline and returned in the Lockheed.

I called at the offices of the Alireza brothers one morning to discuss the concession, and I had been there only a few minutes when Cyril Ousman, the British Consul, put his head in at the door to ask if he could bring in a party who had been shipwrecked farther up the coast. Four weary and bedraggled people were then ushered into the room, chairs were found for them, and they told their story. The party consisted of John Francis, part owner of a fishing ketch called the *Bessie*, and his lovely young Greek wife; the pilot, who had accompanied the yacht from Suez; and a member of the crew. The yacht was jointly owned by John Francis and his wife and a Major and Mrs Barker, who were still aboard the *Bessie*. These two couples, domiciled in Athens, had decided to seek a new life in Kenya and had spent their spare time in the previous twelve months fitting the trawler out as a yacht for the voyage to Mombasa. They had got as far as Suez but had then had to effect some repairs and had run short of money. Eventually an agency in Suez had agreed to clear their repair bills in exchange for the transport of a quantity of freight to Jedda. As part of the deal the Suez firm had insisted on providing them with a pilot. The voyage had gone well until two days earlier, when the yacht had been wrecked on a reef fifty miles north of Jedda.

'After we ran on the reef,' John Francis told us, 'we waited until daylight and then, not being able to see any land, decided there was no chance of anyone seeing us, so four of us decided to row ashore in our leaky boat. We rowed for seven or eight miles, baling all the time, and finally we came to another reef which we couldn't get over or round, so we abandoned the boat and swam the last mile ashore. Then we walked straight inland until we struck the Medina Road and got a lift here.'

'Don't you know the water is full of sharks up there?'

'We had to take a chance. There are still six people on the *Bessie* and they've got no boat and no food. There's a heavy swell running and I've come to ask your help to get them off before the yacht breaks up.'

Ali Alireza produced a chart and handed it to Francis. 'Where is the boat located?' Francis passed the chart to the pilot and after some hesitation he marked the yacht's position. I offered to go out in the *Amazone* to get the rest of the party off, but Ali said he would arrange the rescue at once with the coastguard. The next priority was to get Francis and his wife on board the *Amazone* for a bath and food, and to help in any way I could to get the others off the *Bessie*. I decided to fly out in the Lockheed to find out exactly where she was. In running the yacht on the reefs the pilot had proved that he didn't know his position, and I had noticed that he marked the chart without much conviction. John Francis insisted on coming with me, and when I told Ali Alireza what I planned to do he lent me his own sea pilot, Mohammad, who knew the reefs in that area well.

It took us about an hour to find the *Bessie*. She was about eight miles off-shore, on a reef which was not shown on the charts and about ten miles from the spot marked by the pilot who had brought her down from Suez. I circled the wreck several times at two or three hundred feet and we could see that it was being pounded heavily by seas coming up under the stern. As each wave hit the stern and lifted the yacht it covered the whole vessel with spray. We could see six people on deck waving to us and we knew they were all right for the moment, but it didn't look as if the vessel would last much longer. We headed back for Jedda.

I called on the Ambassador, reported that we had located the wreck, and offered to leave immediately in the *Amazone*. If we left at once we could just get there before dark. But he rejected my offer. 'The authorities are getting a boat organized,' he said, 'and I can't do anything at this stage.' I went on to the Alireza's office and found nothing had yet been arranged, so back I went to the Ambassador, repeating my offer. 'The authorities said they were making plans,' he said, 'and we must be careful not to offend them.'

'But these people are British subjects and it's a British yacht. Can't we make a decision?' The answer, it seemed, was no. 'The coastguard told me they were laying on a vessel,' said the Ambassador, 'and I can do nothing for the moment.' In vain did I point out that they had no vessel capable of reaching the wreck before dark.

I returned to the *Amazone*, where I found Francis and his wife in much better shape, though they were very distressed to hear that no rescue party had yet gone out. We waited up until midnight thinking that I might be sent for, and early next morning I went to the Alireza's office, but the answer was still that the coastguard authorities had the matter in hand. I knew it would be risky to go out without permission, as I would need coastguard authority as well as having to rely on Mohammad's help, but I was determined to take matters into my own hands within the next few hours if no one else went out. I went back to the *Amazone* and told Captain Monti to make ready to cast off at a moment's notice.

While we were at lunch, one of the Alirezas came aboard in great agitation and told me that the coastguard couldn't arrange a rescue party after all; was I still ready to go? I said we would go at once. Mohammad, the pilot, arrived at the same time, and we began to discuss a plan of action. Mohammad said we should go up outside the reefs and then turn in towards the wreck, but it was too late for this. 'It would take at least six hours that way,' I said, 'and we shouldn't reach the *Bessie* until dark. I'm certainly not going to risk lying off those reefs all night. Our only chance of getting them off quickly is to go up inside the reefs. That shouldn't take us more than four hours and it will leave us an hour's daylight to get them off.'

'Those waters are uncharted and full of reefs,' said Mohammad. 'It's bad water.'

'I'm prepared to risk it if you think you can get us through.'

'I think I can.'

Meanwhile the British Ambassador had arrived, also in some distress, but he calmed down as he listened to my conversation with Mohammad. 'Thank you very much, Mr Cotton,' he said at length, 'I'll cover you against damage with my Admiralty funds.' This was an unexpected gesture and as handsome an assurance as I could wish for. I then asked the Alirezas to provide me with another pilot: my idea was to send him up into the cross-trees to look out for reefs while Mohammad stayed on the bridge with Captain Monti and me. The others then went ashore, the second pilot appeared, and we got under way.

I decided it was time to check up on Mohammad. 'Here,' I said, 'you take her.' After a few minutes he turned to the helmsman. 'Steer 340 degrees.' This course, I knew, would take us right over the reef, and we drew ten feet of water. I pointed this out to Mohammad and he laughed. 'There's a gap seven metres wide at one point,' he said. '*Amazone* is six metres so there's enough room to get through and it will save us half an

K

hour.' He paused for a moment and his eyes twinkled. 'That's if I can find it.'

Mohammad, I decided, was all right—he had a sense of humour. I said as much to Captain Monti and I think Mohammad overheard. 'I received my pilot's training in Liverpool,' he said, 'and if I could find my way about there in the fog I can find it through these reefs!'

For the rest of us, though, it was a terrifying experience to look over the side as we passed through the gap in the reef. There was only three or four feet of water on either side and the rippling of the water made it seem as though the coral was stretching out long fingers to clutch us and rip our plates open. But once through the gap we had a long run northwards of thirty miles parallel to the coast in deep water. Two hours later we reached a region of increasing reefs and soon we saw the silhouette of the *Bessie* on the horizon. We signalled with a mirror and received their return flashes with relief. After twisting and turning and corkscrewing through the reefs off Las Hatiba, we eventually reached a pool on the lee side of the reef on which the *Bessie* was aground. The water was smooth behind the reef and we were able to get within about two hundred yards of the *Bessie*. There was just enough room in the pool to put two anchors out wide apart to prevent the *Amazone* from swinging on to the reef.

It was five-thirty and there was only half an hour before dark. The swell was still breaking heavily over the *Bessie* and the work of taking a small boat across to her was going to be tricky. I had had many years of experience with small boats and I decided to go over myself, taking two of the crew. We all wore Mae West lifebelts.

Major Barker had detached the yacht's gaff to start cutting it up to make a raft and it was sticking out about three feet over the side. I called to them to make the gaff fast to the rail and let me have a rope, which I passed through the jaw of the gaff, holding the loose end in my hand. It was essential to keep our tender from touching the side of the *Bessie*; otherwise it would be smashed to pieces. We were going up and down six or eight feet every time the rollers came in, and our own painter snapped immediately. However, by holding the *Bessie*'s line in my hands and letting it out as we dropped in the trough and then pulling it in as the next wave came in I was able to keep the tender in roughly the same position. Had I not been able to hold on to this second line we should have been dashed against the reef when our painter snapped.

As we came up with each roller the crest brought us level with the deck of the *Bessie*. I shouted to Major Barker, who was standing on the deck facing me, that we proposed to take off everyone as quickly as possible before it got dark and that we should have to make three trips. I asked him to make sure that everyone did exactly as I said. Then we began the first rescue. They had run out of water on board the *Bessie* and all they had had to drink for some hours was spirits so it was not surprising that some of them were in a state of collapse. I shouted to Barker to get his wife on the rail of the *Bessie* and to push her over when I gave the word, trusting to us to catch her. Barker agreed and as we came up on the crest of the next roller I shouted and he toppled her over. She fell into the bottom of the boat like a sack and I immediately put my weight on her to stop her from jumping up suddenly and capsizing the boat. We took one crew member as well and then made our way back to the *Amazone*. This process was repeated twice more. Just before we left the *Amazone* for the third time Mrs Barker called out, 'What about the dogs?' They had two dogs aboard. 'I can't get them off tonight,' I said, 'but we'll take them some food.'

The steward quickly brought some pieces for the dogs and we set off. Night was closing in as the tender cleared the reef at the end of this final trip but with the help of the *Amazone* searchlight we drew safely alongside her. Food had been prepared and hot baths made ready, and that night we managed somehow by putting up camp-beds and generally making do. I spent quite a passable night myself on the sofa in the lounge.

Next morning both families asked if we could get as many of their things off as possible when we returned for the dogs. All the possessions they had in the world were on the *Bessie*. I agreed, and we made three more trips back and forth. By the third trip, however, the seas had roughened again and while we were alongside the *Bessie* a wave broke over the tender and the engine stalled. It was impossible to bale the tender without first getting her out into smoother water so we started to row. Within half a minute we had broken both oars, but by using the broken blades as paddles we eventually got into smoother water. When we reached the *Amazone* both Francis and Barker insisted that we attempt no more trips. The risks were too great.

We had spent several hours in unloading the *Bessie* and it was now too late to get back to Jedda before dark, so we stayed where we were for a second night and left for Jedda next morning. As we left the *Bessie* we saw the tug from Jedda arriving from out to sea, towing a barge. She had come to do some salvage work and had timed her arrival well. There being nobody left aboard the *Bessie*, she and her contents were legally anyone's prize. Fortunately we had had time to clear almost everything of value that could be moved except the freight, which belonged in any case to the Alirezas.

We got back to Jedda at noon. The *Amazone*, with two double and two single cabins, now had eight extra people on board and we were hard pushed for space, but Cyril Ousman asked me to keep them all for a day or two while he found accommodation, and I readily agreed. John Francis, however, said this was an intrusion after all we had done for them, and he went ashore to search for accommodation on his own. We mentioned his plight to the head of an American gold-mining company, and after a few days he got himself a job in charge of the company's road between Jedda and the mining area 250 miles to the north. Francis was Canadian born, spoke Arabic, and seemed able to turn his hand to anything. He was a qualified architect and civil engineer. The rest of the party stayed on board for about three weeks, which caused a certain amount of friction amongst my crew. Apart from the accommodation difficulties, there was much extra work. Eventually, and without my knowledge, my daughter went ashore to see the British Ambassador. She told him she thought it was his duty to provide accommodation for the shipwrecked Britishers and not leave them with us indefinitely. This stirred the Embassy and next day Cyril Ousman came aboard and said he had found accommodation and could now take care of everyone.

All the shipwrecked party wanted to go on to Mombasa, but British regulations could not be bent or varied or humanized to allow them to do so. Francis and his wife were allowed to stay in Saudi Arabia, but Barker and his wife had no wish to stay there and they were sent back to England. These two people who had lost so much were told that their passports would be retained after their arrival in England until they had refunded the cost of their passages to the Foreign Office. In vain did they point out that it would be much cheaper for them to go on to Mombasa or back to Greece than to London, where in any case they had far less chance of getting jobs. The Embassy was adamant; to England they must go.

Francis did an indefatigable job on the mining company's road, keeping it in good condition until eventually the mine was closed down. He then got an option on the whole of the mining company's assets and induced some local businessmen to buy them and give him 10 per cent of any profits, which they accepted. They then negotiated the sale of these assets to other interests in Saudi Arabia for a very large sum. The properties were sold for $1,500,000, but Francis never received the full commission which was due to him. So after four years hard work in Saudi Arabia he returned to Greece. Our paths were destined to cross again ten years later.

When Barker got back to England he was given a job by the Government and in a year he had paid off his debt. Two years later, as we were lying at anchor in Piraeus, the yacht harbour at Athens, we were hailed from the dock and to our great surprise recognized Major and Mrs Barker. They had just arrived from England and had been telling friends their story when someone said that a yacht called *Amazone* was in the harbour and they raced down to see us. Major Barker had landed a good job as manager of the Ford Motor Agency in Salonika, and both he and his wife looked happy and well.

In 1952, forty-eight hours after I arrived in Jedda on another visit, the British Ambassador came aboard with a nicely printed parchment from the Ministry of Transport in London thanking us for having saved the lives of six people in the Red Sea the previous year.

24

I Meet Ibn Saud

O NE morning at Jedda Airport I was striding across the tarmac
towards the Lockheed when a strangling pain seized me across
the back and right up both arms from the wrists. I could not move and
I had difficulty in breathing. I stood still for some minutes until the
pain subsided and then turned and walked very slowly back to the car
which Prince Abdulla Faisal, a son of Prince Faisal, had put at my
disposal only a day or so before. I drove back to the *Amazone* and
went to bed. Next day I felt better but as soon as I walked about the
pain returned. I took things quietly for a few days, and then one
morning Captain Monti called me from the lounge to see a giant ray
that was almost alongside. Without thinking I rushed down to the
cabin for my elephant rifle and then raced up to the upper deck. As I
got there the pain seized me again and I collapsed. There was no doubt
that I had been doing much more than Tom Creighton had advised,
and with the aid of the car that had just been lent to me I took things
more easily.

At the end of January the Alirezas handed me a note which informed me that they had decided not to go on with the partnership
agreement. Meanwhile Abdulla Suleiman and Najib Salha became
more and more elusive, and eventually I announced that I could not
stay in Jedda after the middle of May. This brought no response so,
after I had flown the Lockheed back to Cairo, we duly sailed in the
Amazone on 15th May. Later I wrote to Najib Salha saying that I
couldn't understand why there had been so much difficulty after they
had invited me to Jedda and the Finance Minister had agreed my
proposals in principle, and he replied assuring me of their continued
interest, so I decided that I would probably go back to Jedda in the
autumn.

After my second marriage had broken up I had become very much
a bachelor, and I had no thought of marrying again. I had always had

an ideal about marriage, and I had begun to feel that the possibility of finding someone who fitted harmoniously into my way of life was too remote to be considered further. However, after the year which Bunty Brooke-Smith had spent with us aboard the *Amazone* we thought that we knew both the worst and the best about each other. I believed that in Bunty I saw an ideal partner. However, I was now fifty-seven, Bunty was very much younger than me, and I hesitated. It soon became evident, though, that Bunty had similar feelings, and we became engaged.

Some weeks later I was having lunch in London with Tom Creighton when he asked me how I was feeling. 'A hundred per cent,' I said – and then I remembered those rather frightening bouts of pain which had caught me in Jedda, so I told him about them. 'While you're here,' he said, 'I'd like you to see a specialist.' I was subjected to a number of tests, and several days later Creighton came round to my hotel to see me. 'I've got the results of your tests,' he said, 'and I'm not happy about them. You'll have to take great care of yourself.' I asked him what was the trouble and he said it was my heart. 'Strangely enough the cardiogram is good, but you have all the symptoms of Angina and you will have to learn to live within your capacity. You've got to slow down the whole tempo of your life.'

'How about flying?'

'There's no reason why you shouldn't go on flying the Lockheed. Nothing sudden will happen to incapacitate you. But if you feel any sort of pain coming on, take one of these pills. And always take one before you come in to make a landing.'

I made up my mind that Tom Creighton's news put firmly out of the question any idea of marriage. It would be altogether unfair to Bunty. I flew back to Cannes and told Bunty of my decision. She had only one argument: my heart condition provided the best possible reason why we should get married, so that she could look after me. This settled it and we were married in Nice on 1st August 1951, immediately after my sister returned to Australia. My daughter, incidentally, had left us to visit her mother in Canada soon after we returned from Jedda, and six months later she married a captain in the Canadian Army, with whom I am glad to say she lives very happily with their two children.

The other outstanding question was whether or not I should return to Saudi Arabia. Tom Creighton advised against it, but I did not like turning back once I had set course on a project, and on receipt of another encouraging letter from Najib Salha, in which he gave me permission to take my own car out to Jedda, I decided to go. After a leisurely cruise we reached Jedda on 20th February 1952. My car arrived a few days later and we were free to go about as we wished.

During the next few weeks I had frequent talks with Najib Salha and with Ahmed Fakhri, Director of Mines, and we made good progress. I was now being offered a concession for the whole of the Hedjaz, from the Jordanian border in the north to the Yemen in the south, including all the islands in the Red Sea, plus preference for all inland areas relinquished by Aramco. This was much more in line with what I wanted. For these concessions I would be asked to make an advance payment of £5 million.

A few days later Najib Salha came on board the yacht with news which seemed to set the seal on my project. 'You can expect an invitation shortly to go to Riyadh to meet King Ibn Saud,' he said. 'The invitation will include your wife. You will have to wear Arab costume,' added Najib. 'Someone will come to the yacht to see what you require.' We were duly measured and presented with the appropriate garments. My wife had to wear the *ayaba* as worn by all Arab women, and she had to be veiled, and as it was very hot she suffered a good deal in the plane on the way to Riyadh. Najib Salha met us at Riyadh Airport.

'I thought you were bringing your wife,' he said. 'Yes,' I said, 'and so I did. This should be her in the *ayaba*. I think I've got the right bundle but I'm not sure.' When we had established that it was indeed Bunty under the *ayaba* he drove us to our quarters.

Next day I called at the old palace and was received by Ibn Saud. I entered the audience chamber with Najib Salha and the King's Chamberlain and we walked slowly up the centre of the long room on the most exquisite Persian rugs. On either side of us was a long line of chairs. Some of the chairs were empty but many were occupied by courtiers and ministers. On the floor sat armed guards in picturesque costume. At the far end of the room, with his secretary squatting on the floor at his right, was Ibn Saud, sitting on his throne. It was an impressive sight. We bowed in front of the King and he held out his hand; I stepped forward and we shook hands. He then motioned me to sit down on the chair to his left and asked me how my health was. He said he himself was in good health, although it was plain that both physically and mentally he was beginning to fail.

I had been told not to say anything but to wait for the King to talk. After I had taken my seat we sat for fifteen minutes before he said anything. For much of this time his secretary was talking to him in a low voice. He then asked me if I was enjoying my visit to Riyadh and I said I was enjoying it very much and that I admired the development work that was taking place. He then turned back to his secretary and it was another fifteen minutes before he spoke to me again. 'I am aware of why you are here,' he said. 'The Finance Minister will talk to you and I wish you luck.' At a sign from the chamberlain I shook hands with him again and we retreated down the full length of the room and out into the bright sunlight.

It seemed that I had the King's blessing; but next day, when I had a long session with Abdulla Suleiman and Najib Salha, it was clear that I was still a long way from the agreement I wanted. The Government, it seemed, were now undecided whether to grant concessions on the areas relinquished by Aramco, some of which were proved areas, but an advance payment of £5 million would be asked for the Hedjaz concession alone.

'No one would come in and pay £5 million for the Hedjaz when the world's leading geologists are very dubious of finding oil there,' I said, 'but such a payment could be made if and when the oil was found.' Later I was told that the Government conceded that my reaction was a logical one.

Crown Prince Saud, Ibn Saud's eldest son, who was to succeed to the throne on the death of his father three and a half years later, had invited me to his Friday tea-party, and Najib Salha called to take me there. I was well received by the Prince and next day, when Najib Salha put us on the plane back to Jedda, he told us he would be staying on in Riyadh to finalize the agreement with the Finance Minister. Meanwhile I wrote a letter to Suleiman agreeing to take up the Hedjaz concession subject to 180 days grace in which to arrange the finance and ratify the agreement.

Several weeks passed and I still did not receive the final agreement. I called again on Ahmed Fakhri, the Director of Mines, in Jedda, and told him I was most unhappy at the delay. With the air of one giving a great confidence he told me that I would never reach the stage of final agreement unless I was prepared to pay a substantial cash sum, quite independent of any oil payments, something in the region of a million pounds. It was a shock to be faced with such a suggestion after nearly two years of striving and I found it hard to believe, even coming from Fakhri, whom I had found to be trustworthy. 'I know them better than you do,' he said, 'you will find obstruction all along the line unless you do it.'

I had one more talk with Abdullah Suleiman and Najib Salha, when I told them that I could not wait about for the agreement any longer. I had previously agreed to lend the *Amazone* to the Duke of Windsor, and I had to get her refitted in Genoa and delivered in Cannes by 1st August 1952. The final agreement was still not forthcoming, but just before I left Jedda Najib Salha sent me a letter dated 17th April outlining his Government's proposals, and these, I decided, would provide a satisfactory basis for my lawyers to work on.

All the way to Genoa, however, I was giving deep thought to whether I should give up the whole project; my friends were urging me to do this, and so was my wife. As we sailed northwards I went up to take my turn on the bridge one evening in a turmoil of indecision. I felt that the Arab had always been exploited and that it was perfectly natural for him to be suspicious of any new approach. I had become passionately interested in Arab problems, yet I did not relish the kind of frustration I had endured in the previous two years.

We were passing Stromboli at the time and as we drew to the north I saw a burning streak of lava pouring down towards the sea. Stromboli was in eruption. It was a beautiful sight, a cascade of fire streaming down, as it seemed, from the heavens. As we drew farther north a jet of lava forced its way out from the main cascade to either side in a narrow channel to form a cross, and a minute later there was a fiery cross of perfect shape and dimensions hanging in the sky. I could not bear to lose the impression of soul-inspiring majesty that the sight of this cross aroused in me, and I decided to take the night watch. All night long the fiery cross hung there in the sky, and it was not until dawn that it faded. By that time I knew that I must go back to Saudi Arabia.

When I got to London my lawyers drafted an agreement based on the Aramco and similar agreements and on Nahib Salha's letter of 17th April, and I sent copies to Najib and to Abdulla Suleiman. I then called on Hafiz Wahaba, the Saudi Ambassador, and told him about the suggested bribe. He was sympathetic. 'Go to Jedda again after the Hadj and you can be sure of a hearing from the Crown Prince,' he said. 'Tell him everything quite frankly.'

In November 1952 I visited Beirut, where I found that Najib Salha had retired from Jedda and was in residence, apparently for good. He told me that the Saudis thought they had struck oil in the Hedjaz and that they were bringing in their own geologists to report; meanwhile my agreement would be held in abeyance. I protested, drawing attention to the promises that had been made, and soon afterwards I got an invitation from Abdulla Suleiman to go to Jedda to complete the negotiations.

I flew down to Jedda, where Suleiman told me that as Najib Salha had gone it would be best to forget all about past negotiations and start afresh. I was so incensed that I threatened to go to the Crown Prince. This seemed to have some effect and Suleiman promised to send a draft agreement on to me in Beirut; the agreement was handed to me by Najib Salha when I got back. With final agreement at last in sight, I decided to return to Jedda in the *Amazone*; I knew from past experience that the negotiations could still take some time, and living conditions in Jedda were primitive. We anchored for our third visit on 5th February 1953.

An invitation to visit the Crown Prince in Dhahran, the Aramco headquarters on the Persian Gulf, was awaiting me, and Bunty was included. The Crown Prince seemed pleased to see us, and I then told him the whole story of the negotiations so far. 'From now on, if ever you want anything in Saudi Arabia, you have only to ask me,' he said. 'I will give orders that you are to be granted the concession. Come and see me whenever you wish.'

But in spite of this I encountered further procrastination from the Finance Minister, and eventually I was calmly told that the Government had made up their minds not to grant any more concessions until they had completed a thorough geological survey of the country. I protested most vehemently. 'I came out here at your invitation,' I said, 'more than two years ago. After protracted negotiations your Government agreed to give me a concession in April last year, and I am here now to finalize that agreement on your invitation. All this must be on your files, and whatever your Government have decided for the future, it is quite impossible to treat their offer of April 1952 and my acceptance as though they had never happened.' I pressed once again to see the Crown Prince but was prevented from doing so, and all my subsequent protests were in vain.

25

Macmillan Changes his Mind

I LET matters rest for a while in Saudi Arabia. But I had developed other business interests in the Middle East, and Bunty and I decided to make our home in Beirut. We lived on the *Amazone* at first, but later I sold the yacht and we moved into a flat.

On 12th November 1955 King Ibn Saud died and the Crown Prince, Prince Saud, came to the throne. I visited him in Cairo soon afterwards and was well received. Then early in 1956 the situation in the Middle East began to deteriorate and my work in Beirut came almost to a standstill. On 29th October 1956 Israel attacked Egypt, and for reasons best known to itself the British Government decided to intervene. The whole Middle East situation became very uncertain and business relations between one country and another virtually ceased. Various Arab states broke off diplomatic relations with France and Britain, and it became impossible for British subjects to get visas for any of these countries. However, three months after the British and French forces were withdrawn I asked King Saud if I could visit him in Saudi Arabia. It seemed to me that my experience of the previous years, and my friendship with King Saud and Prince Faisal, who had now become the Crown Prince, left me in a position where I might be able to do something towards repairing the damage. I got a reply from King Saud by return inviting me to Riyadh.

I decided that I should first try to find out from the Foreign Office in London what prospect there was of reopening the Buraimi question. This was a subject that had bedevilled Anglo–Saudi relations for some years. The Buraimi oasis is a collection of small Arab villages totalling 3,000 inhabitants at the north-east extremity of the Empty Quarter, roughly equidistant from the Persian Gulf to the east and the Gulf of Oman to the West. It was of no importance and little interest until the discovery of oil in adjacent areas, when ownership of and jurisdiction over the various villages suddenly assumed significance. The disputants were Shaikh Shakbut of Abu Dhabi, who claimed six of the villages, the Sultan of Muscat, who pressed a tenuous claim to three of the villages, and King Saud, whose subjects occupied the tenth village. In support of what they felt to be their legitimate rights the Saudis began to consolidate and extend their influence in the oasis in 1952, and the British pushed them out in 1955. There had been several attempts at arbitration but they had failed.

I cabled King Saud thanking him for his invitation and saying that I would visit him immediately after Ramadan, and I then flew to London and called on Lord Bruce. He agreed that an effort should be made to resolve the Buraimi dispute and arranged for me to see Selwyn Lloyd. The Foreign Minister listened to my ideas and said the Foreign Office certainly wanted a settlement. He then passed me on to Harold Beeley, at that time the head of the Middle East section. Harold Beeley had been co-opted to the Foreign Office and was not a career man, so he had a fresh outlook unimpaired by years of close indoctrination. He gave me the Foreign Office view on Buraimi.

I flew to Jedda and then went on to Riyadh, where next day I was granted a personal audience with King Saud. The King said he would like to reach agreement with the British over Buraimi and return to diplomatic relations, and he asked if I had anything in writing from Selwyn Lloyd. 'No,' I said, 'I did not feel that I could ask for this until I had seen your Majesty, but now that I have this message I will return to London and report.' Back in London I discussed the matter with Selwyn Lloyd, but he later sent me a most disappointing memo, as follows:

'We would welcome any solution of the dispute acceptable to the Ruler of Abu Dhabi and the Sultan of Muscat and Oman, *to whom the oasis belongs*.[1] Much as we desire to improve relations with Saudi Arabia, we would not therefore consider any concession which would sacrifice the interests of the Rulers on whose behalf we have been acting.'

It was no good returning to Saudi Arabia with this, and I pointed out to Harold Beeley that since it had previously been agreed to arbitrate over Buraimi it must have been accepted that there was some doubt about jurisdiction in the oasis, so the words 'to whom the oasis belongs' were out of place and even inflammatory. Beeley agreed to ask the Foreign Office to have another try.

Selwyn Lloyd sent me another letter on 12th July 1957 in general terms, referring to Britain's sincere wish for friendship and saying that the first step was a renewal of diplomatic relations, without prior

[1] My italics.

conditions on either side. I went back to Jedda, but for the next six weeks I was prevented by the intrigues of one of the King's advisers, the violently anti-British Youssef Yassin, from seeing the King. Eventually I flew to Lausanne where the King had gone for treatment and made contact with Jamal Husseini, his chief adviser, who gave me a choice of alternatives for a possible settlement, among which were a plebiscite, a return to arbitration, the establishment of a neutral zone, and reference to The Hague International Court.

I said that when I took these suggestions to Selwyn Lloyd I might be asked if they were given to me by the King personally, and next morning I was received by King Saud. The various points were read out, first in Arabic and then in English. 'I personally give you these suggestions to take to the British Government,' said the King. 'Buraimi is my face in the Middle East and you can say that I am most anxious to reach a settlement and return to friendship with Great Britain.'

I flew to London on 23rd September and wrote a report for Selwyn Lloyd, whom I saw on 1st October. Beeley was on leave, but a man named Riches, formerly a secretary at the British Embassy in Jedda, where I had met him several times, was with the Foreign Secretary when I arrived. From my past experience with Riches I had formed the impression, perhaps erroneous, that he was inclined to be of conservative outlook, one of the old school. Selwyn Lloyd, however, was at his most affable, and I thought at first that we might make some progress. But I soon discovered otherwise.

'Can we agree to anything on these lines?' Selwyn Lloyd asked Riches.

'No, sir,' said Riches firmly, 'we cannot.'

I hope I was wrong in the impression I got that the decisive voice was not that of the minister but that of the permanent staff. I could not help reflecting that this might be the reason why the Foreign Office so often seemed to be lacking in imaginative direction. The permanent staff had nothing to fall back on but years of rigid tradition and directives, and were dependent for information and advice on ambassadors and diplomatic staff who were moved elsewhere as soon as they had learnt enough about local affairs to be able to think for themselves.

There was a murmured exchange between Lloyd and Riches, and then Lloyd turned again to me. 'At the present time,' he said, 'I'm afraid I can't agree to any of the things you have suggested. If you are returning to Saudi Arabia you can tell King Saud that we will have nothing to do with Saudi Arabia as long as Youssef Yassin has anything to do with Foreign Affairs.'

'I wonder,' I said, 'if that would be tactful? The King might be tempted to reciprocate.' This brought a sickly grin from Selwyn Lloyd, and I continued: 'I could not return with that message. I must take a reasonable and constructive reply back to King Saud.'

Eventually I was authorized to say that 'if King Saud would meet the Sultan of Muscat and make what agreement he liked with him, then Britain would accept it. If that was not possible, Britain would agree to the creation of a neutral zone or to arbitration. H.M.G. would play any part required of them in arranging a meeting and in implementing any decision reached between the two parties.'

I returned to Riyadh on 14th November 1957 and passed the Foreign Office proposals to King Saud. When he had considered them I was granted an audience. 'I accept the British Government's suggestion of arbitration,' he said, and added: 'If the decision were to go in my favour, I would honour the oil concessions as already granted.' Here was confirmation of the wisdom of offering alternatives, which I had urged on the Foreign Office. One could be rejected and another accepted without any sense of pressure having been applied. 'However,' continued King Saud, 'I am still doubtful whether the British will allow the Sultan of Muscat to return to arbitration.'

'Your Majesty,' I said, rather piqued that the King should question the word of the Foreign Office, 'Selwyn Lloyd has himself made this suggestion and I think you can take it that it was made in good faith.'

I returned to London and told Beeley of King Saud's decision to accept arbitration, and added that formal confirmation of the Foreign Office suggestion would result in a return to diplomatic relations. I was disturbed to find, however, that no approach had yet been made to the Sultan of Muscat to prepare the ground, and I began to wonder whether perhaps King Saud knew the Foreign Office better than I did. Later I learned that Julian Amery, under-secretary at the War Office, who was about to make a tour of the Middle East, would stop off and visit the Sultan. I was refused an opportunity of seeing him before he left.

I saw Julian Amery on his return to London in January 1958 and it was clear that he had made no progress with the Sultan. He admitted that he had not been well briefed. I decided to return at once to Saudi Arabia, and I took with me a letter from Selwyn Lloyd. 'You ask us to demonstrate our good faith,' he said in his letter, 'and I am willing to do that by agreeing that a meeting should take place outside Saudi Arabia between our representatives to discuss diplomatic relations, Buraimi and anything else, provided no conditions precedent are laid down.'

I arrived in Jedda on 9th February and reached Riyadh on King Saud's invitation three days later, although Youssef Yassin again did his best to delay me. I finally saw King Saud on 24th February. It was a long session, the first part of which was taken up in a discussion of Youssef Yassin's attempts to sabotage a meeting. 'Don't worry,' said His Majesty at length, 'we all know Youssef Yassin.' He then asked me what I advised him to do. I suggested that the best way of avoiding further plotting and interference was for the King to have a personal meeting with a Foreign Office representative in Riyadh, in the same way as he was meeting me. 'I am sure that if you will do this, agreement on all points can be reached.'

'Very well,' said the King, 'but you must not say I have asked for a meeting. You can say I have agreed to meet a British representative here at your suggestion.'

Selwyn Lloyd and Harold Beeley were away when I returned to London and I was directed to see Commander Noble and Sir William Hayter, Minister of State for Foreign Affairs and Deputy Under-Secretary Foreign Office respectively. I recommended giving King Saud the choice of three alternatives: a meeting in a neutral country, a meeting in Riyadh, or, as I was now suggesting, a private meeting at a convenient rendezvous. To this they agreed.

I went back to Riyadh with these proposals, and after much further intrigue was taken secretly to the Palace for a private audience. 'I have sent for you,' said King Saud, 'because I wanted to see you personally, to tell you that owing to a change for the worse which has taken place in the Middle East, it would be better if the British did not now come to Riyadh, as our enemies would make adverse propaganda of it at this time.' I gathered that he was referring to Nasser. 'I have ordered Hafez Wahaba to go to Switzerland and meet the British there, and he is now in Geneva. I ask you to go to Geneva and help Hafez Wahaba in any way you can.'

'Your Majesty,' I said, 'now that I have succeeded in bringing about a meeting I am afraid I shall have to drop out of the picture. In any case the Foreign Office doesn't really like outsiders meddling in what they consider to be their own affairs.'

'I know it is difficult,' he said, 'but I know you will find a way of continuing to help. Will you promise to do so ? ' I gave him my promise.

I asked after the health of Prince Faisal. 'The Prime Minister,' he said, 'is well enough to return to his duties, and I have given orders for him to take over immediately and carry out his responsibilities as Prime Minister, the same as Prime Ministers do in other countries of the world.' Rumours were already current that, following pressure from Nasser, King Saud had abdicated his powers to Prince Faisal, but this put a different complexion on things. The King then adopted a more confidential tone. 'There are some very secret things I want to tell you,' he said, 'because I trust you.' He then gave me a confidential and personal message for Harold Macmillan, and made me promise not to divulge it to anyone else. He put his hand over mine and said, 'I trust you. Deliver that message to Mr Macmillan, and bring me his reply.'

Earlier that day, I discovered, the King had issued a proclamation delegating authority as Prime Minister, Foreign Minister and Finance Minister to Prince Faisal. Before his illness the Crown Prince had held the first two offices, so the only additional task was that of Finance Minister. Nevertheless the news, coming so soon after the trouble fomented by Nasser, gave rise to widespread reports that King Saud had abdicated to Prince Faisal. I did what I could to correct this impression in British diplomatic circles, with, I'm afraid, little success.

My first task on arriving in London was to pass on the special message King Saud had given me for the Prime Minister, and on 2nd April, the Wednesday before Easter, I got a telephone call to say that Mr Macmillan would like to see me at 5.30 the following day at 10 Downing Street. I was shown into the Cabinet Room, where the Prime Minister and Sir William Hayter were awaiting me. Sir William introduced me, and Mr Macmillan asked me to sit at the table opposite him and beside Sir William. I apologized for troubling him personally but explained that I had been asked to deliver the message only to him. He said it was quite all right and spoke of his appreciation of what I was trying to do to bring about a *rapprochement* with Saudi Arabia. I then handed him my report. When he had read the first page I interrupted. 'Prime Minister,' I said, 'I understand you are leaving for the country this evening, so please don't feel that I expect you to read my report

L

now. Perhaps you would like to consider it over the holiday.' He accepted my suggestion, and a few minutes later I took my leave.

A fortnight later Sir William Hayter gave me a memo, which he said the Prime Minister had himself dictated, outlining the Cabinet's ideas. I asked for time to study it. Later I had another meeting with Sir William, when I showed him a suggested new clause that I had drafted. This was agreed next day by Mr Macmillan. It now seemed that a meeting with King Saud would soon result, and I asked Sir William if he could make arrangements to have a suitable representative available. I then went back to Riyadh to see King Saud. I had the Prime Minister's memo and Sir William Hayter's covering letter translated into Arabic and written in large legible handwriting so that the King could read it himself, and I handed these papers to him. He held them very close to his eyes, reading slowly.

It occurred to me what a tremendous handicap his bad eyesight must be to him. It was said that he could only recognize people six feet away, and it was obvious that he found great difficulty in reading. Fate had certainly dealt him a cruel blow. I sensed the tremendous responsibility that lay on his shoulders, through the need for his country to shake off its medieval trappings in abnormal haste in order to adjust itself to the sudden acquisition of great wealth. I felt very deeply for him. He had had no real preparation for his task, as his father had brought him up in the rigid tenets of the old Arabian autocracy and unlike his brother he had not been permitted to travel widely.

After reading several paragraphs the King handed the papers to his son, Prince Mohammed, who was in attendance. The Prince read the papers aloud right through to the end, and when he had finished he talked to his father in Arabic for some time. Then he spoke to me in English. 'His Majesty says he wishes he could believe in the sincerity of the British,' he said, 'but if he accepts Mr Macmillan's proposal and the meeting does not take place he will lose face.'

'Your Majesty,' I said, addressing King Saud, 'Mr Macmillan would not have made that proposal unless he intended to stand by it. He is a man of honour, and will not go back on his word.'

The King exchanged further conversation with his son and then turned to me, putting his hand on my knee. 'I trust you,' he said. 'I will agree to a meeting, but it must be kept secret. It would be bad for me if it were known in the Arab world.' The King then suggested that the most convenient place for a meeting would be Bahrein.

During these negotiations on Buraimi I had allowed the matter of my oil concession to lie fallow, as I did not want any wires to get crossed. But on passing through Jedda I received word from the Finance Minister that the King had given authority for my oil agreement to be signed; I was to see the Minister for Oil next morning. The re-drafted agreement needed re-typing, however, so as my mission was urgent I was obliged to leave with the promise that the agreement would be ready for me when I got back. It would be signed on the King's order. The two propositions–the question of the return to diplomatic relations and the matter of my oil concession–were thus becoming inextricably linked.

I flew to London later that day and had a meeting with Sir William Hayter on 23rd May. I had heard that during my absence the Foreign Office had been in a complete flap about the whole Middle East situation, but I was unprepared for what followed. Sir William broke the news that in spite of the Prime Minister's offer to send someone to see King Saud, and the King's acceptance, the Foreign Office had now decided not to go through with it.

The whole of my time and energies in the previous twelve months had been devoted to bringing about some such meeting, and this *volte-face* was something that I could hardly stomach. All I could say was something to the effect that the Prime Minister and the Foreign Office would be in a very difficult position if they failed to meet King Saud now they had his acceptance.

'We have information on very good authority,' said Hayter, 'that King Saud has abdicated to Prince Faisal. A meeting now would therefore be pointless.'

'I was in Riyadh when King Saud appointed Prince Faisal Prime Minister and delegated certain powers to him, and I can say quite categorically that there is no question of the King's having abdicated.'[1]

I told Sir William Hayter that after Mr Macmillan's offer of a meeting, and King Saud's acceptance, I could not see how the British Government could avoid going through with it. They would have to issue the invitation. If the situation in Saudi Arabia had changed, King Saud would refuse it. But having agreed to arrange such a meeting I suggested with the strongest possible emphasis that they were obligated to make the attempt.

---

[1] This abdication did not come about for a further six years.

Sir William Hayter's answer was to drop a second bombshell: I gathered that in any event the Foreign Office had decided that they did not now wish the Sultan of Muscat to accept arbitration.

'That is exactly what King Saud said would happen,' I observed, 'when I presented him with the Foreign Office's proposal.' In the face of this second reversal I felt that further conversation was useless. 'If this is the situation, I feel I must ask to see Mr Selwyn Lloyd,' I continued. 'I would be glad if you could arrange that for me as soon as possible.'

It was three weeks later, following a number of conflicting reports in the Press about my role as a go-between, that I saw Selwyn Lloyd. It was a lengthy meeting, and misunderstandings were cleared up as far as possible, but it was a depressing occasion for me. Selwyn Lloyd produced a cable from the Saudi Arabian Government which said that I had no authority to discuss anything, and although I pointed out that this was the work of Youssef Yassin, it was clear that the Foreign Office had turned their backs on the Macmillan offer and that nothing would persuade them to take it up again. 'We propose letting matters take their course with regard to Saudi Arabia,' said Lloyd, 'and we do not intend to try to get the rulers to accept arbitration.' I pointed out as discreetly as I could that the view of King Saud, and my own view for that matter, would be that the British Government had failed to keep their word.

The effect on my oil concession, as I had feared, was catastrophic: my requests for a visa to return to Jedda to sign the agreement were ignored.

Many promises have been made to me by visiting Saudi princes in the last few years, but a satisfactory conclusion has never been reached. The only satisfaction I got from my years of effort, involving most of my capital, was the knowledge that, partly as a result of my endeavours, representatives of the British and Saudi Governments had been brought together for the first time since Suez. The gap between the two viewpoints had not been bridged, but a start had been made, and some years later diplomatic relations were in fact re-established. That was a step in the right direction.

It was fourteen years after the Hyderabad operation before I reached a final settlement with the Pakistan Government; so it may still be that the Saudi Arabian Government intend to fulfil the promises they made, or to reimburse me for my heavy losses through having faith in those promises. But that episode of my life is behind me. I have always been fascinated by new things, and at the age of seventy-four I am developing a business which I hope may go some way to recoup my losses and provide for my wife and our two young children. Then I may be able to return with them, as I have always hoped to do, to the country of my birth.

Index